The capitalist mode of destruction

MANCHESTER
1824

Manchester University Press

Geopolitical Economy

Series Editors

Radhika Desai and Alan Freeman

Geopolitical Economy promotes fresh inter- and multi-disciplinary perspectives on the most pressing new realities of the twenty-first century: the multipolar world and the renewed economic centrality of states in it. From a range of disciplines, works in the series account for these new realities historically. They explore the problems and contradictions, domestic and international, of capitalism. They reconstruct the struggles of classes and nations, and state actions in response to them, which have shaped capitalism, and track the growth of the public and de-commodified spheres these dialectical interactions have given rise to. Finally, they map the new terrain on which political forces must now act to orient national and the international economies in equitable and ecological, cultural and creative directions.

Previously published

The US vs China: Asia's new Cold War?
Jude Woodward

Flight MH17, Ukraine and the new Cold War
Kees van der Pijl

Karl Polanyi and twenty-first-century capitalism
Edited by Radhika Desai and Kari Polanyi Levitt

The capitalist mode of destruction

Austerity, ecological crisis, and the hollowing out of democracy

Costas Panayotakis

Manchester University Press

The right of Costas Panayotakis to be identified as the author of this work has been asserted by him in accordance with the Copyright, Designs and Patents Act 1988.

Published by Manchester University Press
Altrincham Street, Manchester M1 7JA
www.manchesteruniversitypress.co.uk

British Library Cataloguing-in-Publication Data
A catalogue record for this book is available from the British Library

ISBN 978 1 5261 4450 8 hardback
ISBN 978 1 5261 4452 2 paperback

First published 2021

The publisher has no responsibility for the persistence or accuracy of URLs for any external or third-party internet websites referred to in this book, and does not guarantee that any content on such websites is, or will remain, accurate or appropriate.

Typeset by Newgen Publishing UK

Contents

Confronting the capitalist virus: a prefatory note

As I was completing this book, I found myself at the latest epicenter of the coronavirus pandemic. As New York City, "the city that never sleeps," was starting to lose its sleep over the blare of sirens announcing the possibility of the city's health system collapsing under the impact of the virus, the contents of this book began to strike uncomfortably close to home. It didn't help that, as I was composing these lines, Anthony Fauci, director of the National Institute of Allergy and Infectious Diseases, was warning, on a TV interview, that "the coronavirus [could] infect millions of Americans and … kill 100,000–200,000" (Perano 2020). Should these projections be confirmed, the virus will claim, in the United States alone, up to 75 times the number of lives lost in the September 11, 2001, World Trade Center attacks. Unlike these attacks, however, no one will dare to blame such stupefying carnage on "Islamo-fascist terrorists who hate America and our freedoms."

There is perhaps no better metaphor for the increasing destructiveness of our capitalist system that this toll, amplified by the losses Covid-19 has inflicted, and will continue to inflict, in China, Italy, Iran, Spain, Britain, Ecuador, and the rest of the world, may have been triggered by routine market-oriented activity. That the site of this activity was a Chinese "wet market," an environment unlike the antiseptic Western supermarkets familiar to Americans, has endowed Covid-19's origin story with an aura of exoticism and inspired President Trump, in a pathetic attempt to divert attention from his administration's woefully inadequate response to the crisis, to describe the lethal pathogen as "the Chinese virus" (Rogers, Jakes, and Swanson 2020).

Appearances often have an uncanny ability to deceive the unwary, however. As an eye-opening article in The Guardian has recently pointed out, the global carnage triggered by Covid-19 can potentially be traced to the fact that "[s]tarting in the 1990s, as part of its economic transformation, China ramped up its food production systems to industrial scale" (Spinney 2020). In a process familiar to farmers around the world, and indeed the United States, the rise of agribusiness that accompanies the industrialization of food production displaced small farmers. Faced with this predicament,

> some of the[se farmers] turned to farming "wild" species that had previously been eaten for subsistence only … But the smallholders weren't only pushed out economically. As industrial concerns took up more and more land, these small-scale farmers were

pushed out geographically too – closer to … the edge of the forest, that is, where bats and the viruses that infect them lurk.

(Spinney 2020)

Moreover, as the article goes on to point out, this chain of events may be symptomatic of a more general phenomenon.

[H]uman [expansion] … into previously undisturbed ecosystems has contributed to the increasing number of zoonoses – human infections of animal origin in recent decades. That has been documented for Ebola and HIV, for example. But behind that shift has been another, in the way food is produced. Modern models of agribusiness are contributing to the emergence of zoonoses.

(Spinney 2020)

In other words, could it be that Trump's racist description of Covid-19 as a Chinese virus has the function – intended or unintended – of disguising the emergence of a new and lethal "capitalist virus"? Could it be that the pandemic-induced carnage is not the product of China's difference from us but a rite of passage, a proof that that country's spectacular recent economic successes are now accompanied by an equally spectacular ability to trigger the kind of large-scale global devastation we have come to expect from more established capitalist powers, such as President Trump's United States of America? In short, could it be that the virus haunting our nightmares is not the product of China being different from us but of that country becoming more like us?

In any case, the link between capitalist development, this development's ecological fallout, and the origins of the coronavirus pandemic is only one of the ways that this pandemic illustrates the growing capitalist destruction, which this book explores. After all, the logic of the capitalist system has not just helped bring about the unimaginable suffering of untold numbers of people around the world. It also amplifies this suffering by turning a serious public health crisis into a massive economic crisis that has begun to deprive millions of people of their livelihoods. According to the International Labor Organization, as many as 25 million jobs could be lost as a result of the crisis (McKeever 2020). And the precariousness of life under capitalism even in affluent capitalist countries, such as the United States, is borne by the sudden and unprecedented increase in the number of Americans filing for unemployment. To really appreciate the significance of the 3.3 million people filing for unemployment in late March 2020, consider the following facts cited in a recent *New York Times* story:

Just three weeks ago, barely 200,000 people applied for jobless benefits, a historically low number. In the half-century that the government has tracked applications, the worst week ever, with 695,000 so-called initial claims, had been in 1982.

(Casselman, Cohen, and Hsu 2020)

Historic, in its bleakness, as the extent of that job loss was, it was soon eclipsed by the numbers announced in subsequent weeks.

The impact will be devastating, even for people who, until recently, enjoyed the solid middle-class American lifestyle millions, if not billions, of people around the world used to envy. Consider "Olivia Fernandes, 26, and her husband, Fabio, … [who] went from earning $77,000 a year to frantically trying to file for unemployment":

> Before the outbreak, they had used much of their savings to chip away at student loans. Their health insurance coverage runs out at the end of March. Rent is due on April 1, and their landlord has made it clear that no extensions will be granted. By Ms. Fernandes's calculations, they will have almost nothing left after April's bills.
>
> (Tavernise et al. 2020).

Not so long ago Adam Seth Levine (2015: 2) had warned that "almost half of Americans are now one financial shock away from poverty." Unfortunately, for Mr. and Ms. Fernandes, as well as for millions of others in the United States and the world, this financial shock has now arrived.

The effects of this calamity are intimately linked to capitalism's pre-existing destructive practices, which this book analyzes. As we will see, the staggering amount of resources spent on ever more lethal weapons emerges as the "rational" and predictable outcome of a capitalist economic system that has long linked economic success to military might. For now, consider the fact that "2019 saw the biggest increase in global military spending in a decade" (Germanos 2020). Leading the charge were two major epicenters of the pandemic, the United States and China: "The US continued to claim top spot in military expenditures, spending $638 billion in 2019. China was the second biggest spender at $185 billion" (Germanos 2020). And, in the case of the United States at least, this largesse was accompanied by an egregious nickel-and-diming attitude when it came to procuring the desperately needed protective gear and ventilators that public health officials and health care professionals have been begging for.[1] As the magnitude of the pandemic in New York City and elsewhere in the country was becoming ever more clear, The New York Times was reporting that, "[a]fter considering $1 billion price tag for ventilators, White House has second thoughts" (Sanger, Haberman, and Kanno-Youngs 2020). And, even as one branch of the federal government was taking its time to assess whether it could afford to pay $1 billion for "80,000 desperately needed ventilators" (Sanger, Haberman, and Kanno-Youngs 2020), the self-same federal government was rushing through Congress an economic relief bill "delivering trillions in bailout funds to corporations" (Higgins 2020). Admittedly, the bill also included just enough "relief to working families" and funds for hospitals to give cover to progressive Democrats, whose vote was needed to pass the bill. As Economic Policy Institute president Thea Lee pointed out, however:

> The single biggest tranche of money goes toward industry bailouts without adequate safeguards to ensure that taxpayer dollars are used to save the jobs and wages of typical workers, rather than to preserve the wealth of shareholders, creditors, and corporate executives … It also egregiously fails to include protections for worker safety during this epidemic in industries seeking federal relief.
>
> (Higgins 2020)

The message of the bill seems to be clear enough: spending federal money to protect human well-being and lighten the capitalist devastation facing working people and ordinary citizens is a necessary evil to be tolerated as long as (and not a day longer than) this expedites the generous flow of corporate welfare. Clearly, some things never change. Would anyone be surprised if, as soon as the loot is distributed among the capitalist interests vying for it, these interests start attacking big government and its spend-thrift ways, eventually forcing it to reimpose austerity on a population already ravaged by decades of neoliberal policies, a global financial crisis, and a staggeringly lethal pandemic accompanied by yet another massive economic crisis? Should that occur, much of this book's discussion of austerity and its destructive effects may, unfortunately, serve not just as an analysis of what has been but an anticipation of what the coming months and years may bring to working people and ordinary citizens in the United States and the world.

In fact, the signs that this latest crisis may aggravate the capitalist destruction that this book analyzes are already emerging. Even as he was being lionized by liberal media as the anti-Trump exemplar of rational leadership in the fight against the pandemic, New York's Democratic governor, Andrew Cuomo, signed a budget that cut health care spending (Lewis 2020). And in another part of the world, Greece, the government has used the coronavirus crisis as an opportunity to render the conditions of Greek workers, who are already reeling after ten years of brutal austerity and drastically reduced incomes, even more precarious, allowing employers to reduce the hours and pay of their workers to half what they were before the crisis.

In an article written before the pandemic, Wolfgang Streeck (2014: 64) argues that capitalism may be in the process of undoing itself, and that

> [w]hat is to be expected, on the basis of capitalism's recent historical record, is a long and painful period of cumulative decay: of intensifying frictions, or fragility and uncertainty, and of a steady succession of "normal accidents"—not necessarily but quite possibly on the scale of the global breakdown of the 1930s.

The coronavirus pandemic may be the kind of "normal accident" that Streeck's analysis anticipates. Nevertheless, the argument in this book refuses to accept Streeck's assumption that capitalism has definitively triumphed over its left-wing political opponents. Although Streeck's anticipation of the end of capitalism may seem the antithesis of the "end of history" thesis advanced by Francis Fukuyama a short generation ago (Fukuyama 1992), this is only partially true. The current state of the political left in most parts of the world may be dispiriting for those of us sympathetic to its goals and ideals. But Streeck's view of the defeat of the anti-capitalist left as a terminal *fait accompli* is no less premature than Fukuyama's earlier pronouncement of the end of history. Given the well-known impossibility of predicting popular upsurges against economic inequality and social injustice, Streeck's pronouncement may very well be disproved by events as rapidly as the "end of history" thesis (Kolko 1999: 294). After all, if the aftermath of the current crisis turns out to be at all similar to that of the Great Recession, popular movements may rise up as unexpectedly as the Arab Spring and the Occupy movement did in 2011.

In any case, the least compelling aspect of Streeck's analysis is the expectation that capitalism is coming to an end because, in permanently neutralizing its political nemesis, it has destroyed the only countervailing force that could check its excesses and keep it from destroying itself. The end of capitalism can come and, most importantly, lead to a better future *only* as a result of a majoritarian anti-capitalist movement fighting for the kind of democratic classless society that this book is arguing for. It is to the formation of such a movement and to the elucidation and removal of the obstacles that capitalism places in its way that this book hopes to contribute.

Note

1 On US health workers' desperate pleas for "protective gears and protocols to keep themselves and their patients safe," see Stockman and Baker (2020).

Introduction

Looking at the world today, it is hard to believe that not long ago pro-capitalist ideologues were announcing "the triumph of … free-market capitalism as the most effective way to organize a society" (Friedman 2000: xxi). To be sure, the first twenty years of the last century, featuring World War I and the Russian Revolution, may have arguably represented even greater setbacks for capitalism than the beginning of our century. Nonetheless, even we have experienced a series of developments that make capitalist triumphalism seem a quaint relic of the past: the brazen attacks on the capitalist world's paramount superpower on September 11, 2001, and the military fiascos in Iraq and Afghanistan that resulted from that superpower's response to those attacks; a major financial crisis erupting in that self-same superpower less than a decade afterwards and its rapid escalation into a global economic crisis, the reverberations of which we still feel today; the sudden eruption across the world of major waves of protest, such as the Arab Spring and the Occupy movement, which were a response to the failings of the neoliberal economic model, the direct and indirect consequences of the global economic crisis, the blatant failure of political elites to deal with that crisis in an equitable and socially defensible fashion, and to the geopolitical strategies through which the United States has long sought to control an oil-producing region of paramount importance for the global capitalist system; and, last but not least, a global pandemic, which is taking a terrible human toll, triggering a massive economic crisis, while also exposing the palpable effects of austerity as doctors, nurses, emergency medical technicians even in wealthy capitalist countries such as the United States – the very people whom the hypocritical austerity-dispensing political elites hail as heroes – often have to fight the lethal virus without health insurance and/or adequate protective equipment, thus attempting to save lives wearing home-made masks, swimming goggles, or even trash bags. One would probably have to go back to the age of Auschwitz and Hiroshima to find a time in which capitalism's destructive and crisis-ridden nature was as blatantly obvious as it is today. It is hardly surprising, then, that, even before the most recent global pandemic, with its massive economic fallout, scholars were comparing the earlier global economic crisis to the fall of the Berlin Wall and the collapse of the socio-economic regimes that ruled the Soviet Union and its satellite states (Vattimo 2010: 206; Holmes 2009: xiii). But compounding the effects of the economic and global health crisis triggered by Covid-19 is a deepening ecological crisis, most manifest in the ongoing process of climate change and in the obvious unwillingness of the powers that be to take the immediate steps scientists are urgently calling for. In the face of public opinion, the ruling elites do not just refuse to take climate change and the deepening ecological crisis seriously. Instead, they continue to pledge allegiance to the pursuit of economic growth, through economic policies that continue to award bailouts to mega-corporations and the wealthy few even as they leave everyone else to fend for themselves. Within the span of a short generation capitalism's claim to represent democracy and progress seems more dubious than ever.

In fact, in addition to the economic and ecological crises it has created, capitalism is increasingly leading to a crisis of democracy. The signs of this crisis are abundant and take different forms. It is not just the polls that reveal the disconnect between the views and priorities of ordinary citizens and those of their "representatives" (Borosage 2017; Post 2012: 76; van Gelder 2011: 189; McAllister and White 2009: 194). Accompanying, and fueled by, this disconnect are the falling participation rates, especially of low-income groups, which mean that "those who actually vote are not a cross-section of 'the people' but tend to be better off economically" (Markoff 2014: 119).

It would be a mistake to blame this state of affairs on popular apathy, however. Not only do ordinary people the world over consistently participate in political processes when they feel that doing so will indeed make a difference to their lives (Avritzer 2005: 393–94; Sader 2005: 464; Wainwright 2003: 109; Tilly and Albelda 2002: 231). In addition, capitalism's multidimensional crisis has given rise to movements of resistance in all corners of the world. Most recently, of course, workers at Amazon and Instacart have struck over the hazardous conditions they have to labor under, as their employers have sought to reap maximum benefit from a global pandemic that has led more and more people to shop online (O'Brien 2020). As the pandemic claims the lives of hundreds of workers, not just in the health care sector but also in other sectors of the economy, more and more workers mobilize against the often life-endangering conditions in which their essential work to contain the impact of the virus is currently taking place (Kim 2020; Almasy and Razek 2020). Even before these pandemic-induced struggles, however, people were on the move against austerity, rising up against the hollowness of political "democracies" intent on sacrificing ordinary people's needs and aspirations to the interests of capital, while also mobilizing against the capitalist system's ongoing depredation of the planet (Gebeloff 2018; Sitrin and Azzellini 2014; Graeber 2013; Mason 2012; Solomon and Palmieri 2011b). Even in traditional strongholds of capitalism, such as the United States, "socialism" was gaining popularity, especially among the young, and leading to electoral successes for self-described socialist politicians (Appelbaum and Tankersley 2018; Newport 2018; Goldberg 2018). No wonder an increasingly beleaguered Trump administration was warning about the specter of socialism threatening economic prosperity (Appelbaum and Tankersley 2018). How ironic, then, that economic crisis has arrived not because of a Sanders presidency. Instead, it follows capitalism's transformation of a public health crisis into a massive employment and demand crisis that denies millions of working people in the United States and the world the only way to survive within capitalism, namely through the sale of their labor power in the market.

All in all, people's general sense of malaise has been unmistakable for some time now. This malaise does not just take politically progressive forms, however. More ominously, it has also led to the rise of racist and xenophobic forces on the far right, even neo-Nazi, end of the political spectrum. These forces have grown by scapegoating immigrants and racialized minorities for the problems that neoliberal capitalism continues to impose on ordinary people even in the most affluent parts of the planet (Horowitz 2018; Bittner 2018; Baier 2016; Watkins 2016: 20; Hildebrandt 2015: 31). Although they present themselves as "rebellious outsiders," their "'anti-system' rhetoric is not aimed against capitalism, but against the system of liberal representative democracy" (Baier 2016: 51).

Both the rise of these forces and capitalism's multidimensional crisis I have just sketched bear witness to an ever more unmistakable reality: capitalism's increasing destructiveness. This destructiveness takes different forms. Economic crisis leads to a multitude of social problems, which destroy people's lives, their health, and their families (Bakalar 2018; Wolff 2012: 53; Panayotakis 2011a: 22–23; Ghosh 2011: 26; Lichtman 2009: 19–21). By assaulting people's right to education and healthcare, the austerity policies the economic crisis has triggered amplify such destruction further. In combination with the ecological destruction that capitalism inflicts on the planet, this destruction endangers the lives of millions, if not billions, of people around the world. So do the geopolitical rivalries for control of economically important regions of the world, such as the "Middle East war zones the Western powers ha[ve] been stoking for decades" (Watkins 2016: 10). By fueling deadly wars, such rivalries push millions of people to migrate to other parts of the world. As the numbers of refugees from military, economic, and ecological devastation continue to increase, the backlash against them in the receiving countries mounts (Fisher and Taub 2018; Kingsley 2018; Badiou 2016: 26–38; Watkins 2016: 10).

All this destruction is not a mistake. It is a predictable consequence of capitalist rationality, which consists in the pursuit of profit and capital accumulation by any means necessary. Supporters of the capitalist system going back to Adam Smith have long claimed that capitalist competition is able to subordinate capitalist rationality to the common good. Even capitalism's greatest nemesis, Karl Marx and the intellectual tradition he pioneered, have seen capitalism as a progressive historical force because of the impressive productive development it is able to generate. This work will not question capitalism's ability to develop the forces of production. It chooses to highlight the sordid underside of this development, however; what it describes as capitalism's equally awesome forces of destruction. The development of capitalism's forces of production and that of its forces of destruction are both the product of the same capitalist rationality. Both are inseparable from the development of science and technique in pursuit of capitalist profit. As we will see, it is this overriding goal of capitalist profitability that explains why developments in science and technique are increasingly leading to destruction rather than simply boosting the productive potential at our disposal.

The result is a new contradiction, a tug-of-war between capitalism's ongoing development of productive forces and its equally dramatic development, and deployment, of its forces of destruction. Productive development under capitalism may increase material consumption among the most fortunate. As the literature indicates, however, the compulsive increase of material consumption does not just contribute to a deepening ecological crisis. It is also increasingly futile, as it distracts people from the things that really make a contribution to people's life satisfaction and happiness, namely free time and the quality of one's relations with other people (Jackson 2017: 49, 126; Layard 2005; Lane 2000; Durning 1992).

In short, this is the capitalist contradiction that this work highlights: the benefits from productive development tend to decline over time while the threat to humanity and the planet from capitalism's escalating forces of destruction continues to grow. As this contradiction emerges from the coincidence of these two trends, I will be referring to it as "capitalism's cost–benefit contradiction." Primarily focusing on the implications of capitalism's productive dynamism, Marxists have long identified the system's waste of the productive potential it creates as a reason to replace it with a classless society. This reason is as operative today as ever. And yet, a new, and no less compelling, reason for such an alternative society is now clear: far from simply representing a waste of productive potential, not replacing capitalism with a classless alternative can lead only to a truly dystopian future. The dilemma "socialism or barbarism" is no less relevant today than when Marxist theorists first articulated it over 100 years ago (Angus 2014).

Central to this work's analysis of capitalist destruction is a rethinking of the concept of economic surplus: after all, it is the use of the surplus to pursue profit and reproduce the prevailing order that fuels capitalism's cost–benefit contradiction. One task of this work therefore is to trace the connection between capitalism's destructiveness and its use of the surplus it extracts from workers. Another, no less important, objective of this work, however, is to broaden our understanding of the forms that the surplus takes and the sites in which its production occurs. In particular, this work builds on the feminist tradition's recognition of housework's contribution to the (re)production of labor power. After all, as Nancy Folbre (2009: 126) rightly reminds us, "[t]he wages that a worker earned never provided his or her subsistence ... [because t]hese wages were transformed into services—such as meals—and into replacement workers—namely children—by women's unpaid work." Taking this insight to heart, this work identifies households as potential sites of surplus. Similarly, the growing role that the state has over time assumed in the (re)production of labor power suggests the need to recognize the public sector as another potential site of surplus production (Folbre 2011: 42; Folbre 2009: 125–26; Folbre 2008: 14; Gardiner 1979: 180–81; Weinbaum and Bridges 1979: 196–97).

Rethinking the surplus in this way has important implications for our understanding of social and class struggles over the surplus, as well as over the distribution of the burden of producing this surplus among the producers populating the capitalist, household, and public sectors of the economy. Tracing the connections between these three different sectors of the economy is especially important at a time of capitalist austerity, which often proceeds by "creat[ing] a wedge between public and private employees" (Fabricant 2011: 236) and by cutting public services in ways that increase necessary housework (Yeginsu 2018; Elson 2017: 55; Fraser 2016: 104; Abramovitz 2012: 34). These connections are also important to recognize, however, because they highlight the inseparable connection between class exploitation and racial and gender inequalities. Not only do neoliberal attacks on the welfare state increase the amount of housework, which, in male-dominated societies around the world, primarily falls on the shoulders of women. Often relying on racist stereotypes that stigmatize low-income receivers of welfare benefits, such attacks have an established record of depressing wages for everyone by increasing the competition for low-wage labor (Badger 2018; Abramovitz 2002: 219, 225; Zweig 2001: 78–79). As Mimi Abramowitz rightly points out, the purpose and effect of such attacks is to "[increase] the profits for those at the top by imposing austerity on nearly everyone else" (Abramovitz 2002: 225).

If capitalism's destruction stems from its use of the surplus, reversing this destruction presupposes an alternative, classless society that allows all people to democratically decide over the size and use of the surplus they will collectively produce. If the end of the Cold War did not send this idea to the dustbin of history, this is because, as we will see, the fall of the Berlin Wall simply signified the triumph of one type of class society, capitalism, over the *sui generis* class society that eventually consolidated itself in the Soviet Union, only to be transplanted later on to the Soviet Union's satellite states. There is a clear lesson that an observer willing to go beyond the propagandistic platitudes of mainstream political discourse can draw from the experience of the twentieth century: a better world is not possible by going back. In particular, the neoliberal fantasy of a return to the free market, which nevertheless always includes a generous dose of government intervention when that suits the interests of huge capitalist corporations, has brought upon us a multitude of crises (Jackson 2017: 189; Wright and Rogers 2011: 392; George 2001: 12). Similarly, social democracy's claim, during capitalism's post-war golden age, to have subordinated capital to democracy and to ordinary people's needs and aspirations has proved to be a cruel hoax ever since the rise of neoliberalism. Thus, this work holds on to the vision of a democratic classless society. Because of the way it rethinks the surplus, however, this work also redefines this vision by recognizing the abolition of racial and gender inequalities as a necessary condition for its realization.

At the same time, this work does not underestimate the obstacles that the realization of such a vision would need to overcome. Although the contradiction it identifies creates the possibility of an anti-capitalist coalition, capitalism's operation regularly creates divisions within the ranks of this potentially anti-capitalist constituency. As this short overview has so far intimated, capitalism regularly divides working people along racial and gender lines, along economic sector lines (for example, private versus public sector workers), along geographic lines (workers in the global North as against workers in and immigrants from the global South), and so on. A democratic classless society is more necessary than ever. But it is not a causal/mechanical necessity that is at issue here. In other words, a democratic classless society will not ineluctably emerge from the dynamics and contradictions of the capitalist system. The necessity of a democratic classless society is a conditional one and, ultimately, amounts to this: if we want to use the productive potential at our disposal in a way that promotes human development, and if we want to avert the dystopian future that capitalism has in store for us, then we have to overcome the obstacles to the realization of an alternative society that capitalism continually raises.

The book's structure

In developing this argument I begin, in Chapter 1, by rethinking the concept of the surplus. In particular, Chapter 1 proposes a more inclusive conception of the surplus that takes into account the wealth and surplus production that take place not just in the capitalist workplace but also in households and the public sector of the economy. Chapter 1 also illustrates the interconnections between the capitalist, household, and public sectors of the economy, through an (admittedly partial) overview of the socio-economic processes and developments that have accompanied neoliberal restructuring and the waves of austerity that this restructuring generates. This overview also illustrates one of the important advantages of our more inclusive concept of the surplus: its demonstration that the exist-ence of distinct sites of wealth and surplus production within contemporary capitalist societies is itself a source of divisions within the ranks of the producers. By adding to our understanding of how capitalism keeps producers divided, this aspect of the argument will be taken up again later in the book, when I examine why it has proved so difficult for capitalism's increasing destructiveness to meet with a strong and unified challenge.

Chapter 2 focuses on the questions of justice and freedom that exploitation and the existence of a surplus raise. Against the contention, advanced by some Marxists, that the surplus at the disposal of a society reflects its freedom to pursue the goals that it sets for itself, Chapter 2 argues that such a connection between surplus and freedom is very problematic within class societies. Capitalism, for example, may raise the pro-duction of surplus to unprecedented heights but its use of that surplus is subject to the compulsive pursuit of capital accumulation. Thus, Chapter 2 argues that the production of surplus can enhance human freedom only in a classless society that allows all people to democratically decide on the size and use of the surplus they collectively produce. As Chapter 2 points out, moreover, the fact that meaningful democratic deliberation is impossible as long as racist and gender inequalities persist indicates that abolishing such inequalities has to be a defining characteristic of such a society.

Chapters 1 and 2 introduce and further develop the concepts of class exploitation and surplus. Chapter 3, by contrast, initiates this work's analysis of the destructive ways that capitalism uses this surplus. In particular, Chapter 3 builds on Marx's distinction between the formal and the real subsumption of labor to capital to analyze the rise of consumerism as a shift from the formal to the real subsumption of consumption to capital. Similarly to the shift that Marx originally described, this latter shift goes beyond turning the means of sub-sistence necessary to satisfy people's pre-existing needs into capitalist commodities. Over time capital uses the surplus it extracts from workers to build a consumerist culture that goes beyond the originally formal subsumption of consumption to capital. Instead, this con-sumerist culture uses science and technique to subordinate consumer needs and consumer rationality to a capitalist rationality intent on pursuing profit. Capital thus refashions our culture in its own image, with destructive effects for human well-being and the ecological integrity of the planet. As Chapter 4 points out, however, this new consumerist culture also erodes democracy by increasingly turning media into vehicles for advertising. This skews political debate by privileging interpretations of the world most congenial to corporate advertisers and the often affluent segments of the population their advertising targets.

Whereas Chapters 3 and 4 begin the discussion of capitalism's destructive uses of the surplus, Chapter 5 formally introduces the concept of "forces of destruction." In par-ticular, the chapter analyzes the connections between the operation of capitalist society and the rapid development of ever more lethal military technologies, as well as of tech-nologies that contribute to the deepening ecological crisis that casts a menacing shadow over human beings and our planet. By contrast to the traditional analysis of history in terms of a dialectic between forces and relations of production, Chapter 5 shows why a more complex understanding also requires an analysis of how forces and relations of production interact with the development and deployment of capitalism's forces of destruction. Departing from a critique of the hegemonic, market-oriented stream of the environmentalist movement, Chapter 5 also begins to make the case that "new social movements" will be unlikely to achieve their emancipatory objectives without making themselves part of a broader anti-capitalist coalition.

Building on the discussion, in Chapters 3 through 5, of capital's destructive uses of the surplus, Chapter 6 formulates the contradiction in contemporary capitalism between the declining benefits of ongoing productive development and the growing threats from the equally dramatic development and deployment of the system's destructive forces. Chapter 6 argues that this contradiction refutes the false and facile dichotomy in the literature between the supposedly material orientation of the labor and socialist movements making up the "old" left and the supposedly post-materialist concerns of new social movements. On the contrary, this contradiction creates the potential for an anti-capitalist coalition fighting for a democratic classless society, which, in addition to ending class exploitation, would also abolish racial and gender inequalities while reversing the forms of capitalist destruction that many new social movements (for example, the environmental and peace movements) fight against. Having identified this potential for convergence, Chapter 6 also analyzes, however, the differing vantage points from which people around the world experience this contradiction, thus also highlighting the obstacles to this convergence that capitalism also erects. No mechanical necessity guarantees the overcoming of these obstacles. Overcoming them can result only from collective political practice cutting through the fragmenting effects of capitalism's operation on the majority of the population suffering from capital's wasteful and destructive uses of the surplus.

In its emphasis on the need for a democratic classless society, this work also attempts to challenge the popular association of the concept of communism with the oppressive and undemocratic class systems of the now defunct Soviet Union. Chapter 7, in particular, challenges pro-capitalist ideologists' equation of capitalism with democracy and of communism with dictatorship in two ways. Showing that both systems have fallen short of the democratic ideal, it traces this failure to the fact that, although they were different from each other, both were exploitative class orders. In addition to explaining why the system that prevailed in the Soviet Union and its satellite states was an exploitative class order, Chapter 7 also explores the ways in which its undemocratic trajectory was partly the product of the forces of destruction that its capitalist nemesis had developed. Having explored the links between class exploitation and the lack of democracy in the Soviet system, Chapter 7 also explores how the link is currently playing out throughout the capitalist world. In particular, it analyzes the hollowing out of democratic institutions that increasingly leads to popular disenchantment with a political system scandalously more attuned to the interests of capital than to the needs and aspirations of ordinary citizens.

Having laid out capital's destructive uses of the surplus and the multiple crises it creates, the book concludes by reasserting the need for a democratic classless society, defining such a society as the essence of the communist ideal. The book's conclusion also recapitulates some of the implications of such a redefinition of the communist ideal, pointing out how integral to this understanding of the communist ideal is the abolition of racial and gender oppression. In this respect, as well as in its promise to reverse capitalist destruction, this rethinking of the communist ideal has the potential to bring together the movements of the "old" left with a multiplicity of new social movements, which, each in its own way, confront capitalist destruction and/or the system's regular reproduction of long-standing forms of social oppression.

1

Rethinking the surplus

Using Marx's analysis as its starting point, this chapter argues for the need to define the surplus in an inclusive way that takes into account the wealth and surplus production taking place not just in the capitalist workplace but also in the household and public sectors of the economy. Such a rethinking allows a fuller understanding of the interconnections between these different economic sectors and of the ways the capitalist economic system creates divisions within the producers' ranks. In particular, a brief overview of some of the dynamics of neoliberal restructuring and austerity shows that labor market competition is not the only structural feature of the capitalist economic system that keeps producers divided. To understand the dynamics that keep producers divided, one has to pay at least as much attention to another structural feature of contemporary capitalist economies: the existence within them of distinct sites of wealth and surplus production.

Marx and the surplus

The concept of the surplus refers to the product above and beyond that necessary to meet the customary subsistence requirements of the producers. One reason for its significance is the contribution the use of the surplus can make to social and technological change. For example, capitalism's unprecedented technological dynamism, which Karl Marx and Friedrich Engels (1978 [1848]) praise in the *Communist Manifesto*, stems from the fact that capitalists, who receive the surplus, have to use a big portion of it productively, thus contributing to productive and technological innovation (Marx 1977 [1867]: 739; Wright and Rogers 2011: 43; Bonaiuti 2012: 30–32). Such innovation represented for Marx (1977 [1867]: 739) the progressive moment of capitalist development, since it created "those material conditions of production which alone can form the real basis of a higher form of society … in which the full and free development of every individual forms the ruling principle."

As this work will show, however, capital does not use the surplus simply to promote productive development. On the contrary, capitalism's destructive use of the surplus is central to the human suffering and the escalating threat to the planet that result from capitalism's economic and ecological crises as well as from the hollowing out of democratic institutions. As we will see, the risks to humanity and the planet that result from capitalism's destructive uses of the surplus add to the urgency of replacing capitalism with a society that will allow both the democratic control of the surplus and its use to secure human well-being and the ecological integrity of the planet.

In any event, the existence of a surplus implies that producers within a society produce more than the output necessary to meet their subsistence requirements and reproduce their labor power. As Marx (1977 [1867]: 275) recognizes, however, that necessary output is not a biological but a social datum. "The number and extent of [the worker's] necessary requirements, as also the manner in which they are satisfied, are themselves products of history," and thus the product of social processes and struggles. Marx (1977 [1867]: 324–25) calls the amount of labor necessary to produce "the means of subsistence necessary for [the worker's] own preservation or continued reproduction" as necessary labor, and adds that part of the reason this labor merits the designation "necessary" is that this amount of labor is "necessary for the worker, because independent of the particular social form of his labour." The existence of a surplus means, however, that producers expend more labor than necessary to reproduce themselves and their labor power. This extra labor can be designated as surplus labor, and its product is the surplus. By the same logic, Ernest Mandel (1973: 8) uses the term "necessary product" to refer to the product of necessary labor.

Surplus production has up to now been carried out in class societies. Such societies divide the population in two main classes: the producers of the surplus; and the ruling class, which receives the surplus, thus living off the work of the producers. This arrangement involves class exploitation, insofar as it denies the producers control over part of the wealth they produce. The struggle that ensues between the exploited producers and the exploiting receivers of the surplus accounts for Marx and Engels' (1978 [1848]: 473) description of "[t]he history of all hitherto existing society [a]s the history of class struggles."

One of the ways exploitation is enforced in class societies is through the use of a coercive state apparatus. The existence of such an apparatus implies that the surplus receivers are not the only group that gets away with not contributing to production. A part of the population, including, for example, police officers, soldiers, and so on, makes a living not by contributing to production but by enforcing the rules of the class order within which production takes place. This also means, however, that receivers cannot use all of the surplus they extract from producers for their own consumption. They have to distribute at least a portion of it to the state personnel who enforce the rules of the class order from which the receivers benefit (Engels 1972 [1848]; Harman 2008: 22; Nolan and Lenski 1998: 151; Russell 2009: 46–47).

The reproduction of class societies has never depended exclusively on the club of the state, however. An exploiting class whose rule depends on fear alone is treading on thin ice. No police force or army would be large or powerful enough to overpower a society's entire class of producers, should the latter feel that they are unjustly exploited. Thus, the continued ability of the surplus receivers to exploit the producers has always also relied on ideologies, or sets of ideas that obscure and justify the existence of class exploitation, and social inequalities more generally. Religious ideas have often in the past served this function (Markoff 2014: 74; Losurdo 2011: 193; Keen 2001: 161; Held 1996: 38; Davis 1998: 59; Nolan and Lenski 1998: 157). In contemporary capitalist societies the most important ideologies justifying class exploitation are often more secular in nature: for example, neoclassical economics, with its portrayal of capitalism as an economic system that efficiently serves consumers' needs even as it ensures that "each [individual] gets his or her just deserts" (Wolff and Resnick 1987: 246); or the set of ideas associated with the "American dream," and its portrayal of capitalism as a system that rewards hard work and talent.

The existence of an armed state may intimidate producers and deter them from rebelling against the meager existence that their hard work affords them and the lavish way of life (by comparison) of the surplus receivers not contributing to production. But the existence of effective ideologies capable of justifying class exploitation in a way that is credible and compelling to producers will reduce the likelihood that producers, or a dangerously large number of them, will even feel that they have a reason to rebel.

But, just as the state depends on police, army and other personnel tasked with enforcing the rules of the prevailing class order, the dissemination of ideologies justifying class exploitation depends on ideological apparatuses peopled with religious officers, journalists, economists, and so on. And, just as in the case of the state, what makes it possible for these ideological institutions to perform their function is that they too receive a portion of the surplus.

One of the important contributions of Marx's analysis was to pierce through the ideological appearances of the capitalist economic system. This is a system that appears to be based on freedom, equality, and justice. Whereas, in previous class societies and systems, producers (for example, slaves or serfs) had limited control – if any – over their labor power, capitalism turns a worker's labor power into a commodity that he or she legally owns. This means that workers can dispose of their labor power as they see fit, deciding whether to sell it to a capitalist employer or not and, if so, which capitalist to sell it to. Although in past class societies slaves or serfs could not choose who they worked for, workers do have that choice. If they work for a particular employer, this is because they have freely chosen to do so. And, since employers are as free to choose their workers as workers are to choose their employer, it would appear that the capitalist–worker relationship is not exploitative but mutually beneficial. In view of all this, it is tempting to regard capitalism as "a very Eden of the innate rights of man," operating under the exclusive sway of "Freedom, Equality, Property and Bentham" (Marx 1977 [1867]: 280).

Marx pierced through this appearance by exposing the underside of the worker's freedom. As this freedom was accompanied by the worker's separation from the means of production, which were concentrated in the hands of capitalists, the worker cannot produce for herself the means of subsistence she needs to survive. These means of subsistence having become commodities, which the worker needs to purchase in the market, she can do so only if she can pay the requisite amount of money. Thus, the commodification of the means of subsistence in combination with the worker's separation from the means of production force her to seek the money she needs to survive by selling her labor power. Thus, her legal freedom notwithstanding, "the worker, whose sole source of livelihood is the sale of h[er] labour power, cannot leave the whole class of purchasers, that is, the capitalist class, without renouncing h[er] existence. [S]he belongs not to this or that capitalist but to the *capitalist class*" (Marx 1978c [1849]: 205, emphasis in original).

Moreover, as Marx (1978c [1849]: 205) also points out, it is the capitalist's pursuit of profit that determines whether to hire or discharge a given worker. This means that, although a capitalist buying a worker's labor power has to pay the wage socially deemed necessary for the reproduction of the worker's labor power, she has an incentive to extract as much labor from the worker as possible. In other words, the capitalist seeks – and, because of capitalist competition, indeed must seek – to make the worker produce during her workday more wealth than the necessary product that corresponds to the wage the worker receives. Thus, the pursuit of capitalist profit forces the worker to produce a surplus, which stays with her capitalist employer. In short, exploitation is the price a worker has to pay in a capitalist society, if she is to stay alive.

The need for a more inclusive conception of the surplus

Marx's important contribution to our understanding of surplus production and exploitation within capitalist societies is not without its weaknesses. In particular, Marx's analysis does not pay sufficient attention to the dependence, emphasized by feminist scholars, of the reproduction of labor power on work within households (Federici 2012: 96; Folbre 2009: 125–26, 130; Folbre 2008: 14; Fox 1980: 13–14; Blumenfeld and Mann 1980: 285). In *Capital*, for example, Marx's (1977 [1867]: 274–76) analysis of the reproduction of labor power makes reference only to subsistence goods that the worker purchases in the market. This reproduction depends as much on the work of cooking the steak the worker buys in the store, however, as it does on the work of raising cattle for their meat. Both types of work produce wealth and are, irrespective of class relations, necessary if the producers are to support themselves. Thus, both types of work deserve to be recognized as part of the necessary labor, just as their respective outputs deserve to be recognized as part of the necessary product. In other words, our concepts of necessary labor and necessary product have to take into account the fact that "the reproduction of labor power involves a far broader range of activities than the consumption of commodities, since food must be prepared, clothes have to be washed, bodies have to be stroked and cared for" (Federici 2012: 96).

A similar argument applies to many of the activities of the public sector. As Marx (1977 [1867]: 275–76) himself recognizes, "[i]n order to modify the general nature of the human organism in such a way that it acquires skill and dexterity in a given branch of industry, and becomes labour-power of a developed and specific kind, a special education or training is needed." The important role of education in the (re)production of labor power has, moreover, increased over the course of capitalist development, since "[t]he permanent revolutionization of the productive forces that characterizes the capitalist mode of production necessitates the continuous revolutionization of its living productive force, labour power, above and beyond its household maintenance" (Seccombe 1980: 237–38). Thus, from the point of view of this work, the work of a public school teacher or a public college professor forms part of necessary labor no less than the work of the farmer raising cattle or the household member cooking a steak at home. The same applies for all the other public sector activities that contribute to the reproduction of labor power through the provision of health care services, the building of infrastructures, and so on.

This suggests a need to enlarge our view of wealth and surplus production by recognizing sites of wealth and surplus production other than the capitalist workplace. Thus, for this work, surplus is the difference between the total wealth produced in the various (private capitalist, public, household) sectors of the economy and the product necessary to reproduce the producers' labor power. Expressed in a simple formula,

$$S = W(cw, h, st) - np(cw, h, st)$$

where s stands for the surplus product, w stands for wealth, np refers to the necessary product, and the parentheses highlight the fact that both the total wealth produced and the product necessary to reproduce workers' labor power are made up of goods and services produced not just in the capitalist workplace (cw) but also in the household (h) and the public sector (st).

Adopting a more inclusive view of wealth and surplus production in contemporary capitalist societies is important for two reasons. To begin with, United Nations Development Programme estimates that, "if unpaid activities were valued at prevailing wages, they would amount to … about 70 percent of total world output" demonstrate that the magnitudes of wealth produced in the non-capitalist sectors of the economy are far from negligible. These magnitudes are becoming increasingly visible thanks to feminist scholars' long-standing critiques of sexist and money-centered measures of economic activity (Benería 2011: 114; MacDonald 2003: 26; Bennholdt-Thomsen 2001: 218). Indeed, studies attempting to measure the value of wealth produced in households have become increasingly common and mainstream. Although feminist economist Nancy Folbre (2008: 127) has made the case that "these estimates significantly undervalue family work," even the value these studies assign the output produced within households does not lag far behind the more conventional gross domestic product (GDP) measure (Yeginsu 2018; Benería 2011: 119; Folbre 2008: 60).

The same is true for the amount of labor expended within households, with

> [a] nationally representative sample of time-budget diaries for US residents show[ing] that in 2003, individuals fifteen years or older spent about the same amount of time in nonmarket work (household activities, purchasing goods and services, caring for and helping household and nonhousehold members, and educational activities) as they did in market work—about four hours a day on average for each.
>
> (Folbre 2008: 14)

And, although the amount of labor expended within the public sector of the economy is significantly lower, both the size of the public sector and its role in the reproduction of labor power have increased significantly over time (Bowles, Edwards, and Roosevelt 2005: 132, 506–13; Briskin 1980: 168).

But, magnitudes aside, there is another, arguably more important, reason to adopt a more inclusive view of wealth and surplus generation within the economy. This has to do with the divisive effects that the existence of distinct sites of wealth and surplus production has on producers. Marx and Engels recognized labor market competition as a structural feature of the capitalist economy that contributes to divisions between workers, while progressive economists and scholars after them have described how this labor market competition has often in the past fueled sexism and racism among male white workers, making the latter complicit to practices of racial and gender discrimination (Marx and Engels 1971 [1846]: 79; Marx and Engels 1978 [1848]: 480–81, note 1; Amott and Matthaei 1991). These discussions of the links between labor market competition, on one side, and the persistence of racial and gender divisions within the working class may help to explain why the *Communist Manifesto's* optimism regarding the tendency of long-term capitalist development to unify the workers has yet to be vindicated. As the discussion that follows will suggest, an analysis of the interactions between the different sites of wealth and surplus production can enrich our understanding of capitalism's divisive effects on producers even further.

This is an important advantage of our inclusive analysis of wealth and surplus production. After all, one of the tasks of this book is not just to add to our understanding of the contradictions underlying contemporary capitalist development but to help explain capitalism's divisive effects over the producers. As we will see, these divisive effects help to explain why, despite capitalism's escalating destructiveness, producers and ordinary citizens the world over have found it so difficult to converge into an anti-capitalist coalition capable of averting the dystopian future that, unless challenged, capitalism has in store for us.

Mapping the interaction of capitalism's distinct sites of wealth and surplus production: the case of neoliberal restructuring and austerity

Accordingly, the brief overview of neoliberal restructuring and the waves of austerity this restructuring has periodically generated is not intended as an exhaustive account of the neoliberal phenomenon.[1] Rather, it seeks to illustrate both how the interaction between capitalist society's distinct sites of wealth and surplus generation influences this society's trajectory and the contribution to the divisions between producers that this interaction also makes.

Among the widely recognized effects of neoliberalism is its increase of economic inequality (Markoff 2014: 170; Schaefer 2013: 180–84; Albo and Evans 2010: 291–92; Bagchi 2005: 302–3). Partly the product of economic policies, involving the deregulation of labor and financial markets as well as the adoption of free trade policies, growing inequality also reflects the increase in capital's bargaining power, which is itself the product of the greater mobility capital has enjoyed thanks to neoliberal policies (Mishel, Schmitt, and Shierholz 2014; Dullien, Herr, and Kellermann 2012: 59; Elson and Pierson 2011: 212–13, 223, note 2; Gunawardana 2011: 432). These policies, and the rise of neoliberalism more generally, were themselves the product of the exhaustion of the post-war model of development and the reduction in capitalist profits that had set in by the time the post-war boom gave place to economic crisis in the 1970s. This constellation of forces meant that wages even in high-income societies, such as the United States, stagnated, even as labor productivity continued to increase (albeit more slowly than during capitalism's post-war "golden age"). In view of all this, it is not surprising that, although, "[f]or the first three-quarters of the twentieth century, income inequality fell," with neoliberalism's "subsequent move towards freer markets ... [i]ncome inequality began to rise, first in Anglo-Saxon countries and later in almost all other countries" (Schaefer 2013: 180–81).

In terms of our formula, these developments signified a widening of the difference between w(cw) and np(cw), and therefore a tendency for the surplus [s(cw)] retained

by capitalists to increase. An additional neoliberal policy that has sought to restore cap
italist profitability is the lowering of taxes. The pattern of tax cuts in the neoliberal era
has tended to primarily benefit capitalist corporations and the most affluent segments
of the population. In the United States, for example, "the annual share of after-tax profit
as a proportion of total profits rose from 54–55 percent in the 1960s and 1970s to
two-thirds in the 1990s and 2000s" (Moody 2011: 222).

Nonetheless, the stagnation in working people's incomes increased the appeal of tax
cuts for many working-class people. Reporting on the United States, Johanna Brenner
(2002: 342–43) has, for example, traced "the beginning of a successful conservative
mobilization around the issue of taxation and spending" to the fact that "[d]uring the
1970s, while median and family income declined by 16 percent, taxes increased as a proportion of workers' income." In any event, the result of such tax cuts has been a chronic
state of austerity for the public sector in many capitalist countries. This austerity reached
new heights when, in the aftermath of the global financial crisis more than ten years ago,
ordinary people were presented with the bill for a crisis they had not caused.

Public sector austerity can take a number of different forms. It can involve pay cuts
for public sector workers, intensification of their work, or both (Miller 2015: 47; Lav
2014: 52–53; Pashkoff 2014: 59; Pollin 2013: 86). Pay cuts, or wage freezes that erode
the real value of public sector salaries, amount to a redefinition of the standard of living
socially deemed necessary to reproduce the labor power of such public sector workers
as teachers, doctors, nurses, and so on. If they are expected to provide the same amount
of services as before, public sector workers would continue to produce the same level of
wealth [w(st)], even as their shrinking salaries allow them to lay claim to a smaller portion
both of the wealth produced in capitalist workplaces and of any services produced in
the public sector that involve a charge. Thus, the surplus these public sector workers
produce has increased. Meanwhile, reduced taxes increase the portion of the total wealth
produced that stays with capital and individual taxpayers, especially the most affluent ones.

But public sector austerity can also take the form of layoffs and attrition, which lead
to understaffing and an intensification of the work the remaining public sector workers
have to perform. The austerity program imposed on Greece in the aftermath of the
eurozone crisis has even implemented a formal "one to five" rule, which dictates that
"for every … five people leaving [the public sector] one would be hired" (Zygoulis and
Zagou 2014). Even if public sector layoffs are not accompanied by salary cuts but salaries
remain the same (something certainly not true in the Greek case), the result is that the
same amount of services [w(st)] now has to be produced by fewer workers. As all the
public sector workers increase the w(st) they produce even as their salaries do not keep
up with their increased productivity, the result is similar to the previous scenario, with
public sector workers producing a higher surplus, which benefits corporate and individual (especially affluent) taxpayers. In this sense, Susan Pashkoff's (2014: 59) account of
British "public sector workers … working longer and harder, due to job cutbacks, for less
pay, and for a pension that is actually going to be worth less" has much wider relevance.

Thus, the effects of public sector austerity illustrate how an increase in the surplus public
sector workers produce can benefit not only capital but, to some extent, even ordinary
workers in the private sector. Thus, the fact that the private capitalist and public sectors of
the economy are distinct sites of wealth and surplus production creates the possibility of

a division between private and public sector workers. Both groups may find themselves under pressure to increase the amount of surplus they produce, and yet this common predicament will not necessarily bring them together but can, potentially, drive them apart. In our example, workers in the private capitalist sector may perceive the lower taxes that public sector austerity makes possible as a way of coping with the stagnant wages and intensified exploitation they face in the capitalist workplace. Increasing the likelihood of significant numbers of workers joining the pro-austerity coalition are concerted ideological campaigns seeking to demonize supposedly "greedy public employees exploiting their job security to get higher pay and benefits than hard-working taxpayers" (Weiner 2018: 3).

This demonization of public sector workers forms part of neoliberalism's vilification of the public sector more generally. This demonization facilitates the privatization of public assets, a mainstay of the neoliberal playbook and of the "structural adjustment programs" in the global South, but more recently even in countries of the global North, such as Greece (Khalil 2015: 80; Desai 2013: 207). Such privatization allows capital access to the surplus that the workers in the privatized companies produce. And, given the fact that the privatization of public assets often amounts to a fire sale in which these assets are sold for a pittance, what this means is that even much of the surplus wealth that public sector workers may have created in the past now passes over to capital (Jackson 2017: xxxvii; Elson 2011: 302).

But there is also a racial and gender dimension to neoliberal privatization. This is because the public sector's record in avoiding racial and gender discrimination is better than that of the private capitalist sector (Bowles, Edwards, and Roosevelt 2005: 336; King 2003: 229; Amott and Matthaei 1991: 187). What this means, of course, is that neoliberal privatization may actually worsen racial and gender discrimination, thus both aggravating the waste of human skills and talent that gender and racial discrimination entail and contradicting neoliberalism's claim to promote economic efficiency.

Now consider the effects of public sector austerity on households. If austerity leads to a reduction of the services the public sector provides to its citizens, this can increase the work burden of household members. Given, moreover, the fact that contemporary capitalist societies are still male-dominated, this additional burden is likely to be disproportionately borne by "low-income women, as these women produce caregiving services formerly provided by the public sector" (Elson 2017: 55). In terms of our formula, this would entail a shift of wealth production from the public sector to households; in other words, a decrease in w(st) that is accompanied by a corresponding increase in w(h). To the extent that this additional burden would fall on women, both the wealth and the surplus the latter would be producing would now increase. This would aggravate the time squeeze that women faced with a double day already face, thus undercutting their health and well-being (Gornick and Meyers 2005: 375).

But the burden that the double day inflicts on women is not only the product of public sector austerity. It is also partly the result of women's increased participation in the paid labor force. This growing participation is one of the ways that working-class households have attempted to cope with the stagnant wages and growing inequalities that neoliberal policies have produced (Ehrenreich and Hochschild 2011: 238; Fraad 2008: 25–26; Jacobs and Gerson 2004: 295–96). At the same time that their growing participation in the paid labor force increases the work burden that working-class women face, it also reduces their economic dependence on men, thus increasing their bargaining power within the household (Bergmann 2003: 105; Stacey 2002: 93–94; Amott and Matthaei 1991: 311). This is, after all, why one factor contributing to the increased participation of women in the paid labor force was the feminist movement's emphasis on "the need for women to increase their financial autonomy, bargaining power, and control over their lives" (Benería 2003: 319). Women's growing assumption of paid labor could potentially equalize the distribution of caring work within the household, if gender discrimination in the workplace did not mitigate the increase in bargaining power that women experience when joining the paid labor force (Folbre 2008: 83; Fraad 2008: 27; Amott and Matthaei 1991: 313). The fact that this asymmetry between men and women was not erased by women's mass entry into the paid labor force may help explain why the inequality between men's and women's contribution to housework has decreased somewhat but not disappeared (Gornick and Meyers 2005: 374).

This means that gender inequalities in the capitalist workplace and the household imply that public sector austerity will not affect men and women in the same way. If most of the burden of that austerity falls on the shoulder of women, it is not surprising that it is not they, but men, who would be more willing to be recruited to conservative, pro-austerity coalitions. Thus, the existence of distinct sites of wealth and surplus production can contribute to the division of producers in yet another way. This is no longer the case of producers in one sector of the economy being turned against producers in another. Rather, the existence of households as a distinct sector of wealth and surplus production means that some of the loss of services that public sector austerity entails can be made up by the increased work burden of women in the household sector of the economy. Thus, austerity policies can compound the division between private and public sector workers with that between male and female producers.

As the analysis above suggests, this latter division is fueled by the way neoliberalism's intensification of exploitation in the capitalist workplace reverberates in the public and household sectors of the economy. Stagnant wages in the context of rising productivity does not just increase the surplus produced within the capitalist workplace, which stays in the hands of capital. It has also triggered a set of processes that disproportionately burdens women. By making it increasingly difficult for families to survive on a single income, neoliberalism's intensification of capitalist exploitation adds to the services that women have to produce within the household those goods or services that they also have to produce within the capitalist workplace. As their total output in these two sectors goes up, so does the difference between this output and the portion of this output necessary to reproduce their own labor power. In joining the paid labor force, therefore, women have mitigated the effects that more intense capitalist exploitation has on their male partners' standard of living, while increasing both their own workload and the total amount of surplus they have to produce.

Partly counteracting this dynamic is the greater economic independence that results from women's entry in the paid labor force. This increased economic independence can enhance women's bargaining power within the household, but this welcome development is undercut by the persistence of gender discrimination and the segmentation of labor markets along gender (and racial) lines (Folbre 2009: 295; Acker 2003: 16–17; Stacey 2002: 94; Hartmann 1979: 229). The gender wage gap that these phenomena imply does not just mean that they have to generate more surplus in the capitalist workplace than male workers. The latter benefit from the fact that the lower wages and "superexploitation" that female workers encounter in the capitalist workplace render them more economically dependent on their male partners than they would otherwise be (Curtis 1980: 124). This helps to explain why many men have still not stepped up to do their fair share of housework, when their female partners join the paid labor force. Equally, it explains why it is also women who disproportionately bear the burden of the added housework that becomes necessary when neoliberal austerity cuts publicly provided child care, health care, and other social services. In other words, it is not possible to understand the distribution of the burden of exploitation among the producers within a capitalist society without paying attention to gender dynamics. In this respect, what Rosalind Petchesky (1979: 381) has said about periods of economic crisis is also true for the capitalist system more generally. When austerity forces women to "take up the slack" by "tak[ing] over the state's job" and its responsibility for social services, the extra housework women find themselves performing has the effect of "smoothing [capitalism's] rough edges … and making it humanly endurable," both for their male partners and all other members of the household receiving their services. In another way, of course, these gender inequalities may be counterproductive even from the point of view of male workers. In particular, in facilitating capital's long-standing cultivation of gender, racial, and other divisions between workers, such inequalities also make it harder for the entire working class to unite in a common struggle against the capitalist exploitation that (to a greater or lesser extent) affects them all (Panayotakis 2011a: 59; Bowles and Edwards 1993: 218–20; Hahnel 2002: 251–52).

Conclusion

This chapter has introduced a concept of the surplus that takes into account the wealth and surplus production taking place not just in the capitalist workplace but also in the public and household sectors of the economy. This more inclusive conception of the surplus enhances our understanding of the ways capitalism generates divisions between the producers who, through their work, allow human life to continue, even as they themselves struggle to make ends meet. In particular, this analysis shows that labor market competition is not the only structural feature of capitalist society that divides producers. At least as important is the existence of distinct sites of wealth and surplus production. This chapter has illustrated this finding through an overview of some of the links between neoliberal restructuring and austerity, on one side, and the generation of divisions among producers, on the other. Without pretending to offer an exhaustive account of the neoliberal phenomenon, this overview nonetheless initiates a process that will be taken up again later in this book. This is the task of explaining why, despite capitalism's increasingly destructive consequences, the formation of an effective anti-capitalist coalition has proved much more elusive than Marx and Engels (1978 [1848]) had foreseen.

Note

1 For useful overviews of neoliberalism, on which I draw in what follows, see Harvey 2005, Steger and Roy 2010, and Saad-Filho and Johnston 2005.

2

Surplus and freedom

Chapter I offered a more inclusive reformulation of the surplus, one that takes into account production not just in the capitalist workplace but also in households and the public sector. By contrast, this chapter pays more attention to the practical significance of this concept. It begins by examining the questions of justice that class exploitation raises and continues by addressing the relationship between surplus production and human freedom. Responding to the view of surplus as a society's "index of freedom," this chapter argues that only a classless, non-exploitative society can make use of the surplus at its disposal in a way consistent with human freedom. To do so, such a society would need to subject decisions regarding the size and use of the surplus to democratic deliberation. In making such democratic deliberation over the surplus central to the communist ideal, this chapter also begins a process of reconceptualizing communism that later chapters continue. Since democratic deliberation over the surplus – or over any other matter of public concern, for that matter – is inconceivable in the presence of racial and gender inequalities, however, this chapter also introduces a recurrent theme in this work, namely that abolishing class exploitation is not possible without also abolishing gender and racial oppression.

Class exploitation as a question of justice

The concepts of surplus and exploitation are important for a number of reasons. First of all, the presence of exploitation raises questions of justice (Wolff and Resnick 2012: 8–9; Hahnel 2002: 20–32; Roemer 1988: 52–71; Wolff and Resnick 1987: 9). Exploitation represents an expropriation not only of part of the wealth that results from the work of direct producers (Ollman 1998: 89) but also of their "time to live" (Ahrne 1988: 62). In other words, in addition to leaving workers with less wealth than they produced, exploitation also forces them to spend more time at work than necessary for the reproduction of their labor power. Both of these implications of exploitation stem from the fact that "[a] portion (often called the 'surplus') of the goods and services produced by some gets transferred to others even though they did not participate in producing any of those goods and services" (Wolff and Resnick 2012: 8).

It is not only the capitalist receivers of the surplus whose survival depends on the exploitation of surplus-producing workers, however. The same is true for those workers who do not directly contribute to the production of wealth and the surplus. Instead, these "unproductive" workers are paid to contribute to the reproduction of the dominant class order by enforcing the rules of producing, expropriating and distributing wealth, by providing ideological legitimization for the exploitation that these rules facilitate, or, more generally, by performing socially – as opposed to materially – necessary activities.

Designating these workers as unproductive does not, therefore, change the fact that their work is necessary for the survival and the reproduction of the existing class order. The point of this designation is to distinguish them from workers who directly add to the production of wealth and surplus. Whereas the latter produce both the wealth necessary to reproduce themselves as workers and a surplus that they do not keep, the former do not add to the surplus but, instead, receive a slice of it in exchange for facilitating the reproduction of the existing class order.

The questions of justice that exploitation raises are not always obvious when one compares the "productive" and "unproductive" segments of the working population. After all, many unproductive workers have to work hard and long for wages and salaries that are often no less meager than those of most productive workers. The injustice of exploitation becomes clearer when one compares the productive workers to the members of the exploiting class who receive the surplus and determine how to use it. The latter group's control of the surplus does not necessarily presuppose long hours of hard work, nor is it accompanied by incomes so meager as to hardly differentiate them from productive workers. The ability of surplus receivers to live in luxury without having to contribute to production highlights the fundamental injustice of class exploitation. This injustice also means that it is the exploiting class that mainly benefits from the existence and reproduction of any class society.

Productive workers, by contrast, do not benefit from an arrangement that exploits them by condemning them to perform more labor than is necessary to produce their means of subsistence. This judgement does not assume that all work is by definition a distasteful burden. As Marx (1973 [1861]: 611) has pointed out, work can be "the individual's self-realization, which in no way means that it becomes mere fun, mere amusement ... Really free working, e. g. composing, is at the same time precisely the most damned seriousness, the most intense exertion."

Nonetheless, even Marx differentiates between what he calls the "realm of necessity" and the "realm of freedom" in a future classless society. The former would be the realm of producing the material necessities of life. Everybody able to do so would contribute to such production, and this contribution would be a means to an external end, namely the production of material goods and services without which people's pursuit of activities for their own sake would be inconceivable. The realm of freedom, by contrast, would involve "the development of human powers as an end in itself" and would have "[t]he reduction of the work day [as its] basic prerequisite" (1981 [1894]: 959).

Marx's vision of a realm of necessity and a realm of freedom in a future classless society does not mean, of course, that this duality has not been operative in class societies up to now. In class societies, however, this duality does not assume the democratic form that Marx envisages. Indeed, whereas in Marx this duality assumes that all human beings would be active in both realms, in class societies the realities of exploitation for the most part exclude the majority of the population from the creative and fulfilling activities that characterize the realm of freedom (Cohen 2000: 204–5).

Instead of equal participants in the activities of the realm of freedom, the majority of the population primarily labors within the realm of necessity to produce the material goods and services necessary to support not just themselves but society as a whole. In other words, by forcing them to perform more than the labor necessary to reproduce themselves and their labor power, class exploitation inevitably prolongs the time that direct producers have to toil in the realm of necessity. Conversely, by relieving members of the exploiting classes from the need to produce their own means of subsistence, class exploitation also increases the amount of time they can spend in the realm of freedom as well as their ability to produce "high culture" and "[h]istorical works of art and thought" that represent "an expression of the highest human faculties" (Cohen 2000: 204–5).

Predictably, this class segregation of human activity can easily lead to ideological justifications of class inequality. If instrumental activity within the realm of necessity is primarily the domain of ordinary workers while the "higher," more fulfilling, activities that build "culture" are primarily the domain of the exploiting class, it is not hard to see how these two different groups of people might come to appear as two different kinds of people. In other words, this class segregation of human activity is likely to appear not as an injustice but as a manifestation of the natural superiority of the members of the exploiting class over those of the producing class. And this leap would be all the more difficult to resist in view of the fact that members of the exploiting classes have, in class societies, either monopolized thinking on such matters or, at the very least, controlled through "the material surplus which enables the human spirit to flower" (Cohen 2000: 205) the institutions in which such thinking takes place.

It is interesting, for example, how many experts and supporters of the capitalist order have in the past agonized over the problem of the "free time" that capitalism supposedly threatens us with (Keynes 1963 [1930]: 367–69; Rostow 1990: 91; Schor 1991: 4). Extrapolating from the reduction of the working day in the late nineteenth and early twentieth centuries, such thinkers have wondered whether ordinary people would find a way to occupy themselves once the working day had been reduced to a minimum. Apart from the fact that the rosy assumption regarding capitalism's ability to deliver permanent and steady progress in this respect has not materialized, the very question itself is instructive (Schor 1991; Basso 2003). What this question bears witness to is the conviction of many intellectuals that their ability to thrive in the realm of freedom makes them special and superior to common mortals, who supposedly would not know what to do with themselves if they no longer had to waste their life toiling in the realm of necessity.

It is also interesting to observe how warnings regarding the problem of boredom that will supposedly confront ordinary people once capitalism delivers us from scarcity have at times been accompanied by assumptions regarding the inevitability and permanence of a gendered division of housework. Thus, for example, W. W. Rostow (1990: 91) tempers his warnings about the potential "problem of boredom" with the reassuring note that, when this problem materializes sometime in the future, "we doubt that half the human race – that is to say, women – will recognize the reality of this problem; for the raising of children in a society where personal service is virtually gone is a quite ample human agenda, durable consumers' goods or no. The problem of boredom is a man's problem, at least until children have grown up."

A number of assumptions stand out in this statement. Beyond the most obvious of these, namely that raising children is women's work, another assumption, implicit in other theorists' warnings regarding the threat of a future filled with boredom, is that the only source of boredom one has to fear is the one that will supposedly result from not having to work as much. The actual (rather than hypothetical) drudgery and boredom that result from a capitalist labor process that, as Harry Braverman (1974) has described, often has the effect of deskilling workers are completely absent from such warnings.

Thus, on the one hand, this peculiar conceptualization of the problem of boredom consecrates the capitalist present as the only one capable of providing working people with interesting, meaningful lives. On the other, this way of thinking also seems to suggest that Marx's vision of a society using modern society's technological resources to drastically reduce the necessary amount of labor would, should it become a reality, inflict on people only the "curse" of boredom (Schor 1991: 4). Thankfully, as Herbert Marcuse (1969: 91) has pointed out, "there is an answer to the question … : what are the people in a free society going to do? The answer which … strikes at the heart of the matter was given by a young black girl. She said: for the first time in our life, we shall be free to think about what we are going to do."

Second, the indiscriminate treatment of all work as a cure to boredom leads Rostow to treat all the work that raising children involves as basically the same. Thus, changing diapers is as good for relieving boredom as talking to and playing with one's children. So, just as most intellectuals' lack of familiarity with ordinary people's work makes them overestimate the ability of such work to relieve boredom, so does Rostow's thinking of raising children as a woman's job prevent him from realizing that some of the tasks that raising children involves are better cures for boredom than others.

In fact, recognizing this difference can open the way to a rethinking of which kinds of activities belong to the realm of necessity and which belong to the realm of freedom. Marx himself may not have thought of housework and changing diapers when he thought of the kind of work that the realm of necessity of a future classless society would include. This work's rethinking of the surplus, however, certainly makes it possible and necessary to think of the realm of necessity in such broader terms. Combining the democratic spirit underlying Marx's vision with this broader conception of the realm of necessity then makes it possible to envisage what Rostow apparently cannot, namely an egalitarian division of housework, including those of its tasks that are not likely to protect those performing them from the scourge of boredom.

But Rostow's undifferentiated treatment of all housework as the same also obscures the extent to which some of the activities that the raising of children entails may be meaningful and enjoyable enough in their own right to help even the "bored" men of the future overcome their unfortunate predicament. In other words, we may need to broaden our conception of the activities that people would pursue in the "realm of freedom" no less than we need to broaden our conception of the activities that the "realm of necessity" in such a society would encompass. By foregrounding the importance of the household sector of the economy and the housework that takes place within it, this work makes it easier to avoid imagining the "realm of freedom" of a future classless society in gendered terms. In other words, this realm of freedom would not exclusively consist of activities in arenas such as science, art, literature, and so on, in which men have often in the past monopolized public acclaim. It would also include private activities, such as talking to one's children, teaching them and playing with them, which male-dominated societies have often defined as women's work.

This chapter has so far focused on the inequalities in material standards of living and free time that the extraction and expropriation of surplus from its producers imply. Although these inequalities, as we have seen, raise important questions of justice, so does the way class societies, in general, and capitalist societies, in particular, use this surplus. As we will see later in this book, the use of the surplus in capitalist society has important implications for the kind of culture we have, the quality of our democracy, and the integrity of the ecosystems on which our survival depends. In short, insofar as the use of the surplus shapes in many ways the future of the human species and the planet, the existence of exploitation means that people's influence over the world they live in and how this world develops crucially depends on their position within the current class order. And, insofar as it distributes this influence unequally, class exploitation raises questions of democracy and justice in yet another way.

Is the surplus an index of a society's freedom?

That the way a society organizes the production and use of the surplus has implications for justice should, at this point, be clear enough. Marxist theorists have sometimes also treated the economic surplus and its size as an index of a society's freedom and cap- acity to achieve its goals, however. Thus, for example, Richard Wolff and Stephen Resnick (1987: 148) have described the surplus as "the discretionary fund of the society," while Paul Baran and Paul Sweezy (1966: 9) have claimed that "[t]he size of the surplus is an index of … how much freedom a society has to accomplish whatever goals it may set for itself. The composition of the surplus shows how it uses that freedom."

In one sense this argument is plausible, since the surplus represents production over and above society's most indispensable material requirement, namely the cost of repro- ducing the direct producers' labor power (Wolff and Resnick 1987: 148). It is tempting to assume, then, that, after meeting this requirement, society is free to decide what to do with the remainder of the wealth that direct producers have generated. It is, in other words, tempting to see the use of the surplus as akin to a society's "realm of freedom" and the production of the indispensable material minimum a society needs as akin to its "realm of necessity."

Such an interpretation of the surplus would, in an important way, be misleading, however. Indeed, even the Marxist thinkers who have represented a society's surplus as an index of its freedom recognize that it is not society in the abstract – at least in the case of class societies – that receives and controls the surplus. It is the exploiting class that receives and controls the surplus, and even this class does not have a completely free hand when determining what to do with this surplus (Wolff and Resnick 1987: 149).

To be sure, its members are able, thanks to this surplus, to finance personal lifestyles much more luxurious than anything the average worker producing this surplus could ever dream of. Even this luxurious consumption by the members of the exploiting class represents only one (and often not the largest) portion of the surplus, however. In deciding how to use the rest of the surplus, the exploiting class and its members need to secure the conditions for the reproduction of the established class order (Wolff and Resnick 1987: 149). As the earlier discussion makes clear, for example, one portion of the surplus has to support unproductive workers who perform repressive, ideological, and other social functions that help to reproduce the current class order.

Moreover, capitalism differs from previous class societies insofar as the economic competition central to its operation magnifies the constraints over the surplus receivers' use of the surplus. It is important to understand, therefore, the nature of these constraints. The motivation behind capitalist production and exploitation is profit. This is, after all, why capitalist businesses hire labor power and other factors of production (Robbins 2005: 41–43). To turn the labor power and the means of production at their disposal into profit, capitalists have to ensure two things: that the commodities their employees produce will find willing buyers; and that the sale of these commodities will generate revenues higher than their cost of production. What makes this difference possible is, of course, the surplus their workers produce while working for them.

This does not mean, however, that the amount of surplus a capitalist receives is equal to that of his or her profits. One reason for the discrepancy is that part of what capitalists experience as "costs of production" and thus not as a part of profit are really payments that capitalists have to make out of the surplus they receive. This is the case, for example, for their interest payments on loans they have received from banks or for the salaries of managers and supervisors who facilitate the extraction from workers of as much labor as possible (Robbins 2005: 42). Being not materially necessary activities for the production of wealth but socially necessary ones, stemming from the social organization of production within capitalism, both the services provided by banks and those provided by supervisors do not produce new wealth but are financed out of the surplus.

Moreover, just as part of the surplus capitalists receive goes to support unproductive workers in the private sector (as well as the means of production these workers require), another part goes to support unproductive workers in the public sector, including those in the repressive state apparatus, workers in state-owned financial institutions, and so on. Although this means that a portion of "[c]apitalist surpluses [is] distributed to government in the form of taxes" (Wolff 2012: 148), it is also true, as Chapter 1 showed, that part of these taxes finances the wages and salaries of productive public sector workers who either build labor power or add to the production of wealth in other ways (for example, by building and maintaining public infrastructures). And, just as in the private capitalist sector the wages and salaries of that sector's unproductive workers (as well as the cost of the means of production they require) soak up part of the surplus while the wages and salaries of that sector's productive workers facilitate the further expansion of that surplus, so in the public sector the portion of the taxes paying for the wages, salaries, and means of production of unproductive workers soaks up part of the surplus, while the portion of the taxes paying productive workers facilitates the further expansion of the surplus produced within the economy.

But the necessity of taxes, of wages and salary payments to unproductive workers, and of interest payments is not the only constraint on capitalists' use of the surplus. After all, capitalist businesses have to compete for customers. One way they do so is through costly technological and product innovations. Such innovations give them an advantage over competitors by allowing them not only to develop new and more attractive products but also to reduce their costs of production. A reduction in the costs of production in turn makes it possible for innovating companies to reduce the prices they charge for their products, thus allowing them to undersell their competitors, gain market share, and increase their profits. The competitors, on the other hand, will see their market share and profits dwindle and could potentially find themselves making losses and having to go out of business (Wolff and Resnick 2012: 188–89; Wright and Rogers 2011: 43; Bowles, Edwards, and Roosevelt 2005: 148–52; Bowles and Edwards 1993: 289).

Thus, it is a matter of survival for capitalist businesses to keep up with or stay ahead of their competitors. Squeezing one's workers is one possible way of pursuing this goal, but at least as important is the reinvestment of a sizeable portion of the profits that capitalist businesses obtain. Only through such reinvestment can capitalist businesses pursue the research and development, modernization of plant and equipment, and growth of scale necessary to keep them competitive. If it is true, however, that the more they engage in such reinvestment, the more likely they are to increase their profits, it is also true that the more they increase their profits, the easier it will be for them to continue engaging in the costly reinvestment and innovation efforts that can keep their profits growing. In this sense, capitalist profits provide "not only the incentive … for individual capitalists to introduce change but also the means for implementing" the dizzying technological advances that continue to distinguish capitalism from previous class societies (Bowles, Edwards, and Roosevelt 2005: 152). All in all, it is this constant drive to reinvest large portions of their profits that explains why capitalists have historically played the revolutionary role that Marx and Engels (1978 [1848]) attribute to them in the *Communist Manifesto*.

In this sense, capitalist competition puts great pressure on capitalist businesses to maximize the surplus they extract from workers and to maximize the portion of that surplus that they reinvest. What results from this pressure is a systematic tendency towards capital accumulation. In fact, as Wolff and Resnick (2012: 188–89) have pointed out, capital accumulation facilitates the survival of the accumulating business while threatening the survival of its rivals. Faced with that threat, the latter can ill afford to fall behind in this race to accumulate. In this sense, capitalists are subject to the capitalist system's impersonal logic of compulsive accumulation no less than their workers (Wolff and Resnick 2012: 187). They function as "personification[s] of capital" (Marx 1981 [1894]: 1021), who have to subordinate their use of the surplus to the logic of capital accumulation.

Capitalism therefore illustrates the fact that there is no simple relationship between the surplus a given society generates and that society's freedom. Indeed, on the one hand, capitalism distinguishes itself from previous class societies by the unprecedented amounts of economic surplus that it makes possible (Cohen 2000: 198–99, 365). On the other hand, this dramatic increase in the production of economic surplus is not an index of capitalist society's freedom but, rather, reflects the logic of compulsive accumulation that imposes itself on capitalists and workers alike. It is because of this logic that capitalist businesses have no choice but to continue accumulating. And, as they do so, they increase the productivity of their workers, thus also increasing the surplus that the workers produce.

Surplus and historical progress

Marx himself does not see the size of a society's surplus as an index of its freedom. He does, however, in the *Grundrisse* turn capitalism's dramatic increase of this surplus into a narrative of historical progress. This is progress from a pre-capitalist past in which people's needs were a reflection of natural necessity, involving no more than the worker's "immediate requirements for keeping himself alive" (Marx 1973 [1861]: 324–25). By contrast to this past, Marx (1973 [1861]: 325) identifies capitalism's creation of "surplus labour, superfluous labour from the standpoint of mere use value, mere subsistence" as well as the embrace, even by workers, of this surplus labor as "[t]he great historic quality of capital." The workers' embrace of – and, indeed, need for – surplus labor is, according to Marx, partly the result of the development of individual needs under capitalism. But it also reflects the fact that "the severe discipline of capital, acting on succeeding generations ..., has developed general industriousness as the general property of the new species."

Thus, according to this passage, capitalism's dramatic increase of the surplus represents more than quantitative change. It has truly anthropological significance, and amounts to a creation by capitalist discipline of a new kind of human being. In fact, Marx (1973 [1861]: 325) continues that

> [c]apital's ceaseless striving towards the general form of wealth drives labour beyond the limits of its natural paltriness ... , and thus creates the material elements for the development of the rich individuality which is all-sided in its production as in its consumption, and whose labour also therefore appears no longer as labour, but as the full development of activity itself, in which natural necessity in its direct form has disappeared.

In other words, the vision of capitalism and its effects that emerges from this passage is one that downplays the continuity between capitalism and previous class societies, namely the fact that surplus labor pre-existed capitalism. But this passage also seems to accentuate the continuity between capitalism and a future communist society. It does so by suggesting that capitalism's compulsive logic of capital accumulation helps to create a new set of human needs that points towards the new, richer individuality that would characterize the classless communist society of the future. With this revolutionization of human nature on track, all it would take to complete this process would be for capitalism's "development of these productive forces [to encounter] its barrier in capital itself" (Marx 1973 [1861]: 325).

By exaggerating the continuity or downplaying the breaks between different historical periods, this passage posits a progressive and teleological history that culminates in a classless society capable of nurturing human beings with a rich individuality. In this picture the compulsive nature of the capitalist accumulation process that makes this culmination possible would represent a necessary, but ultimately subordinate, moment in a "protracted [historical] process of human liberation" (Cohen 1988: vii) from natural as well as social limits.

The point of discussing the passage from the *Grundrisse* is not to claim that it represents the one and definitive view that Marx had on this issue. After all, as Agnes Heller (1976: 22) has pointed out, grasping on to individual quotations makes it possible to attribute to Marx a number of different and mutually contradictory views. Since the rhetoric of capitalism or class society having a mission that helps to advance history towards its ultimate fruition is not uncommon among Marxists, however, it is important to point out that such a teleological interpretation of capitalism's compulsive economic dynamism is not the only possible one.

It is true that capitalism can, thanks to its peculiar structure, which makes its reproduction dependent on intense economic competition between the members of the exploiting class, bring about prodigious technological development, with corresponding increases in labor productivity. It is also true that a post-capitalist classless society could translate these advances into much shorter working days for everyone.[1] Should that possibility become a reality, the "realm of freedom" in such as a society would obviously grow at the expense of a "realm of necessity," which, as many scholars have pointed out, continues to occupy inordinate amounts of ordinary people's time even in our highly productive, highly technological capitalist society (Schor 1991; Basso 2003). This does not mean, however, that capitalism had to exist because of this beneficent potential that it has created. It is, rather, the case that, once, for whatever (causal rather than teleological) reason, a class society emerges that, like capitalism, makes the reproduction of the class order dependent on economic competition between the individual members of the exploiting class, this class society has the unintended effect of making it possible to envisage and pursue a classless society that builds on the accomplishments of its predecessor(s).

The realization of this possibility is not inevitable, however. If it is worth focusing on the passage from the *Grundrisse*, this is partly because there may be ways in which capitalism's use of the higher surplus it extracts from workers negates Marx's optimism. As we will see later in this book, for example, far from representing an unambiguous step in the process of creating a new human being with rich individuality, the multiplication of human needs that capitalism triggers also illustrates how capitalism's use of the surplus often undermines human well-being and the ecological integrity of our planet.

In this respect, far from preparing the new kind of human being that a classless communist society would make possible and call for, the multiplication of human needs by consumer capitalism may, in some respects, prove an obstacle to the realization of such an alternative society. This is especially the case in view of the possibility that any working-class revolution seeking to bring about such a society might require, at least in its early stages, significant sacrifices with respect to the material standard of living that significant segments of the working class, especially in the affluent global North, have enjoyed (Nove 1990: 230). As G. A. Cohen (2000: 244) points out, for example, "[i]f the price of socialist revolution in Britain today would be a substantial immediate reduction in the standard of living, that bears on how much power to overthrow capitalism the working class disposes of."

Some implications of a communist society's democratic control of the surplus

We have already indicated that a classless communist society has to ensure the democratic determination of the size of the surplus and of its disposal (Wolff and Resnick 2012: 29; Ticktin 1998: 73; Ollman 1998: 107; Callinicos 1991: 97–98). There are more than one ways of implementing this principle.

Richard Wolff (2010: 9), for example, has proposed a new strategy for the left that "is micro-focused in two parts. First, enterprise boards of directors must no longer be non-workers or elected by shareholders. Second, their functions—the appropriation and distribution of surpluses—must henceforth be performed instead by the workers collectively." Although Wolff's emphasis is on the democratic control over the surplus on the enterprise level, David Schweickart (1997: 63–64) has argued that it would be possible to supplement democracy on the enterprise level with political mechanisms that used enterprise taxation to pursue democratic control of investment on the macro level as well. One thing that Wolff's and Schweickart's conceptions of a post-capitalist future have in common is that they are compatible with the existence of markets. Other scholars have argued that the persistence of markets would vitiate any alternative to capitalism, proposing instead models of democratically planned economies, in which producers on a society-wide level would decide what to produce and how to distribute it.[2]

Implicit in the requirement that workers democratically control the size and use of the surplus is also the requirement that they also democratically decide on the specific institutional way to implement it. The reason for this is that the different modes of implementing democratic control over the surplus may require socially, rather than materially, necessary activities that do not directly add to the production of wealth but have to be financed through the surplus. For example, both a democratically planned economy and a market socialist economy that involved democratic controls over investment on the macro level might require the work of economists compiling different economically coherent options of allocating investment and economic resources. This work would then make it possible for either ordinary workers or their democratically elected representatives to vote between these different options.

This means a number of things. The choice over the way to implement democratic control over the surplus is not completely independent from the decisions a society would make over that surplus. As we just saw, if the way of implementation involved the necessity of socially, rather than materially, necessary activities, this would mean that the society in question would have to produce at least the amount of surplus necessary to support these activities. It would be up to the members of that society to decide whether to increase the surplus beyond that level and how to use that extra surplus produced.[3]

Making the democratic control of the surplus a defining characteristic of a classless society means that such a society would also have to combat any obstacles to such democratic control. In view of "the powerful influence of status inequality on people's sense of self-respect, on their autonomy, and on their ability to freely participate in deliberations about the public good" (Satz 1996: 85), it is clear that both racial and gender inequality would prevent people from having equal voice on deliberations regarding the size and use of the surplus. In addition, however, the democracy-based definition of a classless communist society also requires combating the "second shift" phenomenon (Hochschild 1989; Wright and Rogers 2011: 316; Dugger and Peach 2009: 143; Gornick and Meyers 2005: 375; Resnick and Wolff 2002: 320; Mies 1986: 192). This is not only because a gendered division of household labor undercuts women's participation in politics, in general (Ginsborg 2008: 99), and in the political processes that, in a classless society, would determine the size and use of the surplus. It is also the case because, since households are themselves sites of production, the continuation of the second shift would in effect force women (in heterosexual households) to spend more of their time producing wealth and surplus than their male partners. If one reason for the superiority of a classless society over capitalism and the class societies that have preceded it is its challenge to the confinement of part of humanity primarily in the realm of necessity while another part can, without any distractions, enjoy the realm of freedom, it is clear that a classless society has to do away with the second shift.

One way to combat the second shift phenomenon would be by increasing the provision of public services that reduce the necessary amount of housework.[4] The fact that such a decision would entail significant costs underlines the importance of making women's equal participation in public affairs a top priority from very early on. Not doing this could trigger a vicious cycle. Indeed, complacent tolerance of the domination of public affairs by men could preclude policies that increased women's political participation, thus perpetuating men's domination of politics into the future. This is more than a hypothetical concern, in view of the contribution of gender inequalities to the eventual failure of the Russian Revolution. As Resnick and Wolff (2002: 183–202) have shown, in its early stages the Russian Revolution did contain utopian impulses and experiments vis-à-vis the provision of services that impinged on housework and gender relations. The eventual abandonment of such experiments, as well as the restoration of patriarchal family patterns, contributed both to the revolution's failure to create a genuinely classless society, however, and to the Soviet system's eventual collapse.

Thus, defining communism in terms of this work's alternative conception of surplus makes racial and gender equality as central to the definition of communism as the absence of classes. In fact, this work's insistence on the importance of sites of surplus production outside the private capitalist economy enriches our understanding of class by underlining the extent to which the multiplicity of sites of surplus production also multiplies the different segments of the working class. It also shows the possibility of contradictions between the interests of these different segments and recognizes sexism and racism as two of the possible sources of such contradictions.

In this respect, this redefinition of communism becomes as much an affirmation of democracy against past undemocratic practices on the part of segments of working people as it is an affirmation of the interests of working people as against those of capitalists. This is an important point, of course, in view of the long history of complicity, by the European and North American working classes and their political and labor union representatives, in racism, sexism, colonialism, and the "exclusion of the unskilled immigrant workers from the trade unions and … the radical movement" (Aronowitz 1992: 151). And this point becomes even more important as the working class across the capitalist world is becoming more and more diverse, thus making working-class unity an elusive goal as long as these undemocratic legacies of the past persist (Schmitt and Warner 2010; Panitch 2000: 369; Sassoon 1996: 658, 669).

In this sense, this redefinition of communism also addresses the understandable suspicion by the feminist and other new social movements of the tendency of left-wing and revolutionary movements in the past to subordinate the struggle against gender, racial, and other forms of social oppression to labor's struggle against capital (Sassoon 1996: 688–89; Cohen 1985: 668). Both this tendency and the discovery by female social justice activists in the past that "their 'revolutionary brothers,' so sensitive to the needs of the exploited of the world, would blatantly ignore their concerns" (Federici 2012: 62) contributed to women's recognition that fighting for gender equality was no less important than other social justice struggles (Federici 2012: 62). The redefinition of communism in terms of people's democratic control of and deliberation over the surplus breaks with any past tendencies to prioritize workers' struggle against capitalists over the struggles against gender, racial, and other forms of social oppression. It does so by virtue of its break from other definitions of communism, which have been influential in the past, notably the definition of communism in terms of property relations (whereby communism is equated to the abolition of private property) or in terms of mechanisms of economic coordination (whereby communism is understood as organizing economic life through central planning rather than through the market). Such definitions make it easier to separate struggles against gender, racial, and other forms of social oppression from that against exploitation, treating the former as a subordinate moment within the revolutionary movement's primary goal of abolishing private property and/or doing away with a market-based economic system. In particular, given capital's long-standing history of reproducing gender and racial inequalities as a means of dividing workers, such definitions lend themselves to the privileging of the goal of abolishing capitalist private property and/or markets and to viewing the pursuit of that goal as prior to that of challenging gender and racial oppression.

Defining communism in terms of a democratic control of and deliberation over the socially produced surplus makes any impediment to democracy an impediment to communism. Thus, this definition envisions a society that is not just classless but is also devoid of gender, racial, and all other forms of social oppression that are incompatible with democracy. It is, therefore, consistent with the socialist feminist insight that the success of "future attempt[s] at creating human liberation" crucially depends on "an integrated revolutionary struggle against class and sex oppression at the inception of revolution" (Eisenstein 1979: 268). Moreover, the redefinition of communism in terms of democracy, rather than in terms of property relations or the replacement of a market-based economy by central planning, not only makes it less likely that post-revolutionary societies in the future will merely duplicate previous "socialist' revolutions" failure to do away with gender inequality; it also reduces the risk of future post-revolutionary societies repeating the experience of the Russian Revolution, which, as we will see, ended up instituting an undemocratic regime that used its nationalization of productive assets and the introduction of central planning as ideological covers for a reconstitution of class exploitation by a ruling political and technocratic elite that appropriated and controlled the surplus produced by ordinary workers.

Surplus and freedom in a communist society

Insofar as it overcame all obstacles, including racial and gender inequalities, to the democratic determination of the size and use of the surplus, a classless society would establish a relationship between surplus and freedom different from the one Baran and Sweezy attribute to society, in general. In particular, although we questioned whether Baran and Sweezy's association between surplus and freedom held in the case of class societies, in general, and capitalism, in particular, the case is different when thinking of a future democratic classless society.

One of the problems with Baran and Sweezy's formulation is its reference to society setting goals for itself. In the absence of democratic deliberation over what these goals are, this formulation is meaningless. In particular, in class societies this formulation is problematic for two reasons: first, because surplus receivers use the surplus to reproduce the conditions of their rule, irrespective of the goals that a democratic deliberative process might have come up with. Second, in capitalism the process of exploitation takes place through an impersonal dynamic of capital accumulation that imposes itself on surplus producers and receivers alike.

In a classless society in which people democratically determined the use of the surplus, by contrast, the idea of society determining its goals would be meaningful. Even in such a society, however, it would not be the size of the surplus that would determine "how much freedom … society ha[d] to accomplish [its] goals" (Baran and Sweezy 1966: 9). On the contrary, the size of the surplus itself would be an expression of that society's freedom to democratically determine that size in the first place. To make that determination, people would select between potentially competing priorities, such as the pursuit of higher material standards of living, more free time to pursue activities in the realm of freedom, the preservation of the ecological integrity of the planet, and so on.

This point has grown in importance since Baran and Sweezy published *Monopoly Capital* more than 50 years ago. Indeed, turning surplus into an index of a society's freedom to accomplish its goals can lead to the misleading conclusion that a higher level of surplus is always preferable. Such a conclusion might seem plausible, if one valued a growing surplus as the means to an acceleration of material consumption. This assumption seems to be lurking in the passage from the *Grundrisse* discussed above and seems to also inform Marx's celebration of the development on the part of workers of a need for surplus labor as such. But such an assumption seems inappropriate, especially at a time when escalating material consumption is contributing to a deepening ecological crisis, which threatens the future of the human species and the planet alike (Kasser 2002: 95; Guha 1994: 288; Durning 1992: 21).

Once again, however, it is worth bearing in mind that this assumption does not necessarily represent Marx's final word on this issue. As some theorists point out (Tanuro 2010: 284), it is possible to interpret Marx's emphasis on the free time that a classless society would make possible as a corrective to consumerism's focus not on "the qualitative development of human beings … [but on] the quantitative growth of things" (Tanuro 2010: 284). Similarly, one can interpret Marx's distinction between a realm of necessity and a realm of freedom as suggesting that material production is only a means that, in a classless communist society, would allow people to focus their time and energy on creative and intrinsically meaningful activities pursued for their own sake. In so doing, such a distinction suggests the possibility of disengaging progress from never-ending increases in material standards of living and of defining freedom not in terms of never-ending increases in material consumption but in terms of having ample time for free, creative, and meaningful activity.

Marx's ambiguity on this issue notwithstanding, questioning the link between the existence and size of surplus within a society and the degrees of freedom available to this society is also important in view of the role that this assumption played in the attempt by the Soviet Union and its satellite states to implement Marx's ideas. Making economic growth and a convergence with Western capitalist consumption standards as one of their overriding goals and standards of success, these regimes ended up imploding when they proved unable to deliver on this promise (Resnick and Wolff 2002: 303; O'Connor 1998: 258; Altvater 1993: 17; Szelényi, Beckett, and King 1994: 247). And, although the socio-economic system such regimes instituted managed for a time to generate surpluses, which were ample enough to turn the Soviet Union into a major industrial power as well as a military and political superpower that played a crucial part in defeating Nazi Germany, the absence of democratic determination of the size and use of these surpluses ended up undermining their sustainability. The ultimate result, as Resnick and Wolff (2002: 310) show, was that

> [t]he Soviet state could neither appropriate enough surplus … nor find other revenues sufficient to secure its own survival even to the end of the 1980s. It was increasingly unable simultaneously to finance industrial expansion, military preparedness, global superpower status, and a rising standard of living for its masses. A population increasingly able and determined to compare the Soviet state's troubles with Western private capitalism's economic boom and political and cultural openness became ever more disaffected as citizens and unproductive as workers. The state and the Party collapsed.

In other words, one (of the many) lessons that future attempts to go beyond capitalism have to draw from the experience of these regimes is this: not only is the democratic determination of the size and use of the surplus a better index of freedom than the size of the surplus; such democratic determination may in fact be necessary to secure the sustainability of whatever surpluses a post-capitalist social order would need to survive.

By contrast to the qualitative sense in which the surplus could serve as an index of a democratic classless society's freedom, in capitalism the geometrical growth of the surplus is not a sign of freedom but, on the contrary, of the compulsive logic of capital accumulation imposing itself even on capitalists. On the other hand, it is true, for capitalism as well as for other class societies, including the Soviet Union and the societies that followed its model, that a higher surplus does make it easier for exploiting classes to meet the conditions for their continued class rule. Thus, with respect to the relationship between surplus and freedom in class societies, the amount of surplus these societies are able to generate is at most an index of the freedom of the exploiting class to perpetuate its exploitation over the direct producers.

Conclusion

This chapter has discussed both the questions of justice that class exploitation raises and the way that the existence of a surplus may or may not enhance human freedom within a given society. It argues that the existence and use of a surplus will be conducive to human freedom only in a society that has abolished class exploitation by subjecting decisions over the size and use of the surplus to democratic deliberation. Identifying such democratic deliberation over the surplus as the essence of the communist ideal, this chapter not only underlines how integral the end of racial and gender inequality is to the realization of this ideal; it also lays the ground for the further discussion, in later chapters of this work, of the relationship between communism and democracy.

Notes

1 Illustrating the rapid productivity increases that capitalism has made possible, Bowles and Edwards (1993: 8) point out that "it took 1430 times as long to spin yarn in 1750 as it does today." As to the ability of a post-capitalist society to translate higher productivity into less work and more free time, Michael Albert (2003: 243) has calculated that, in view of the productivity increases over the last 40 years, "the workweek could [have] go[ne] from 40 hours to about 13, … with no loss in fulfillment or in output earmarked to engender socially beneficial progress."

2 For an example of this approach, see Albert (2003).

3 For the reader interested in this issue, I have discussed the debate between market socialist and democratic planning models in Panayotakis (2011a: chap. 8).

4 To be sure, increasing the provision of public services as a means of reducing the necessary amount of housework would not be a substitute for an equalization of the housework that men and women perform. On the contrary, it might actually help to accelerate the changes in the household division of labor that would bring this equalization about.

3

Capital's real subsumption of consumption

Having examined the relationship between surplus and freedom, I now turn to capitalism's use of the surplus it extracts from producers. All class societies use the surplus to reproduce their conditions of existence (as would a democratic classless society). The specific use of the surplus varies with the specific characteristics of different societies, however. In the case of capitalism, both the way of extracting the surplus and the use of this surplus to reproduce that class order leads to a number of serious problems for humanity and the planet that add to the urgency of replacing it with an alternative classless society. These problems have over time added to the case against capitalism.

In early Marxist approaches, this case focused on economic crises and on capitalism's inability to use modern technology to reduce human suffering and to promote the development of all human beings. As the recent global economic crisis reminds us, these early Marxist concerns are as relevant as ever.

Nevertheless, capitalism's historical trajectory makes it clear that that system's reproduction represents more than a lost opportunity to live a better life in a better society. It also adversely impacts our culture and the ecological integrity of our planet, while also undermining such basic values as democracy and peace. This chapter begins to explore the connection of these problems to the way capitalism pursues and uses the surplus it extracts from direct producers. In particular, it focuses on capitalism's use of the surplus to build up a consumerist culture that undermines human well-being and fuels a deepening ecological crisis.

From capitalism's "golden age" to neoliberalism: the ups and downs of popular consumption

The rosy picture regarding capitalism's multiplication of human needs in the passage from Marx's *Grundrisse* I discussed earlier is to some extent consistent with capitalism's historic ability to raise the material standard of living of significant segments of the working class, especially in the affluent global North. For centuries its supporters have used such improvements to justify capitalism (Smith 1909 [1776]: 18; Friedman and Friedman 1981: 129–30, 138; Hayek 1944: 16–17). Capitalism, they argue, has made it possible for ordinary workers to enjoy a material standard of living that "was previously the exclusive prerogative of the rich and powerful" (Friedman and Friedman 1981: 13) and that might indeed surpass that of mighty pre-capitalist rulers and "many an African king, the absolute master of the lives and liberties of ten thousand naked savages" (Smith 1909 [1776]: 18).

This argument was especially plausible in the period after World War II. During this "golden age of capitalism" the economy grew rapidly and its fruits were distributed relatively widely, especially in the most industrialized countries of the capitalist world (Marglin and Schor 1990; Domhoff 2017; Thompson 2011: 138; Steger and Roy 2010: 7; Harvey 2005: 9–12). One of the pillars of this economic success was the rise of mass consumption among large segments of the working class.

To be sure, even in the United States, where mass consumption developed the most, entire population groups, including those subject to structural racism and sexism, "f[e]ll through the cracks with little to no access to adequate wages and stable jobs" (Van Arsdale 2013: 94). Nonetheless, consumption by many ordinary people grew, thanks to intense class struggles that eventually won workers important collective bargaining rights (Brenner 2016: 11–12; Gude 2016: 64; Mishra 1996: 326). As labor unions' strength grew, growing labor productivity was matched by rising wages.

These developments enhanced post-war capitalism's stability. On the one hand, if the capitalist class ended up, at least for a time, recognizing labor unions as representatives of the workers' interests, this was because it expected that, in exchange for higher wages, unions would contain rank-and-file militancy and the risks it posed for capital's control of production (Friedman 2008: xvii, 157).

From a macroeconomic point of view, moreover, rising wages and mass consumption bolstered the demand for the mass-produced commodities of capitalist corporations (Boyer and Drache 1996: 18; Steger and Roy 2010: 7; Aglietta 1987: 117). In so doing, regular wage increases also encouraged investment, which boosted employment and demand even further, thus giving rise to a virtuous circle.

Representing the golden age of the American middle class, this period led in the United States, the leading example at the time of a mass consumption society, to the redefinition of class in terms of consumption (Lichtenstein 2012: 11). This redefinition obscured the fundamental dichotomy between exploiters and exploited, while suggesting that workers' material gains were a sign of capitalism becoming humane and conducive to upward mobility and constant social progress (Thompson 2011: 126–27; Sassoon 1996: 210). Projecting this optimistic narrative onto the international stage, modernization discourses pointed to rich capitalist mass consumption societies, such as the United States, as the future of all newly independent Third World countries willing to copy those societies' institutions (Rostow 1990).

These optimistic narratives, in the rich capitalist world and internationally, and the concessions to the popular masses accompanying them (the welfare state, international aid, and so on) sought to exorcize the specter of communism and the Russian Revolution. The existence of an alternative socio-economic model that might lead working people in the capitalist world to expropriate the capitalist class from its wealth "ensured that … 'full employment' and welfarist policies … had to be tolerated (Desai 2013: 53).

This golden age did not last very long, as the international capitalist crisis of the 1970s signaled its exhaustion. The crisis gave rise to intense class struggles that shook the faith of the capitalist class in the ability of labor unions and center-left social democratic and labor parties to contain working-class militancy (Friedman 2008: 137, 152). This, along with capital's growing mobility, prompted capitalists to initiate a "class war" against working people and the post-war social and economic model (Albo and Evans 2010: 291; Streeck 2013: 270–71). The result was a systematic dismantling of social gains and protections (Sitrin and Azzellini 2014: 46; Thompson 2011: 190; Yates 2009: 20) as "capitalists and the state redefined the concessions earlier granted workers from being measures of progress under capitalism, to now being problems in need of correction: high wages were uncompetitive; workplace rights undermined productivity; and worker security was a hindrance to enforcing discipline and carrying out economic restructuring" (Gindin 2012: 17).

Moreover, the collapse of Soviet Union and its satellite regimes removed the need for capitalist concessions to the working class, thus fueling the neoliberal counter-revolution that has rolled back the gains that last century's working-class struggles had won (Thompson 2011: 247). As a result, economic inequality grew to "a point … close to that which preceded the crash of 1929" (Harvey 2005: 188). By undercutting ordinary people's purchasing power and thus the demand for the commodities of cap-italist corporations, this development paved the road to a global economic crisis (Kotz 2008: 14; Albo and Evans 2010: 288). The fact that the financial crisis of 2008 was a manifestation of a housing crisis in the United States is itself highly significant (Badiou 2010a: 98). Since homeownership has long been central to the American dream, serving as a marker of middle-class membership, the bursting of the housing bubble highlights the extent to which capitalism is eroding its own ideological supports.

Given the heightened economic insecurity and great economic inequalities generated by the neoliberal model, it is not uncommon for progressive commentators and the labor movement to wax nostalgic about capitalism's post-war golden age (Panayotakis 2014b; Levine 2015; Hacker 2019). After all, this was also social democracy's golden age, since many of the social policies advocated and/or pioneered by social democrats and left liberals in Europe and elsewhere had become part of a political consensus, which was not challenged even by center-right governments (Sassoon 1996: 322, 675; Held 1996: 234; De Jong 2013: 22). The growing influence of Keynesianism, in particular, provided social democrats with an ideological toolkit more appropriate to the task of managing capitalism than the Marxist ideas prevalent during the Second International (Przeworski 1985: 35–37). Indeed, Keynesianism allowed social democrats to argue that a progressive management of capitalism, based on government spending, a wel-fare state, and redistributive full employment policies, could actually improve capitalism's performance while avoiding the kind of severe economic crises, with all the attendant social turmoil, political instability, and human suffering, that had characterized the Great Depression. In this sense, "Keynesianism was not only a theory that justified socialist par-ticipation in government but, even more fortuitously from the social democratic point of view, it was a theory that suddenly granted a universalistic status to the interests of workers" (Przeworski 1985: 36–37).

Thus, the post-war golden age seemed to vindicate the contention that Marx had both overestimated the polarization and misery that capitalism would generate and underestimated the potential for reforming and humanizing that system (Schorske 1955: 17; Nolan and Lenski 1998: 372). This critique was accompanied by the assumption that gains from social democratic reforms would be cumulative and irreversible (Przeworski 1985: 40). The passing of the post-war golden age and its replacement by the much harsher neoliberal model has proved that, despite its function as an ideological cover for social democracy's transformation into a pillar of capitalist society, this view vastly overestimates the ability of political democracy to tame capitalism.

In this sense, although some scholars view the collapse of the Soviet Union and its satellite states as definitive proof of the bankruptcy of Marx's ideas (Nolan and Lenski 1998: 372), the replacement of Keynesian welfare capitalism by the neoliberal model suggests that it may have been Marx, and not reformist social democrats, who had a more realistic view of what is and is not possible under the rule of capital. As we will see later in this book, the outcome of the Cold War did not vindicate the super-iority of capitalism over the vision of a democratic classless society. Instead, the Cold War represented a competition of two different types of class society, in which one of them, capitalism, proved more dynamic and resilient. In fact, as noted above, the political pressure that the Cold War exerted on capitalist classes helps to explain the latter's willingness to tolerate a more humanized model of capitalism as long as they did. Thus, to the extent that, as we will see, capitalism's inhumanity and destructiveness are resur-gent as a result of its undemocratic use of the surplus it extracts from producers, the solution to our current predicament is not a return to capitalism's short-lived golden age. The only lasting solution is a more fundamental transformation, which would lead to a classless society based on people's democratic control of the surplus they produce.

Capitalism's real subsumption of consumption

In any event, the contrast I have drawn between capitalism's "golden age" and our crisis-ridden neoliberal present does not mean that in the former period all was well with capitalist patterns of consumption. The claims of neoclassical economics notwithstanding, capitalism's *modus operandi* is not the efficient satisfaction of pre-existing human needs. Instead, with the help of "more and more sophisticated attempts to awaken wants and to direct preferences" so as to remove them "from the hold of convention and local tradition," capitalism has in effect sought to remake human needs in its own image (McCracken 1988: 18).

And, contrary to Marx's analysis in the *Grundrisse*, this remaking of human needs does not necessarily point towards the rich individuality that human beings would develop in a democratic classless society. In fact, more consistent with capitalism's remaking of human needs may be Marx's (1964 [1844]: 148) warning, in the *Economic and Philosophical Manuscripts*, that "no eunuch flatters his despot more basely or uses more despicable means to stimulate his dulled capacity for pleasure in order to sneak a favor for himself than does the industrial eunuch—the producer—in order to sneak for himself a few pennies." An even better way of understanding capitalism's remaking of human needs, however, is through an adaptation of Marx's distinction in *Capital* between the formal and real subsumption of labor to capital.

Marx (1977 [1867]: 645, 1021) points out that, in its early stages, capital can take over the labor process without revolutionizing it. In other words, the producers con-tinue to produce in the old way but they do so as "as wage-labourers under the direct control of a capitalist" (Marx 1977 [1867]: 645). Thus, in this early stage the subsumption of labor is formal. As capitalism develops, however, the pursuit of profit leads to a revolutionization of the labor process (Mandel 1977: 944). This revolutionization, which includes the spread of ever more elaborate machine-based technologies of production (Marx 1977 [1867]: 1024), increases not just labor productivity but also management's control over workers and the labor process (Marx 1963 [1847]: 167–68; Marx 1977 [1867]: 526, 562–64; Basso 2003: 201).

In other words, as capitalism develops, it increasingly abandons the labor processes it inherited, changing them instead in its own image. As this transformation proceeds, the formal subsumption of labor gives place to its real subsumption. Both the tools the worker uses to produce and the skills that she learns and uses in production bear the stamp of capitalist social relations and capital's compulsive pursuit of profit.

Capitalism's relationship to consumption has evolved in a similar way. Marx (1977 [1867]) along with other scholars have discussed how "enclosures" expropriating peasants from the land they used to work on contributed to the rise of capitalism. Described by Karl Polanyi (2001 [1944]: 37) as "a revolution of the rich against the poor," this development facilitated the rise of capitalism in two ways. First, it created a pool of potential consumers, since, no longer producing their own food and means of subsistence, the former peasants had to turn to the market. To do so, however, these former peasants had to earn the money needed to purchase those means of subsistence. Thus, enclosures also created an available pool of wage workers. This is why Ernest Mandel (1971: 286, emphases in original) identifies "[t]he private appropriation of *all cultivable land*, which prevents free settlement of new peasants on the land, ... [as] an absolutely indispensable condition for the rise of *industrial capitalism*."

Through this double effect, enclosures also facilitated the formal subsumption of consumption to capital. They did so because they made the satisfaction of even people's pre-existing needs (such as the need for food, clothing, and so on) dependent on capitalist markets. Just as its compulsive pursuit of profit leads capitalism to replace pre-existing labor processes with new ones more consistent with its logic, however, so does it lead beyond a market response to a pre-existing set of human needs. And, just as the revolutionization of the labor process depends on the investment of a sizeable portion of the surplus, so has the revolutionization of consumption relied on a diversion of large portions of the surplus into the "sales effort" (Baran and Sweezy 1966: 114–41), which includes the development of grand spectacles and "cathedrals of consumption" (Ritzer 2005: x) and which "gives us what we want—once it gets through ... helping us to want it (that's marketing)" (Barber 2007: 127). Thus, the surplus that workers produce not only increases capital's control over them in the workplace; by facilitating the real subsumption of consumption to capital, it also reconstitutes everyday culture, along with people's consumption habits and desires.

An early, though not completely satisfactory, intimation of this process is present in John Kenneth Galbraith's (1985: 184–85) interpretation of the rise of consumerism as a manifestation of material affluence. According to Galbraith (1984: 129), people's needs were increasingly produced by advertising and techniques of corporate persuasion. What facilitated this process was the growing prominence in affluent societies of "needs that are discovered to the individual not by the palpable discomfort that accompanies deprivation but by some psychic response to their possession" (Galbraith 1985: 184). By contrast to the latter type of needs, "[h]unger and other physical pain have an objective and compelling quality … No one whose stomach is totally empty can be persuaded that his need is not for food but for entertainment" (Galbraith 1985: 184). But, although persuasion might not convince someone hungry to choose entertainment over food, it might convince "a well-nourished man" to trade his perfectly functioning car for a newer model. In short, the growing importance of advertising and corporate persuasion techniques led Galbraith to conclude that much of the output in affluent societies, such as the United States, had zero marginal utility. It was, in effect, useless, as the wants it satisfied were "effectively contrived" (Galbraith 1984: 133).

Meanwhile, people's need for public services and infrastructure did not receive the requisite attention, because the public sector's output did not benefit from the propagandistic advertising and marketing techniques boosting the sale of commodities (Galbraith 1984: 113). The result was a lack of balance in contemporary capitalism, as the composition of output increasingly favored not "the solid needs of the public sector of the economy" but "the tenuous and expensively synthesized wants for private goods" (Galbraith 1984: 240). Thus, economic growth no longer signified a rise in people's well-being, as that well-being increasingly depended not on the size of economic output but on its composition (Galbraith 1984: 241).

The critical analysis, not just by Galbraith but by other economists and social theorists as well, of the rise of consumerism located this phenomenon in the changes that the capitalist system underwent over the twentieth century. Phenomena such as the dramatic growth of the advertising industry, which has easily outpaced the growth of the economy as a whole (Sackrey and Schneider 2002: 170; Charkiewicz 2001: 53), resulted from the movement of the capitalist economy away from the idealized models of perfect competition populating economic textbooks. In such models advertising would be senseless and impossible, for two reasons. In addition to the products of different firms in this model being identical to each other, the different firms do not have to compete for market share. Being price takers, "they can sell as much as they want at the market determined price" as "[t]he quantities that [they] produce and sell depend only on their marginal costs" (Wolff and Resnick 2012: 266).

With the move, in the course of the twentieth century, towards a more oligopolistic model of capitalism, by contrast, the domination of entire industries by a few large corporations became increasingly common. In this new context, the dominant companies in each industry tended to avoid price wars that could leave all of them worse off (Heilbroner and Galbraith 1990: 528; Baran and Sweezy 1966: 58–59). Advertising and branding, by contrast, rose in importance as they allowed companies to compete through product differentiation (Baran and Sweezy 1966: 116). If a company can convince consumers that its product is superior to that of its rivals, it can not only increase its sales but also create a quasi-monopolistic position for itself that allows it to charge a higher price (Baran and Sweezy 1966: 116, 119).

The relationship between the rise of advertising and branding, on one side, and market structure, on the other, points to a weakness in Galbraith's implicit equation of advertising and branding with the creation of unreal or imaginary needs once economic affluence has taken care of real needs, such as the need for food, clothing, etc. Indeed, advertising and branding are present as much in industries that cater to such more basic needs as they are in industries that do not produce basic necessities.

Galbraith (1985: 184) implicitly recognizes this when he claims that, "[t]hough a hungry man cannot be persuaded as between bread and a circus, a well-nourished man can. And he can be persuaded as between different circuses and different foods. The further a man is removed from physical need the more open he is to persuasion—or management—as to what he buys."

Galbraith's contrast here between the hungry and the well-fed man does not convince. The well-fed, more affluent man may indeed have more discretionary income to spend on frivolous products that do not add to his well-being. Thus, he may be more amenable to persuasion simply by virtue of the fact that he can afford more commodities, whether they be basic necessities or luxuries. On the other hand, however, Galbraith implicitly admits that companies selling necessities are as likely to use methods of persuasion as companies that sell luxury products. It is not clear, therefore, why Galbraith assumes that company X will be more successful in persuading a well-fed consumer about the superiority of its cereal than it will be in persuading a hungry one.

Strategies of subsumption

We therefore need to go beyond Galbraith's interpretation of advertising and branding as an invention of unreal needs. In their search for effective ways to push products, whether necessities or luxuries, advertisers often tap into and exploit valued cultures and cultural meanings as well as the fears, insecurities, and real psychological needs of ordinary people.

The former strategy presents commodities in ways that invite the consumer to associate the commodities in question with socially valued cultures (for example, "cool" urban youth cultures) or widely shared cultural values (for example, individuality, love, success, family, and so on) (Barber 2007: 288; Kasser et al. 2003: 18; LaPoint and Hambrick-Dixon 2003: 243; Kilbourne 2003: 265; Goldman and Papson 2000: 81, 91; Gladwell 2000; Frank 2000). This strategy, which amounts to a transfer of meaning from the existing cultural universe to the commercial universe of capitalist commodities, has a double effect (McCracken 1988: 22, 77–80). On the one hand, it instrumentalizes existing cultures and cultural values, feeding off the respect, admiration, and acceptance that cultures and values enjoy within specific communities or society as a whole. In this respect, advertising and branding sanctify capitalist commodities by associating them with cherished cultures and values. It is not a surprise, then, that, for some advertising executives, brands are "the new religion," while "cults are a rich and legitimate source of insight for the creation of brand worship" (Barber 2007: 180).

But instrumentalizing cherished cultures and values in this way also has a second effect. The never-ending association, repeated thousands of times a day, between cherished cultures and values, on one side, and capitalist commodities, on the other, also commercializes culture. As Robert Goldman and Stephen Papson (2000: 91) point out, "[o]nce a sign is appropriated it circulates between advertising discourse and everyday life in a stylized form—this kind of mediation invariably changes the sign's cultural meanings and associations." In other words, although the goal of particular advertisers may be to associate whichever specific product he or she happens to push at a given time with the cultural value of success, or "coolness," or whatever else, the imaginative and well-crafted repetition, in various ways, of the same move by countless advertisers of countless other capitalist commodities will not only change the meanings that people attach to the commodities in question. It will also change the meaning of the cherished cultural values that capitalist commodities seek to parasitically feed on. Just as commodities X, Y, Z, and so on have now become symbols of success, coolness, etc., so do the cultural values of success, coolness, and so on increasingly become equivalent to possessing the appropriate capitalist commodities (Panayotakis 2011a: 48; Levin and Linn 2003: 217). In other words, although the intention of individual advertising and branding efforts may be to sell specific products, their aggregate result is to build a consumerist culture (Bordwell 2002: 238; Durning 1992: 119).

In this sense, the rise of a consumerist culture is one of the results of capital's use of the surplus. Advertising and branding efforts are not productive of wealth but simply seek to secure that the wealth workers produce will find willing buyers. To pursue this objective, such efforts inevitably absorb some of the surplus. As for capitalist companies, since their profit depends on finding willing buyers, it is not surprising that they seek and, under the pressure of competition, indeed have to channel part of the surplus in the direction of a rapidly growing advertising industry (Bowles and Edwards 1993: 166–67). In fact, as a successful brand name is one of the most valuable assets a company can possess, advertising and marketing expenses increasingly appear, from the point of view of capitalist corporations, as an investment no less indispensable than productive investments seeking to modernize a company's equipment or methods of production (Klein 2000: 8; Charkiewicz 2001: 68).

In their accounts of the rise of consumerism, social historians have described the consciousness, on the part of business elites, of the need to nurture a new consumerist culture. Such a culture would make it possible to absorb the growing output that mass production techniques churned out, while addressing a problem Galbraith was later to treat, namely "the fact that workers did not desire new goods and services," such as automobiles, "as spontaneously as they did the old ones—food, clothing, and shelter" (Hunnicutt 1988: 42). The development of a culture in which "excessiveness replaced thrift as a social value" (Ewen 1977: 25) was openly understood by the capitalists pioneering it as "basically a project of broad 'social planning.'" (Ewen 1977: 54).

Instructive and thought-provoking as such historical studies and their findings undoubtedly are, it should be clear by now that the rise of a consumerist culture is not conceivable only as the product of conscious social engineering by a business elite and its willing agents. Such a culture can develop out of capitalist competition. The parties doing their part to build such a culture do not have to consciously plan such an outcome. Their immediate goal is only to increase the sales and profits of specific companies selling specific products. But the aggregate macro-social effect of the microeconomic efforts to associate specific products and brands with socially cherished cultures and cultural values cannot, when they assume the scale that they have over the last hundred years, but commercialize culture and socially cherished values.

This commercialization of culture implies that capitalism is not a benign instrument that efficiently serves people's needs and preferences. By commercializing cherished cultural values and associating them with the possession of commodities, capitalism's use of the surplus also influences ordinary people's perception of how they can partake in these cherished values. And, as people increasingly come to see capitalist commodities as the key to achieving success, coolness, individuality, and so on, the real subsumption of consumption to capital proceeds apace. And the more it does, the longer people have to work in order to afford a higher level of consumption and the more surplus they have to generate for their employers. Further fueling this process, the latter can then use this additional surplus to carry the commercialization of our culture, as well as the real subsumption of consumption to capital, even further.

What results from this process is a "cycle of work-and-spend" (Schor 1991: 126), which dramatically contrasts with ordinary people's attitude towards money and work in many pre-capitalist societies as well as in capitalist societies themselves during their early stages (Biggart 1994: 676–78). Characterizing this attitude is the fact that "[a] man does not 'by nature' wish to earn more and more money, but simply to live as he is accustomed to live and to earn as much as is necessary for that purpose" (Weber 1958 [1905]: 58–60).

Associating specific commodities with socially cherished cultures and cultural values is not the only way that capital's subsumption of consumption takes place. Just as advertisers and marketers tap on cherished cultural meanings, so do they exploit people's needs, fears, emotional insecurities, and unfulfilled longings (Barber 2007: 181, 183; Kasser et al. 2003: 17; Kanner and Soule 2003: 56; Kilbourne 2003: 252; Cross 2000: 34; Ewen 1977: 39). When they do so, advertisers and marketers do not seek to invent needs. Instead, they attempt to take advantage of people's real needs, which often do not find fulfillment because of the economic insecurity, stress, loneliness, alienation, and general unhappiness that everyday living in capitalist societies often engenders. Advertisers and marketers can pursue this objective by constructing an association in consumers' minds between specific commodities and the fulfillment of consumers' deeply felt needs for happiness, security, community, and so on (Barber 2007: 218; Levin and Linn 2003: 223; Kanner and Soule 2003: 57; Postman and Powers 2010).

And, just as capital's first strategy of subsuming consumption can lead to broad cultural changes and the commercial redefinition of values, the successful pursuit of this second strategy affects the way people pursue the satisfaction of deeply felt psychological needs. Although in any specific instance the goal of advertisers and marketers is to establish associations in consumers' minds between a specific product and the fulfillment of a deeply felt need (for companionship, social acceptance, personal happiness, freedom, and so on), the aggregate effect of advertisers and marketers employing this strategy countless times will be to encourage a general perception of commodity consumption as the key to satisfying our deepest psychological needs and urges. As psychologists Allen Kanner and Renée Soule (2003 : 57) point out, people's exposure to "thousands of commercials a day" also exposes them to the consistent "meta-message … that happiness is to be found primarily in material goods and services."

But this meta-message is false. The existing research suggests that, once societies have reached a minimum material standard of living that covers basic necessities, the key to psychological health and a happier life for their members lies not in ever-growing levels of material consumption but in such non-materialistic goods as free time and the quality of one's relationships with other people (Barber 2007: 50; Layard 2005: 6–7, 65–66, 68–69, 176; Kasser 2002: 61–62, 72; Lane 2000: 6–7, 33; Durning 1992: 23).

This also means, however, that, instead of being self-undermining, the false promises that advertisers extend to consumers may, in fact, be self-feeding. The more seriously consumers take the false promises of advertisers and marketers, the less they will be able to satisfy their needs. And the more they fail to satisfy their needs, the more it will pay for marketers and advertisers to employ the strategy of appealing to human needs that their commodities could not possibly satisfy.

"Consumer sovereignty," neoclassical economics, and capitalism's war of rationalities

The false promises of consumerist culture reveal how capital's use of the surplus often does less to satisfy consumers' needs than to boost profit. Recognition of this fact does not only have implications for how we assess consumer culture. It also highlights the broader ideological function of mainstream economics when it "celebrate[s] capitalism as a just economic system that generate[s] incomes according to what people [want] and [contribute]" (Wolff and Resnick 2012: 329). As this assessment of neoclassical economics by Wolff and Resnick suggests, far from offering an honest and realistic analysis of capitalism, neoclassical economics idealizes it by portraying it as a good servant of society. In so doing, neoclassical economics merely updates the old argument going at least as far back as Adam Smith regarding the ability of capitalist competition to serve the common good (Wolff and Resnick 2012: 98).

One neoclassical assumption making it possible to reach this rosy conclusion is that consumer preferences are "exogenous." This technical term refers to the neoclassical treatment of consumer preferences as "fixed and given" data that do not result from capitalism's operation (Costanza et al. 1997: 141; Wolff and Resnick 2012: 39, 59; Bowles, Edwards, and Roosevelt 2005: 36; DiMaggio 1994: 29; Frenzen, Hirsch, and Zerrillo 1994: 404; Bowles 1991: 13; Galbraith 1984: 119; Dobb 1975: 33). This assumption is crucial, because it makes it possible to present consumers as "sovereign" and capitalism as only their efficient servant (Bowles 1991: 15). In this respect, this assumption bolsters the ideological understanding of contemporary capitalist societies as conducive to "individual autonomy and freedom: apparently powerful corporations are really controlled by consumers" (Wright and Rogers 2011: 42).

Against this assumption, Galbraith claims that, beyond the needs for necessities, such as food, clothing, etc., contemporary capitalism synthesizes most of the wants that it claims to satisfy. Because of this, Galbraith argues, capitalism's claim to deliver the goods that people want is not a sign of consumer sovereignty. It is instead a tautological and ideological claim that facilitates capital's management of the consumer and his wants, even as it reassured him that he was the boss while large corporations were his "humble servant[s]" (Galbraith 1985, 200).

Although Galbraith's critique of consumer sovereignty as an ideological concept is sound, one pitfall of his reference to the synthesizing of wants is that it seems to suggest that contemporary capitalists "manufacture artificial wants or desires" rather than satisfying real ones (Friedman and Friedman 1981: 214). This allows supporters of capitalism, such as Milton and Rose Friedman (1981 : 214), to argue that this is not plausible, since it would be cheaper for producers to satisfy real wants rather than to manufacture false ones. What the Friedmans' argument misses, however, is that the critique of the neo-classical view of consumer preferences as exogenous does not necessarily presuppose a Manichean contrast between real needs and false wants. Instead, both the advertising and marketing strategies we have discussed so far can explain how the distortion of con-sumer preferences in line with the requirements of capital can proceed not by ignoring people's needs and fabricating false alternatives but by instrumentalizing both these needs and the cherished cultures and cultural values within a society.

That marketers and advertisers have to resort to such strategies, which sell com-modities by appealing to cultural values and human needs that are very real indeed, is, in fact, a sign that companies cannot fabricate wants for their products out of thin air. In other words, it is because of the difficulty, which the Friedmans correctly recognize, of fabricating something completely unreal that capital colonizes what is very real and important to ordinary people, namely their cultural "lifeworlds" (Habermas 1984) as well as their social and psychological needs. And it is to this colonization of something very real and important to people that such strategies owe their effectiveness. Thus, the reality and importance of people's cultural lifeworlds and social and psychological needs do not only make consumers more receptive to capital's advertising and marketing strategies; they also make it possible to use this receptiveness as a point of vulnerability that capital can exploit.

This analysis also undercuts another assumption central to the ideological mission of neoclassical economics. This is the assumption of rationalism on the part of all eco-nomic actors, whether they be capitalist producers or consumers (Wolff 2012: 64–65; Sackrey and Schneider 2002: 10–11; Desai 1994: 416; Laidler and Estrin 1989: 11–13). It is the combination of this assumption with the assumptions of exogenous consumer preferences and of competitive markets that makes it possible to derive theoretical "proofs" of consumers' sovereignty over capitalist producers.

Indeed, these assumptions make it possible to argue that, in making "choices concerning … their consumption of goods and services available for purchase in the market" (Wolff and Resnick 2012: 64), rational consumers will allocate their scarce resources in line with their exogenous preferences. Similarly, producers will rationally seek to maximize profits. As long as producers face competition, they will succeed only by producing commodities that are desirable to the consumers because they com-bine good quality and an affordable price. Overly greedy producers trying to maximize profits by cutting corners with respect to quality while charging unreasonably high prices will lose rational consumers to rival producers delivering better-quality products for a more reasonable price. Thus, competition disciplines producers by teaching them that the only rational way to pursue profit is by catering to the needs and preferences of the sovereign consumer. In the colorful words of a contemporary popularizer of this argu-ment, competition makes it "wonderful to be a consumer … and … hell on wheels to be a seller or manufacturer" (Friedman 2000: 82).

One of Marx's contributions was to explain how the dynamics of capitalism undermines the very competitive model that allows neoclassical economics to por-tray capitalism as an efficient servant of consumer needs. This contribution raises an interesting contrast between Marx's analysis and that by neoclassical economics. Indeed, Marx (1977 [1867]: 777–81) is able, in his discussion of how capitalist competition contributes to the centralization of capital, "to predict the advent of big business" (Schumpeter 1942: 34) as well as the rise of the more monopolistic forms of capitalism (which have facilitated the marketing and advertising techniques we discuss in this chapter) at a time when the competitive model seemed to prevail.

By contrast, neoclassical economics, which emerges at the end of the nineteenth century and the beginning of the twentieth, foregrounds the unrealistic model of perfect competition (Heilbroner 1986: 175) at a time when the movement of the capitalist economy in oligopolistic and monopolistic directions was becoming ever more obvious (Beaud 2001: 156–57). Bearing witness to its ideological function, neoclassical economics continued to privilege the competitive model by downplaying the presence in contemporary capitalism of economies of scale that favor industrial concentration and the domination of a few large corporations (Wolff and Resnick 2012: 266–67; Bowles, Edwards, and Roosevelt 2005: 541–43; Panayotakis 2011a: 15). In other words, to preserve its assumption of competitive markets, neoclassical economics also had, at a time when a handful of (first national, then increasingly transnational) mega-corporations became dominant in their industries by acquiring smaller companies or driving them out of business, to assume that larger companies did not enjoy a competitive advantage.

The possibility and likelihood of such an advantage shatters the myth of a sustainably efficient free market. Free market competition becomes self-undermining because the ability of winners to reinvest profits and grow will compound their advantage further by undermining the competitiveness and viability of smaller rivals. As fewer and fewer of these small companies survive and as large companies become even larger, industries will move towards monopoly and oligopoly and away from the felicitous efficiency properties of the neoclassical competitive model. Thus, the very assumption that allowed Marx's prophetic (at least in this respect) analysis of long-term capitalist development is the assumption that neoclassical economics has to repress, if it is to perform its ideological function.

Although Marx's analysis anticipates the self-undermining properties of capitalist competition, this chapter's analysis of consumption demonstrates the self-undermining nature of another central element in the ideological arsenal of neoclassical economics, namely the rationality of economic actors within capitalist society. Indeed, the marketing and advertising strategies this chapter discusses in effect seek to assault the rationality of consumers. Their goal is to skew consumers' preferences in an irrational direction by establishing dubious (and often unconscious and, thus, not rational) associations between commodities, on one side, and either cherished cultures and cultural values or deep social and psychological needs that the possession of commodities cannot really satisfy, on the other. And, as we saw earlier, to facilitate such associations, marketing and advertising strategies cultivate and manipulate consumers' fears, insecurities, and longings, thus making it harder for the latter to articulate and pursue the satisfaction of their preferences in a way that is rational and conducive to their well-being.

These assaults on consumer rationality are, of course, not irrational. On the contrary, as Benjamin Barber (2007: 196) notes,

[a]lthough the marketers ... are certainly trying to evoke emotion in consumers, they themselves are actually acting rationally, employing a powerful form of instrumental reason—that is, emotion rationally deployed in the name of profits. Their concern with girls' body image, for example, is the quite rational one (for them, not us) of selling goods and keeping the corporations they serve ... afloat. Producers absolve the consumer from rationality so they can sell her on doing what suits the producer's rationality: making money.

In other words, it is entirely rational for capitalist exploiters to use part of the surplus they extract from direct producers to declare war on consumer rationality. This means that the advance of capitalism gives rise to a war of rationalities. The rationality of profit making can thrive only at the expense of consumer rationality. And in this war the former type of rationality has the advantage because of the superior resources that capital derives from its control of the surplus.

In this sense, the real subsumption of consumption to capital signifies the separation of these two rationalities as well as the subordination of consumer rationality to capital's profit-seeking rationality. This has important implications for the notion of economic efficiency, which is central to the ideological function of neoclassical economics. Because of the multiplicity of the dubious assumptions that, as we saw earlier, underlie the neoclassical edifice, the real subsumption of consumption to capital, with all its implications for the subordination of consumer to profit-seeking rationality, is missing from the neoclassical story. It is this repression of an important feature of contemporary capitalist reality that allows neoclassical economics to equate capitalist efficiency with capital's efficient satisfaction of consumers' needs.

Since the overriding goal of capitalist activity is profit, however, capitalist efficiency involves nothing more than the efficient pursuit of that goal (Badiou 2010a: 94). Thus, if we drop the ideological assumptions of neoclassical economics and acknowledge the real subsumption of consumption to capital, the capitalist economic system emerges not as an efficient servant of consumer needs but, rather, as an efficient machine of maximizing profit through the subordination of consumers and their well-being to the logic of capital accumulation.

It is not surprising, then, that critical psychologists who have studied consumer capitalism have revealed the toxic effects of its materialistic culture. Psychological research, in a number of different societies from different continents and with very different cultures, confirms that the materialistic attitudes that consumer capitalism promotes "are associated with a pervasive undermining of people's well-being, from low life satisfaction and happiness, to depression and anxiety, to physical problems such as headaches, and to personality disorders, narcissism, antisocial behavior" (Kasser 2002: 22).

To be sure, materialistic attitudes and their negative effect on individuals in part stem from other concomitants of the capitalist economic structure, such as poverty and economic insecurity (Kasser 2002: 27–30; Panayotakis 2011a: 50). There is a totalitarian dynamic at play here, insofar as capitalism is able to feed on its own failures. The failure of capitalist societies to fulfill people's social, material, and psychological needs makes people receptive to the false promises of advertisers and marketers. And the materialistic attitudes that, by instrumentalizing socially cherished cultures and cultural values, these false promises generate also replenish the pool of unhappy people vulnerable to these very promises.

In this respect, the analysis of the real subsumption of consumption to capital also enriches our understanding of capitalist competition and its effects. For supporters of capitalism since Adam Smith this competition harmonizes individual self-interest with the common good (Smith 1909 [1776]: 351–52; Friedman and Friedman 1981: xv–xvi). This is because, as we saw earlier, one of the effects of competition is to put pressure on companies to produce good-quality commodities that are also affordable. However beneficial this dynamic may sometimes be for consumers, the real subsumption of consumption to capital makes this rosy picture less tenable. Indeed, as capitalist competition undermines over time the competitive model of capitalism, competition increasingly relies on advertising and marketing strategies that subvert the rationality of consumers while building a consumerist culture that undermines people's well-being.

In the language of neoclassical economics, the microeconomic pursuit of profit produces negative externalities that the traditional model does not take into account. In other words, capitalist enterprises impose costs on third parties that are not reflected in the prices that they charge their customers (Boyes and Melvin 2005: 103–4; Laidler and Estrin 1989: 418–19). Indeed, the price that a consumer pays for a product includes only a fraction of the total costs that the producer's advertising and marketing strategies entail. The price does include the economic costs of these strategies on the producer, who has to pass on these costs to her consumers in order to make a profit.

Nevertheless, a substantial portion of the (cultural and psychological, rather than monetary) portion of "the costs … [is] borne by [people] who are not a direct party to the market transaction" (Boyes and Melvin 2005: 103). Indeed, beyond their immediate economic costs to the producer and consumer of the advertised product, advertising and marketing strategies have, as we explained above, a much more diffuse unintended effect on everyday culture and consumer rationality. This is because, in their attempt to sell a specific product, these strategies also contribute to a consumerist culture, while at the same time encouraging consumers to seek satisfaction of their social and psychological needs in material consumption. Therefore, these advertising and marketing strategies help to build a cultural environment that affects not only the actual customers of the products these strategies push but everybody exposed to them. Thus, even though the economic cost of the marketing and advertising strategies of company X will not weigh on consumers who do not buy company X's wares, the broader cultural effect of these strategies will.

Whether those not purchasing company X's product recognize this effect is, of course, another question. Indeed, it may be tempting for them to conclude that, since they desisted from buying company X's product despite their exposure to this company's marketing and advertising campaigns, such campaigns have no effect on them. And this conclusion could be very widespread indeed. After all, in view of the great numbers of advertising messages that the average person encounters in her everyday life (Townsend 2010: 115; Kanner and Soule 2003: 57), there is no consumer who has not had the experience of not buying a product after being exposed to its producer's advertising and marketing entreaties. This obvious fact has even given rise, especially among supporters of capitalism, to facile "proofs" of the wrong-headedness of those criticizing advertising. For such ideologues, the possibility of citing "numerous expensive advertising fiascos" (Friedman and Friedman 1981: 214) is enough to confirm the consumer's position as the sovereign of the capitalist economic universe.

This rosy conclusion is unconvincing, however, for two reasons. First, it fails to differentiate between the intended and unintended outcomes of marketing and advertising campaigns. The fact that many consumers do not buy a product despite their exposure to its producer's marketing and advertising campaign at most shows that, in their case, that campaign did not produce its intended outcome. This fact says nothing, however, about the campaign's possible unintended effects, including its contribution to an ever more materialistic cultural environment that adversely affects everyone, whether they buy the product in question or not. As Alan Thein Durning (1992: 119) has pointed out, "[e]ven if [commercials] fail to sell a particular product, they sell consumerism itself by ceaselessly reiterating the idea that there is a product to solve each of life's problems, indeed that existence would be satisfying and complete if only we bought the right things."

The conclusion that people are immune to the influence of advertising and marketing campaigns as long as they don't succumb to every marketing or advertising campaign they are exposed to also flies in the face of the willingness of capitalist businesses to spend ever more astronomical amounts on such campaigns (Sackrey and Schneider 2002: 170; Charkiewicz 2001: 53; Durning 1992: 120; Baran and Sweezy 1966: 117–18). As Jean Kilbourne (2003: 252) points out, "[t]here has never been a propaganda effort to match that of modern advertising … More thought, more effort, and more money go into advertising now than have gone into any other campaign to change social consciousness." And, as Kanner and Soule (2003: 58) add, whatever people may tell themselves about their immunity to marketing and advertising campaigns, "corporations would not spend tens of billions of dollars only on marketing if their research … and profits did not confirm its effectiveness."

The reason these campaigns usually produce a return for the companies undertaking them is because, in their war against consumer rationality, it is the companies and not the consumers which better understand their enemy. Indeed, the portions of the surplus funding advertising and marketing campaigns make it possible both to reach such a superior understanding and then to put it to use. To continually refine these campaigns, capital enlists psychologists and social scientists as well as psychological and social scientific knowledge to the cause of uncovering and manipulating the limits of consumer rationality (Kasser and Kanner 2003: 4–5; Kanner and Soule 2003: 56–57; Rosenberg 2003: 112–13; Levin and Linn 2003: 217, 225; Cross 2000: 34). It also relies on the recruitment of talented artists, attractive models, and glamorous actors to translate the scientific insights of psychologists and social scientists into irresistible images and messages capable of manipulating human frailties (Ewen 1977: 66; Kanner and Soule 2003: 57). In this respect, the consumer is more transparent to the producer than the producer's persuasion techniques are to the consumer.

And it is for this reason that the tempting, but ultimately self-deluding, conclusion that one is immune to the influence of marketing and advertising efforts in effect turns reality on its head. It does so by overestimating consumer rationality, while underestimating the rationality of capitalist producers. In other words, this self-deluding conclusion makes two dubious assumptions: first, that capitalist producers waste their money on costly but basically ineffective advertising and marketing campaigns; and, second, that consumers are fully transparent to themselves. In this respect, capital's instrumentalization of consumers' "nonconscious processes" (Rosenberg 2003: 110) is doubly effective. It not only makes it easier to overcome the consumer's resistance; it also makes it possible for consumers to succumb to capital's rationality of profit even as they stick to the illusion (to which neoclassical economics, through its flattering postulate of consumer sovereignty, gives its "scientific" seal of approval) that their individual consumer rationality remains intact.

In any event, the external effects of capitalists' marketing and advertising campaigns on the general culture, as well as the costs on third parties that these external effects impose, further undermine the neoclassical portrayal of capitalism as an efficient servant of consumer preferences. This is the case because this portrayal relies on yet another assumption, namely the absence of external effects on third parties.

The recognition that externalities of all kinds do occur within capitalist economies has long given rise to a debate even within the neoclassical camp. More liberal neoclassical economists are more supportive of government intervention, such as the use of taxes and subsidies, to address externalities. More conservative neoclassical economists, by contrast, counter that government intervention to correct externalities often produces unintended costs that may exceed the costs from the externalities that this intervention seeks to remedy (Wolff and Resnick 2012: 62–63; Wright and Rogers 2011: 390; Boyes and Melvin 2005: 103–4, 311–12; Bowles, Edwards, and Roosevelt 2005: 221).

The argument regarding the use of taxation to address externalities does seem to have some relevance to the question of the effect that marketing and advertising strategies have on our culture. According to this argument, taxation could help to align the private cost facing producers and consumers of a product with the full social cost the production of this good or service entails. The presence of externalities prevents such an alignment (Boyes and Melvin 2005: 310; Hahnel 2002: 93; Panayotakis 2011a: 97–99). Because of this misalignment, "the economic actors' self-interested action will misallocate resources. In the case of goods and services that entail negative externalities … , this misallocation will lead to greater production of these goods than warranted by considerations of efficiency, while in the case of goods and services that entail positive externalities, the opposite will be the case" (Panayotakis 2011a: 97–99).

One way to address this problem is to tax economic activities that generate negative externalities while subsidizing activities that generate positive externalities (Panayotakis 2011a: 98). This would create incentives both to reduce the production of goods and services with negative externalities and to increase the production of goods and services with positive externalities. As a result, the production of both these types of goods and services would converge towards the economically efficient level. For example, this would be the rationale for imposing carbon taxes that raise the price facing the producers and consumers of goods and services contributing to climate change and to all the negative consequences that climate change imposes on third parties the world over (Hahnel 2011: 129–30; Brown 2001: 119). Similarly, this would be the rationale for subsidizing vaccines, which have a positive protective effect not just on the vaccinated but on everybody around them.

One could similarly argue that, because of their negative externalities, activities such as advertising should be taxed (Kasser 2002: 109–10). This argument seems especially appealing in view of the fact that the situation in advanced capitalist societies is often the opposite. Indeed, although some regulations restricting advertising practices exist in parts of the capitalist world (Kasser 2002: 109), government subsidization of advertising expenses is not uncommon (Charkiewicz 2001: 71; Cross 2000: 241).

Nonetheless, my argument so far makes it clear that, however desirable it may otherwise be, the replacement of the perverse subsidies on advertising with taxes that treat advertising as comparable to pollution (Kasser 2002: 109–10) would not address the problem at hand. Indeed, underlying the argument of addressing externalities through the use of taxes and subsidies are the rationalist assumptions at the basis of neoclassical economics. Just as it is rational for profit-maximizing producers and utility-maximizing consumers to overproduce and overconsume products with negative externalities as well as to underproduce and underconsume products with positive externalities, so it would be rational for them to converge towards more economically efficient levels of production and consumption once externality-generating goods or services were taxed or subsidized as appropriate.

It is precisely this assumption of rationalism that the operation of contemporary capitalism questions, however. It does so by making the pursuit of profit dependent on strategies that undermine the rationality of the consumer and her ability to pursue the satisfaction of her needs as efficiently as possible. Indeed, the effect of consumer capitalism is to reorient people's values in a materialistic direction while encouraging them to seek to satisfy their social and psychological needs through material consumption rather than in other more effective ways, including the prioritization of free time and the cultivation of high-quality relationships with other people (Barber 2007: 50; Layard 2005: 6–7, 65–66, 68–69, 176; Kasser 2002: 61–62, 72; Lane 2000: 6–7, 33; Durning 1992: 23). The result is a materialist culture that takes a toll on people's well-being while also giving rise to the paradoxical failure of ever-growing levels of material consumption in rich countries to increase people's happiness and satisfaction with life (Layard 2005: 3; Lane 2000: 4). In short, the well-documented fact that "it is the quality of social relationships rather than money that is more closely related to reported levels of subjective well-being ... [means] that capitalism has become an obstacle to a richer and more satisfying life even for the minority of the world's population living in the affluent global North" (Panayotakis 2011a: 55).

In this respect, advertising and marketing strategies are more than an externality, which leads to a market failure by sending the wrong signal to producers and consumers whose rationality is otherwise left intact. Instead, they are a manifestation of the war of rationalities, which opposes capitalist rationality to that of consumers. And, since the formal subsumption of consumption to capital has long commodified even basic means of subsistence, thus making all of us consumers who turn to capitalist markets to meet basic needs, the assault by capitalism's real subsumption of consumption on consumer rationality is, in effect, an assault on everybody's ability to pursue happiness and the satisfaction of their needs as effectively as possible.

This aspect of capitalist development, which is perfectly intelligible once one analyzes the uses of the surplus that capitalist exploitation makes possible, is completely missing from the neoclassical story. This is hardly surprising in view of the fact that

> the neoclassical explanation for what ultimately determines income and its distribution in society is remarkable both for what it claims and for what it rules out as a possibility.

The claim is that each individual gets back from society a quantum of wealth exactly proportional to what each has contributed to society. This theory of distribution is remarkable for its inherent fairness. It is also remarkable for what it rules out: exploitation. Exploitation, in the sense of some individual or set of individuals receiving some produced wealth from society without giving any in return to it, is clearly not possible.

(Wolff and Resnick 2012: 90–91)

It should be clear by now that this neoclassical refusal to entertain the possibility of exploitation erases the process through which capital increasingly subordinates people not just in their capacity as workers but also in their capacity as consumers. And, in so doing, it also obscures the fact that capitalist exploitation represents not just an assault on workers but on society as such, thus making the interest in a classless society beyond exploitation a genuinely universal interest.

Neoliberal austerity and the role of science, technology, and the arts in capital's subsumption of consumption

Thus, our increasingly consumerist culture is both a product of capitalism's real subsumption of consumption and one of the means through which this subsumption takes place. This culture reflects capitalism's instrumentalization of science, technology, and art.

With respect to science and technology, there is a parallel between capital's real subsumption of labor and its real subsumption of consumption. Marx (1977 [1867]: 1034–35) himself stresses the important role that science and technology play in the former. The real subsumption of labor involved a revolutionization of the labor process, which relied on the systematic promotion and use of scientific and technological advances (Marx 1977 [1867]: 1021–25). The principle animating these advances, moreover, was the pursuit of capital accumulation and capital's control over workers. In fact, technological advances have long served as a weapon of class struggle (Marx 1963 [1847]: 167–68; Marx 1977 [1867]: 489–91, 526, 562–63; Engels 1844; Basso 2003: 201). As Marx (1977 [1867]: 562) argues,

machinery does not just act as a superior competitor to the worker, always on the point of making him superfluous. It is a power inimical to him, and capital proclaims this fact loudly and deliberately, as well as making use of it. It is the most powerful weapon for suppressing strikes, those periodic revolts of the working class against the autocracy of capital.

As we discussed earlier, capital's real subsumption of consumption also relies on an instrumentalization of science and technology. But, beyond this parallel, there is also a parallel between the motivations driving both capital's real subsumption of labor and its real subsumption of consumption. In the former case, the guiding principles of scientific and technological advances contributing to capital's real subsumption of labor is profit rather than the pursuit of truth, the promotion of human well-being, or even technical efficiency (Bowles, Edwards, and Roosevelt 2005: 336–38). Similarly, the scientific and technological advances fueling capital's real subsumption of consumption also subordinate human well-being to the pursuit of profit. This becomes evident when one considers how capitalist society allocates resources for the study of the mechanics of consumer culture but also how it manages the results of such research.

One of the conclusions of critical analyses of consumer culture is that research in this area is primarily the domain of capitalist corporations, which, obviously, do not use the insights from such research to highlight the negative social consequences of capital's real subsumption of consumption. Instead, those insights fuel this subsumption further by refining the techniques capable of eliciting from consumers the desired response (Levin and Linn 2003: 225). These techniques, incidentally, include direct appeals to children, which at times go as far as to turn children against their parents (Schor 1991: 297–99; Levin and Linn 2003: 224–25). In fact, it is not even possible to know the lengths to which advertisers and marketers will go to refine their techniques of subsuming consumption to capital, since they do not make their research public, guarding it instead as a trade secret (Kasser and Kanner 2003: 4–5; Levin and Linn 2003: 224).

And while psychologists, social scientists, computer experts hired by corporations to push capital's subsumption of consumption to new heights have all the resources they need to pursue this goal further, academic researchers focusing on consumerist culture's negative effects on human well-being and the ecological integrity of the planet find themselves at a serious disadvantage (Levin and Linn 2003: 225). As Levin and Linn (2003: 227) report, "very little research has examined how the rapid escalation of marketing to children is affecting them. Our colleagues who conduct research point to a lack of funding as the primary reason for this dearth of information."

This underfunding becomes even more acute in periods of austerity, whether it be the austerity spreading throughout most of the capitalist world since the global financial crisis or the chronic austerity that has plagued the public sector during the decades-long reign of neoliberalism. First of all, by slashing the funding of public universities and the amount of money governments devote to research and development (Soederberg 2015: 13; Berry and Worthen 2012: 19–20; Albo and Evans 2010: 291), such austerity inevitably makes researchers more dependent on the private capitalist sector. This means that their projects have to align more closely with the interests of their corporate funders than with the interests of the general public. In addition, researchers who are dependent on corporate support "are unlikely to examine the problems associated with consumption, because doing so might be seen as 'biting the hand that feeds me'"(Kasser and Kanner 2003: 5). In this respect, just as austerity policies tend, through the unemployment and economic insecurity they increase, to enhance capital's control over workers, so do they bolster capital's use of scientific and technological research to subordinate consumers and their well-being to capitalist profit.

Second, the chronic underfunding of public schools, which is another form that chronic austerity has long assumed, forces many of them, at least in the United States, to make up the missing funds by forcing their students to watch television programs that also contain advertisements targeting school-age children (Barber 2007: 147; Schor 1991: 292; Kasser 2002: 107; Consumer Reports 2000: 385). This is just one illustration of how neoliberalism and the chronic public sector austerity it imposes have altered the flows of surplus through capitalist economies. On the one hand, lower taxes for corporations and the very wealthy mean that capital has to bear less of the cost of reproducing the socially available labor power. To the extent that public sector underfunding adversely affects public sector salaries and staffing levels, it also increases the surplus that public sector workers have to produce, thus also increasing the level of exploitation they face. And, to the extent that accompanying this more intense exploitation are measures such as the transformation of schools into platforms for capitalist advertising, the contribution of capitalist corporations to the costs of reproducing labor power now becomes contingent on the more full subjection of children and ordinary people not only as workers but also as consumers.

Thus, austerity forces educational institutions, such as public schools, to become complicit in capital's war against consumer rationality. Instead of empowering children to pursue their well-being and happiness in the most effective way possible, schools often turn children into fodder for capitalist branding efforts. In so doing, of course, schools do not empower children to protect themselves from the toxic consumerist culture these efforts create but, instead, socialize them to become the kind of human subject this culture demands.

This social function, which austerity policies and the capitalist pursuit of profit force upon schools, adds yet another dimension to schools' "hidden curriculum." This latter concept "refers to the way in which cultural values and attitudes (such as obedience to authority, punctuality, and delayed gratification) are transmitted, through the structure of teaching and the organization of schools" (Scott and Marshall 2005: 267–68). Since the teacher is "effectively the infant's first boss" (Scott and Marshall 2005: 267), the hidden curriculum also prepares students to become docile workers. This work's analysis, therefore, complements the implications of the "hidden curriculum" concept by highlighting the role of schools in capital's real subsumption of consumption.

In any event, one of the reasons corporations target children, whether in school or outside, is the financial benefit that corporations can reap from an early establishment of brand loyalty (Schor 1991: 287–92; Consumer Reports 2000: 384). In addition to providing a life-long base of customers, targeting children exploits their great vulnerability to advertising (Levin and Linn 2003: 217, 223; Kilbourne 2003: 252) by establishing associations in their minds between corporate brands, on one side, and cherished cultural values or the satisfaction of deeply felt needs, on the other. Thus, although, from an ethical point of view, the manipulation of children is especially reprehensible, from the standpoint of capitalist corporations it is an irresistibly promising investment of the surplus at their disposal. In fact, the appeal to capitalist corporations of a world full of children consumers is such as to lead some scholars to analyze the evolution of capitalist consumer culture in recent decades as a project of infantilizing adult consumers (Barber 2007).

There is another way that neoliberal austerity fuels corporate branding efforts, however.

> In Canada under Brian Mulroney, in the US under Ronald Reagan and in Britain under Margaret Thatcher (and in many other parts of the world as well), corporate taxes were dramatically lowered, a move that eroded the tax base and gradually starved the public sector ... As government spending dwindled, schools, museums and broadcasters were desperate to make up their budget shortfalls and thus ripe for partnerships with private corporations.
>
> (Klein 2000: 30)

Thus, our society's most venerable cultural institutions slowly but surely transform themselves into "brand-extensions-in-waiting" (Klein 2000: 30). In other words, neoliberal austerity allows capitalist corporations to pose as generous patrons of the arts magnanimously making the highest achievements of the human spirit available to the masses.

Thus, the lightening of capital's tax burden also makes it possible for capitalist corporations to channel a portion of the additional surplus they retain to cultural initiatives that burnish their brands and carry capital's real subsumption of consumption to the next level. In this respect, assessments of austerity's negative effects on human well-being have to take into account not just such obvious, albeit serious, consequences of austerity as unemployment and the assault on ordinary people's access to education, health care, and so on. Also important is the way austerity undercuts human well-being by fueling capital's real subsumption of consumption.

Conclusion

This chapter has interpreted consumerism as a process of real subsumption of consumption to capital. It has traced this process to the dynamics of capitalist competition and the pursuit of profit, while also discussing its negative impact on human well-being and the ecological integrity of the planet. In this sense, this chapter represents a first step in the analysis of the destructive ways that capitalism uses the surplus it extracts from workers. The chapters that follow develop this theme further: they explore capitalism's rapid development of the forces of destruction at its disposal, paying special attention to the incessant development of ever more lethal military technologies as well as to the ways that capitalism's deployment of technological advances is contributing to a deepening ecological crisis that endangers humanity and the planet. Before exploring these aspects of capitalist destruction, the chapter that follows examines how the financial dependence of contemporary media on advertising skews media coverage in ways congenial to the sensibilities and interests of capitalist advertisers and the affluent strata they often target. In other words, the real subsumption of consumption to capital does not just undercut human well-being and the ecological integrity of the planet. It also erodes democracy.

4

Consumerism and capital's use of science and technology to undercut democracy

Departing from Marx's distinction between capital's formal and real subsumption of labor, Chapter 3 applied an analogous distinction to analyze the rise of contemporary capitalism's consumerist culture. Capital's real subsumption of consumption refers to the fact that capital does not simply force people to satisfy their needs through the purchase of commodities in the market. Instead, in a way parallel to its real subsumption of labor, capital's real subsumption of consumption reconstitutes consumers' preferences in ways that serve capitalist profit. As we saw, by commercializing our culture and encouraging the futile attempt to pursue happiness and satisfaction through ever higher levels of material consumption, capital's real subsumption of consumption subverts consumer rationality and assaults human well-being and the ecological integrity of the planet.

Serious as this indictment may be, it is not yet complete. As this chapter will show, capital's real subsumption of consumption, as well as its use of science and technology more generally, also undercuts the conditions for meaningful democratic debate. This chapter examines this negative consequence of the real subsumption of consumption to capital by examining the role that the media play in this process. On the one hand, this chapter completes this work's account of the destructive effects of contemporary capitalism's consumerist culture. On the other hand, it forms part of this work's discussion of the ways that contemporary capitalism undercuts political democracy, a theme also explored later in this work.

In particular, this chapter examines how the increasing dependence of the media on advertising skews their coverage to suit the sensibilities and interests of capitalist advertisers and of the affluent audiences these advertisers often target. This means that the dynamics of competition within an increasingly monopolistic capitalist system contributes in yet another way to the difficulty of perceiving the exploitative nature of capitalist society. In this respect, this chapter adds another dimension to classical Marxism's account of the reasons that make exploitation in capitalist societies so hard to recognize.

Finally, the chapter also discusses other ways that capital's use of science and technology undermines democracy. These include its adoption of technologies that confine large numbers of people to routine, repetitive jobs that do not encourage them to develop the skills and self-confidence necessary for effective political participation, as well as capital's use of parts of the surplus to bankroll "scientific" research and lobbying campaigns designed to promote capitalist profit rather than our knowledge of the world.

The role of the media

Any discussion of capital's real subsumption of consumption would be incomplete without some reference to the role of the media in this process as well as to the related question of how the media fit into contemporary capitalism's surplus flows. On the one hand, media workers do contribute to the production of wealth and socially available surplus. Educational programs contribute to the reproduction and expansion of socially available labor power while entertainment programs also represent additions to the production of wealth and surplus. On the other hand, other aspects of media work, such as news programs, often offer a view of the world that tends to justify the capitalist status quo. Insofar as this is the case, such programs are not an addition to socially available wealth and surplus but creations that absorb part of the socially available surplus in exchange for contributing to the capitalist system's reproduction.

To be sure, these distinctions are only indicative. First, any given product of one or more media workers may not be easily classifiable as belonging to the educational, entertainment, or news categories. Second, even products within each of these categories may contain elements that both add to the production of wealth and perform an ideological function. All in all, this ambiguity means that media workers are themselves not easily classifiable as either surplus producers or workers who receive part of the socially available surplus for helping to secure the current class order's ideological conditions of existence.

The ideological role of the media in contemporary capitalist society takes at least two forms. Both these forms are inseparable from the economic dependence of media, in general, and privately owned media, especially, on advertising. Since privately owned media corporations are profit seeking just like any other capitalist corporation, they have to ensure that their revenues exceed costs. Such revenues increasingly depend on advertising, making advertisements both "the lifeblood of the traditional media and ... the Internet" (Ritzer 2005: 30) and "[t]he backbone, the heart, the soul, the fuel, the DNA ... of nonpublic television in America" (Postman and Powers 2011: 33). Thus, the media have an incentive to generate as much revenue from advertisers as possible by broadcasting as many commercial messages to their audience as they can get away with.

This points to the first ideological effect of contemporary media. This effect, which emerges as the unintended consequence of the media corporations' profit-seeking strategies, operates in the same way that capital's subsumption of consumption emerges as the unintended consequence of regular corporations' profit-seeking strategies. In Chapter 3 we saw how regular corporations' intentional microeconomic strategies unintentionally add up to the creation of a toxic materialistic culture and an assault on consumer rationality. Similarly, media corporations' profit-seeking intentions have the unintended effect of transforming media into an ideal platform through which this materialistic culture invades consumer consciousness, modifying it in a direction that does more to serve capital accumulation than human well-being. It is through this competitive process, then, that advertising increasingly dominates the content of many media sources (Bordwell 2002: 240; Cross 2000: 34). At the same time, substantive content becomes almost an afterthought and a means to attract an audience that is large and affluent enough to keep advertising revenue flowing. In fact, as one advertising executive admitted as early as 1907, "a magazine is simply a device to induce people to read advertising" (Cross 2000: 34).

The second ideological effect of contemporary media also stems from the growing financial dependence of the media on advertising revenues. This dependence means that the media are not interested in attracting any kind of audience. They are mostly interested in the audience most attractive to advertisers. The latter are, of course, especially interested in consumers with high purchasing power. This means that the safest course for profit-seeking media corporations is to avoid points of view that antagonize the economically affluent strata of society and the large (often transnational) corporations with large advertising budgets (Wright and Rogers 2011: 401; McChesney et al. 2009: 19).

It is hardly surprising, then, that the contrast between academic research and media propaganda that Moshe Lewin (2005: 2–3) has noted with respect to the representation of the Soviet Union in the West survives in a different form after the end of the Cold War. In particular, with the defunct Soviet Union no longer serving as the bogeyman of choice, Marx and Marxism are more likely today to illustrate the contrast between serious academic research and media propaganda.

On the academic side, even scholars who do not necessarily share Marx's analysis and politics locate him "in the great line of economic viewpoints that have successively clarified, illuminated, and interpreted the world for us" (Heilbroner 1986: 139). It is not controversial, among scholars, to regard Marx as a "pivotal" figure within the discipline of sociology (Collins 1985: 490), whose "theories have produced one of sociology's most productive and significant research programs" (Ritzer 2008: 44), while also helping to "transform the social philosophy of earlier centuries into the modern discipline of sociology" (Pampel 2007).

On the other hand, corporate media treat Marxist views, when they acknowledge their existence, as marginal and beyond the pale. When it comes to discussions of Marxist views in the corporate media, it is not knowledgeable analysis but caricature and propaganda that are the norm. Thus, the unsuspecting audience member usually remains blissfully unaware of the great ideological and political diversity within Marxism (Wolff 2012: 107–8; Collins 1985: 49; McLellan 1979), concluding instead that the only Marxism that has ever existed is that of Stalin. Thus, communism in this ideological narrative becomes as synonymous with one-party dictatorship as capitalism is with multi-party democracy and freedom (Resnick and Wolff 2002: 98–99).

In other words, the process through which capital's real subsumption of consumption takes place does not just divert part of the surplus towards the advertising and marketing industry. It also has to divert another part of the surplus towards the creators of the ideological substantive content that delivers an audience to the advertisers and marketers who keep their employers afloat.

What emerges from this analysis is the interaction between the exploitation of workers and capital's real subsumption of labor, on one side, and capital's real subsumption of consumption, with its assault on consumer rationality, on the other. These two processes feed on each other: the exploitation of workers through capital's real subsumption of labor generates a surplus that finances, among other things, capital's real subsumption of consumption; and the role of the media in the process through which capital's real subsumption of consumption proceeds promotes an ideological representation of reality that facilitates the reproduction of capitalism's exploitative class relations.

This macro-social effect of the media on the public's consciousness does not imply a vast conspiracy to indoctrinate the general public. Rather, it emerges as the mundane and understandable product of the microeconomic strategies that profit-seeking media corporations understandably adopt. Because of their dependence on advertising, it makes economic sense for these corporations to adapt their message to the tastes of corporate advertisers and the affluent segment of the public that advertisers are most interested in.

But, since the audience consuming the media content produced is broader than the audience advertisers target, the ideological effect of media content is to encourage everyone in that broader audience to understand reality just as beneficiaries of capitalist exploitation do. And this effect is probably more, rather than less, potent precisely to the extent that it does not rely on any kind of blatant censorship by a heavy-handed state clumsily restricting free expression. Emerging from mundane economic competition, this effect is correspondingly more subtle and harder to detect.

Capital's subsumption of consumption as an assault on democracy and citizen rationality

This insight has implications for the long-standing debate regarding the supposedly democratic effects of market capitalism. The treatment of the latter as akin to democracy is clear, for example, in the popular platitude regarding the ability of consumers to "vote with their dollars." In fact, some writers go even further than attempting to invest capitalism with the positive aura of democracy. In their argument, capitalist markets are superior to democracy because

> [m]ajority rule is ... very different from the kind of freedom you have when you shop at the supermarket. When you enter the voting booth ... , you almost always vote for a package rather than for specific items. If you are in the majority, you will at best get both the items you favored and the ones you opposed but regarded as on balance less important. Generally, you end up with something different from what you thought you voted for. If you are in the minority, you must conform to the majority vote and wait for your turn to come. When you vote daily in the supermarket, you get precisely what you vote for, and so does everyone else.
>
> (Friedman and Friedman 1981: 57)

Critics of the treatment of capitalism as a kind of consumer democracy have rightly pointed out that, whereas democracy relies on the principle of "one person, one vote," market capitalism relies on that of "one dollar, one vote." This means that markets are less democratic insofar as they give the rich more "votes" than the poor (Hahnel 2005: 79–80). And, of course, numerous scholars have pointed out the corrupting effect that capitalism and growing inequality have on democracy, as a very affluent tiny minority can use its money to influence policy and public opinion (Crouch 2012: 80–81; Wolff 2012: 150; Wright and Rogers 2011: 351; Nichols 2011a: 7; Nichols 2011b: 274; Engler 2010: 21; Dowd 2000: 208; Bowles and Edwards 1993: 428–29; Block 1994a: 375).

In fact, the influence of money on politics can give rise to a vicious cycle, whereby growing inequality makes it possible to change policies in ways that fuel the growth of inequality even further (Graeber 2013: 39; Crouch 2012: 80–81; Chomsky 2011: 153; Sackrey and Schneider 2002: 114). In the neoliberal era, in particular, "[m]oney became the key to political influence as never before," with the result that "many citizens lost interest in politics and a general mood of disenchantment if not alienation in regard to the whole political process became common" (Munck 2005: 66).

The analysis of capital's real subsumption of consumption advances beyond the argument that capitalist markets' dependence on the "one dollar, one vote principle" makes them less democratic than democracy. Capital's real subsumption of consumption also undermines the democratic nature of political democracy itself. It does so through its ability to skew the public debate that shapes the citizens' perception of social reality.

In particular, by privileging some perspectives over others, capital's real subsumption of consumption has a differential effect on the ability of different classes and social groups to articulate their respective interests. Since the representation of reality most consistent with the pursuit of advertising revenue and profit is also the one most consistent with the interests of those benefiting from capitalist exploitation, the benefits that different groups accrue from the media content broadcast will depend on where they stand in the class pyramid. The discretionary income at the disposal of those on the top provides the media with an economic incentive to become that particular group's advocate. By painting a picture of social reality that is not offensive to that group, the economic incentive of the media to please corporate advertisers and the most affluent segments of society makes it more difficult for exploited groups to recognize the connections between exploitation and the hardships and social problems they face in everyday life. Thus, for example, the same media that stifle meaningful debate on economic policy by presenting the neoliberal agenda as a self-evident solution to economic and social problems often invent dubious debates about environmental problems by treating the fossil fuel industry's obfuscation and denial of climate change as no less credible than the overwhelming consensus among natural scientists regarding the grave risks for humanity and the planet that this crisis entails (Tanuro 2010: 254; Hoggan 2009: 151–67; Simms 2005: 122).

In this respect, capital's subsumption of consumption also has the effect, via the influence it exerts over media content, of making working people's recognition of capitalist exploitation even more difficult than it already is. As Marx points out, by contrast to exploitation in pre-capitalist societies, capitalist exploitation

> is not directly visible. Surplus labour and necessary labour are mingled together … It is otherwise with the corvee. The necessary labour which the Wallachian peasant performs for his own maintenance is distinctly marked off from his surplus labour on behalf of the boyar. The one he does on his own field, the other on the seignorial estate. Both parts of the labour-time thus exist independently, side by side with each other. In the corvee the surplus labour is accurately marked off from the necessary labour.
>
> (Marx 1977 [1867]: 345–46)

As Marx's discussion reveals, the obscurity of capitalist exploitation stems from the fact that there is no clear spatio-temporal separation, within capitalism, between the wealth that workers produce for the reproduction of their labor power and the economic surplus they are forced to generate for their employer. The existence of these two different parts of the wealth they produced was readily visible

> [i]n civilized pre-capitalist society [, in which] agriculture constitutes man's chief economic activity. Ground rent is therefore the essential form of society's surplus-product. It is produced by agricultural producers who ... surrender part of their labour-time (labour-service) or of their production (rent in kind) to the property-owning classes. This division of the peasant's product into necessary product and surplus-product (ground rent) takes place wholly outside the market, in the sphere of the production of use-values.
>
> (Mandel 1971: 272)

In capitalism, by contrast, the fact that workers receive their hourly wage for each of the hours they work prevents them from recognizing, as peasants in pre-capitalist societies easily could, that they do not reap the full benefit of the work they perform.

The source of obscurity Marx discusses predisposes workers to view capitalist societies as fundamentally free and fair. This makes them more receptive to media content that, as a result of the process through which capital's subsumption of consumption proceeds, paints a similar picture. And the ideological representation of capitalist reality and its critics that advertising-dependent media in capitalist society have an incentive to adopt tends to discourage an understanding and appreciation by working people of critical discourses, such as Marxism, that show capitalism to be no less exploitative than other class societies of the past.

In view of these effects on social consciousness and democracy, capital's real subsumption of consumption is an assault not just on consumer but also on citizen rationality. Funding both these assaults, moreover, is the surplus that capital extracts from the direct producers. Thus, the effect of exploitation on the latter is not just to deprive them of part of the fruits of their labor. It is also to use that surplus to distort their preferences and values in a materialistic direction that is inimical to their well-being and to skew their understanding of social reality in a way that obscures the class exploitation they are subject to.

Thus, instead of the growing economic productivity at the basis of the growing surplus becoming a means to the enhancement of human well-being and democracy, it turns into its opposite. As many scholars, in line with Marx's (1981 [1894]: 959) vision of an enlarged "realm of freedom," have pointed out (Wright and Rogers 2011: 115–17; Schor 1991: 2; Albert 2003: 239, 242–43), this growing productivity could be used to reduce the amount of time people have to spend at work. Instead, capitalism tends to channel growing productivity into a direction more conducive to profits and capital accumulation (Panayotakis 2006; Schor 1991: 120–22; Cross 1988; Hunnicutt 1988: 42), namely the expansion of production and consumption. And, notwithstanding the claims that in capitalism people are "free to choose" (Friedman and Friedman 1981), the reality is that

> [c]onsumerism is also generated by what can be called a failure in the "market" for leisure. If we had a perfect market for leisure, then people would be able to easily choose the amount of work and leisure they preferred. This is not the case. Labor

> market and employment in the United States are organized in a way that makes it dif-
> ficult for individuals to choose a less consmumerist lifestyle in favor of more free time.
>   (Wright and Rogers: 2011: 112–13)

Referring to this effect of contemporary capitalism as a market failure may be a little misleading, since the term suggests that it is the product of a mistake when, in fact, it is the predictable product of capital's profit-seeking rationality (Panayotakis 2006). In any event, what is clear is that contemporary capitalism prevents people from increasing their well-being by choosing more free time over the consumption of more commod-ities (Wright and Rogers 2011: 112–17; Schor 1991: 3; Durning 1992: 114). This lost opportunity is a manifestation of capitalism's assault on consumer rationality, if we con-sider, as mainstream neoclassical economics does, free time as one of the goods that rational consumers can choose from when they try to maximize the satisfaction of their needs and preferences (Laidler and Estrin 1989: 69–71).

Moreover, the channeling of growing productivity into consumerism rather than add-itional free time undercuts democracy in two ways. The first way, as we have already discussed, has to do with the obstacles it places to the ability of the exploited to recog-nize their interest in abolishing exploitation. In addition to the injustice that they intro-duce in the nominally democratic political systems of many capitalist societies, such obstacles also impoverish the democratic debate. They do so by making it more difficult for a full articulation of all the contradictory interests existing within society and by therefore preventing a full articulation of and vigorous debate between all the different possible interpretations of social reality as well as the different possible responses to the various problems plaguing society.

The second way that the channeling of growing productivity into consumerism undercuts democracy is by unnecessarily depriving people of a resource indispensable to democratic participation, namely time (Panayotakis 2011a: 63; Bookchin 1986: 234; Wainwright 2003: 218–19, note 7). As labor and social historians have shown, one of the first rationales underlying the labor movement's struggle for shorter work hours was precisely the contribution that more free time would make to working people's ability to function as full citizens (Friedman 2008: 98; Sirianni 1991: 249; Cross 1988: 9; Behagg 1988: 64; Weaver 1988: 88). In particular, more free time could empower ordinary people to build their political and democratic skills and self-confidence through partici-pation in local politics, community groups and labor unions (Panayotakis 2011a: 69–70). And, last but not least, more free time would also increase people's ability to study the complexities of political debates and social phenomena. This would empower them "to participate capably in public and civic affairs" (Weaver 1988: 88) by making them less vulnerable to capitalism's systematic assaults on their citizen rationality.

In this respect, capital's real subsumption of consumption only amplifies an undemo-cratic effect inherent in all class societies. In such societies the presence of exploitation in effect divides the population into "a class proprietor of social time, of 'everyone's time, of time *tout court*, and the class whose time has been dispossessed, the class of those 'without time'" (Basso 2003: 199). In so doing, it also divides the population into a minority, which, not having to work for a living, is able to dominate public affairs by mon-opolizing the debates and decisions over matters of common concern, and a majority, which, knowing only "a lifetime of toil" (Bookchin 1986: 234), finds it much more difficult to intervene in political affairs and make its voice heard. In this sense, Basso (2003: 199) is right to point out that the control by the exploiting class of everyone's time secures its dominance over society's political as well as economic life.

Re-empowering ordinary workers and citizens in the face of capital's disempowering use of science and technology

But the process through which capital's real subsumption of consumption proceeds is not the only way that capitalism's instrumentalization of science and technology undermines democracy. As Braverman (1974) has shown, capital's real subsumption of labor often proceeds through technologies that deskill and disempower large segments of the working class by confining them to work that does not engage their critical faculties. This lack of participation in decision making and creative problem solving in the workplace means that workers lose the opportunity to develop, in their daily activities, skills crucial to democratic participation. It is not surprising, then, that class struggle under capitalism has for a long time also involved a struggle over the right of workers to become masters of the labor process rather than serving as passive, subordinate cogs within it (Ness and Azzellini 2011).

That this is the case becomes manifest in the regular recurrence of spontaneous movements of worker self-management during most waves of social protest and revolution since the rise of capitalism (Cohen 2011: 63; Wallis 2011: 12; Markovic 1991: 494; Rothschild and Whitt 1986: 10, 188). These movements have often sprung up even in opposition to the official leaderships of the labor movement and of socialist and communist parties alike (Ness and Azzellini 2011: 2; Cohen 2011: 53). To the extent that this is the case, such leaderships have been complicit in the reproduction of capitalism's undemocratic tendencies. And, although they have often exerted this role in the hope of gaining material benefits for workers, the long-term decline of the labor movement in most of the Western world and beyond suggests that this strategy is becoming ever less viable and effective (Friedman 2008: 22–23). The labor movement can no longer afford to confine itself to an "agenda of getting more crumbs from capitalists" (Mulder 2015: 3). As Gerald Friedman (2008: 163) argues,

> [o]ver a century of the reformist Labor Movement teaches one lesson: if we do not demand what we want, then we are sure to get something else. Enriched by a century of struggle, the Labor Movement can only be reborn, even reignited, as institutions for revolutionary struggle rather than reform, but only if its means reflect its ends, its democratic aspirations. Either labor acts on its belief that all are entitled to an equal voice, or we accept autocracy; either autocratic institutions are revolutionized and democratized, or they remain autocratic; either we are revolutionaries, or we are conservatives who believe in divine right.

This is an argument for the labor movement to reinvent itself as part of a broader movement to democratize society as a whole (Friedman 2008: 161–62). This self-reinvention would require the labor movement to radicalize itself, however, and to embrace again the ideal of communism, with its imperative that working people gain control over the decisions that determine the size, allocation, and use of the economic surplus they produce. Its abandonment of a radical anti-capitalist stance has over time led to the labor movement's "portray[al] as an exclusive 'special interest,' concerned only with the interests of those lucky few who belong to unions or, even worse, the interests of a few leaders" (Friedman 2008: 12). By contrast, its return to its past radicalism would associate the labor movement with the increasingly universal interest both in making a better use of contemporary productive forces and in doing away with the grave threats for humanity and the planet that, as this work shows, capitalism generates. Last but not least, the labor movement's self-reinvention would also have to include a challenge to capitalist consumer society's long-standing premise that rising levels of material consumption could serve as a substitute for workers' control over the organization of the workplace (Cross 2000: 53).

Abandoning this premise is necessary not only because in the neoliberal era capital has itself abandoned its own part of the deal, no longer sharing productivity gains with the workers (Bowles, Edwards, and Roosevelt 2005: 162–63, 167–69; Friedman 2008: 162). It is also objectionable because it leads working people to hand over to the functionaries of capital a number of decisions that greatly affect not only their lives at work and outside but also the skills they develop in their everyday life and the kind of people they can become (Dahl 1989: 324–32; Bowles and Gintis 1986: 130, 204–5). This last point is especially important, moreover, in view of its implications for working people's ability not only to achieve fulfillment inside and outside work but also to have a voice in the political deliberations and struggles that will shape their own future as well as the future of humanity and the planet.

No longer prioritizing higher standards of living over workers' control over the production and distribution of the surplus is not just a break with the past, and ultimately self-defeating, practices of organized labor within the capitalist world. This prioritization also characterized the class system that eventually emerged out of the Russian Revolution and that elevated catching up with the material living standards of advanced capitalist societies into a central criterion of success (Resnick and Wolff 2002: 303). This class system, in the Soviet Union and elsewhere where it was transplanted, did to some extent advance people's standard of living (Lewin 2005: 366–67; Lovell 2009: 72). But even such advances were undercut by the promise, by ruling elites, that the post-capitalist class societies they were presiding over would deliver material standards of living higher than those in advanced capitalist societies. By setting up a geographical and systemic comparison of material standards of living, ruling elites inadvertently diverted their population's attention from such temporal advances in domestic material consumption as their class societies had achieved (Brown 2009). Thus, when the post-capitalist class societies failed to deliver living standards higher than those in advanced capitalist societies, the blow to their legitimacy hastened their eventual collapse (Brown 2009; Resnick and Wolff 2002).

In this sense, the decline of organized labor in the capitalist world and the eventual failure of the Russian Revolution both teach a similar lesson. Treating the pursuit of higher standards of living as an alternative to a democratization of the economy and the production and distribution of the surplus can, in the long run, neither challenge capital nor even lastingly mitigate its exploitation of workers. In this sense, there is an affinity between the vision of a democratic classless society and the autonomist/horizontalist tradition's challenge of the logic of political representation (Sitrin and Azzellini 2014). Indeed, by requiring the general population's democratic control over the surplus, the vision of a democratic classless society challenges the division of the population into a directive, technocratically sophisticated and politically skilled elite receiving and managing the surplus and a subordinate majority implementing the decisions that the elite makes in the name of the masses.

So, to the extent that there is a parallel between the long-term decline of organized labor within the capitalist world and the ultimate failure of the social model that ultimately emerged from the Russian Revolution, Friedman's diagnosis of what it would take to reignite organized labor within capitalist societies has implications for the discussion of what it would take to resuscitate the search for a democratic classless alternative to capitalist society. To possess any kind of credibility and to combat the demonization of communism that the Soviet experience has fueled (Badiou 2016: 22), the movement for a democratic classless society will need to adopt the kind of prefigurative politics that autonomous and horizontal movements are known for. In other words, such a movement would have to break with the rigid hierarchical political model characteristic of many of the organizations of the traditional left. Instead, it would have to learn from and build on the insights and experience of new social movements and the tradition of horizontal and autonomous politics, placing special emphasis on the development of political and other mechanisms that nurture the democratic skills of the rank and file. Such mechanisms can take different forms, ranging from participatory budgeting to occupied and worker-managed factories in Latin America and elsewhere (Magnani 2009; Santos 2005b; Avritzer 2005; Trigona 2008).

At the same time, however, a project for a democratic classless society has to avoid the temptation, to which the autonomist tradition sometimes succumbs, of assuming that people can effect fundamental change by "circumventing [the state] to go straight to becoming other people doing other things without state permission" (Solnit 2009). Supporters of horizontal models of politics rightly point to the delegitimization of mainstream electoral politics, as electoral campaigns increasingly degenerate into "fairytale contests" (Sitrin and Azzellini 2014: 42), which take a toll on political elites' credibility and ability to represent their constituents.

But the most promising of the experiments informed by the horizontalist impulse have shown that the state has to be engaged, even if that has to be done in a different, less hierarchical way. Participatory budgeting, for example, challenges the hierarchical and technocratic logic that usually informs the allocation and use of the taxes collected by the state. And, if the crisis of representation that contemporary advocates of autonomous and horizontal politics rightly deplore leads to lower popular interest and participation in politics, innovative attempts that, like participatory budgeting, magnify the influence of the most disenfranchised segments of the population on state processes have shown their ability to enhance ordinary people's political engagement (Avritzer 2005: 393–94; Sader 2005: 464; Wainwright 2003: 109). Similarly, even occupied worker-managed companies have not had the luxury of sidestepping and ignoring the state but, in their quest to survive, thrive, and serve as a living proof that another way is indeed possible, have often pressured the state to recognize their right to operate and control the businesses that their previous capitalist bosses had run into the ground (Panayotakis 2011a: 136–37).

In this sense, the project for a democratic classless society can perhaps benefit from a potentially virtuous circle between mechanisms that democratize the state, such as participatory budgeting, and practical examples of democratized production, such as occupied worker-controlled factories (Panayotakis 2011a: 137). As the experience of participatory budgeting demonstrates, the democratization of the state can enhance the democratic skills and participation of the most disenfranchised groups in society (Menser and Robinson 2008). This shows two things: first, as Hilary Wainwright (2003: 109) has pointed out,

> [t]he problem with present forms of political power is not people's apathy or an unwill-
> ingness to participate. When there is a chance of having a real influence over the allo-
> cation of resources, a real chance to improve the quality of life of a neighborhood,
> and when people are aware of it and are at least half convinced that it could make a
> difference, then they engage.

Second, the more a democratized state encourages disenfranchised groups to partici-pate, the more their participation will close the gap of participation between privileged and underprivileged groups, which political theorists and sociologists have often described (Markoff 2014: 119; Schaefer and Streeck 2013: 13). In so doing, however, the enhanced participation of underprivileged groups could not but help to democratize the state even further.

Moreover, the more the state becomes democratized, the more likely it will be to provide support for democratic alternatives to capitalist production, including worker-controlled businesses. Such support would be valuable, given the great obstacles that worker-controlled businesses have to overcome in a capitalist society, including the fact that such businesses are often hard-pressed to find the lines of credit that would allow them to survive (Dominick 2008: 384; Schweickart 1996: 240). Such support is also feasible to the extent that, even in the hardly radical United States, there is widespread support for worker-owned and -controlled companies on both sides of the political spectrum (Alperovitz 2011). Thus, any advances in the democratization of the state would also make it more likely that this popular support for democratic alternatives to capitalist production would actually shape state economic policy.

Conversely, the expansion of democratic forms of production, such as worker-controlled companies, would turn the workplace from an enemy of ordinary people's ability to develop their democratic skills into its greatest friend. As Robin Hahnel (2008: 255) has pointed out,

> [w]orker-owned firms ... afford workers important opportunities to participate in eco-
> nomic decision-making unavailable to them in capitalist firms. They train workers to
> make decisions collectively, together with their co-workers. When they compete suc-
> cessfully against capitalist firms, worker-owned firms challenge the myth that workers
> cannot govern themselves effectively, and therefore require bosses to decide what they
> should do and compel them to do it.

In performing all these functions, the expansion of democratic forms of production could also empower people in their capacity as citizens, helping them to more effectively participate in the political process and in innovative experiments, such as participatory budgeting. Thus, a positive synergy could be established between the democratization of the state and the expansion of democratic forms of production, with each of these elements in the project for a democratic classless society gaining strength from its interaction with the other (Panayotakis 2011a: 141).

Capital's use of science to mold the public agenda

I have argued that both capitalism's subsumption of labor and its subsumption of consumption undermine democracy itself when they undermine working people's ability to develop the skills, knowledge, self-confidence, and autonomous class consciousness they need to participate in the democratic debate more meaningfully and effectively than they currently do. Similarly, I have discussed how capitalism's undemocratic implications, in this regard, are crucially dependent on an instrumentalization of science, technology, and the production of information. In a capitalist society all these crucial aspects of our culture become means of generating profit, even at the expense of human well-being and development.

And yet the list of capital's techniques for instrumentalizing science, technology, and the production of information is still not complete. No less important, and no less detrimental to democracy, is the ability of capital to sponsor scientific research, policy agendas, and an elaborate network of institutional apparatuses, such as think tanks, research centers, foundations, and so on, that shape the public debate, thus altering social consciousness and public policy alike. To pursue that objective,

> [c]apitalists ... devote portions of their surplus to sustaining allied political, economic, and cultural organizations ... This especially includes the cultural organizations that originate and/or disseminate theories, religions, and other ways of understanding how the world works that serve their interests. To control politics requires shaping how the mass of people understand the workings of the world, what the Marxian theorist Antonio Gramsci analyzed as building a "hegemonic bloc."
>
> (Wolff 2012: 150)

Building a hegemonic bloc favorable to capital entails the subordination of both science and the production of information to the pursuit of capital accumulation. As a result, the intellectual products of the institutional apparatuses involved in the hegemonic project are as, if not more, likely to obfuscate the issues confronting society as they are to shed light on them (Hoggan 2009; Union of Concerned Scientists 2011).

The great social importance that this use of the surplus can have becomes evident when we consider the role that it has played in the rise of the neoliberal consensus (Wolff 2012: 150; Mason 2012: 118; Steger and Roy 2010: 23; Harvey 2005: 43–44; George 2001: 18–19; Clarke 1996: 299–300). Representing the intellectual moment in capital's "counterrevolution" after the exhaustion of the post-war model of development in the 1970s, the mobilization of intellectual forces in support of neoliberal policies has not only facilitated the generalization of these policies (Duménil and Lévy 2005); it has also contributed to the vicious cycle whereby neoliberal policies increase economic inequality, which in turn increases the resources that corporate interests and the wealthy can devote to influencing public policy and public debate, thus also further fueling the redistribution of resources from the bottom to the top (Graeber 2013: 39; Crouch 2012: 80–1; Chomsky 2011: 153; Sackrey and Schneider 2002: 114).

As the analysis of the last two chapters shows, therefore, the surplus that capital extracts from workers, and the growing productivity that keeps this surplus increasing, do not enhance people's well-being and happiness. Neither do they make cultural activities and human interactions in an expanding "realm of freedom" the means to a more fulfilling life for all working people. Instead, capital uses culture, science, technology, and the dissemination of information to promote a consumerist way of life that adversely affects people's well-being, while also contributing to the ecological devastation of the planet. And, last but not least, these processes subordinate science and the dissemination of information to the interests of capital rather than to the pursuit of truth and the deepening of democracy.

Conclusion

This chapter concludes our account of the destructive effects of capitalism's consumerist culture. The role of the media in promoting this culture, in combination with the media's dependence on advertising, contributes to a problem that we are going to revisit, namely capitalism's erosion of democracy. But this chapter also traces capitalism's erosion of democracy to other ways that capital uses science and technology. In particular, it examines how the profit orientation shaping capitalism's division of labor confines large numbers of people to jobs that do not encourage the development of the skills necessary for effective political participation. Similarly, this chapter demonstrates how its pursuit of profit also encourages capital to bankroll "scientific" research and public campaigns that do less to promote human knowledge than to misrepresent reality in line with the interests of their capitalist sponsors.

5

Capitalism as a force of destruction

In line with the discussion, in the last two chapters, of the negative effects of capitalism's consumerist culture, this chapter continues the analysis of capital's destructive uses of the surplus. Introducing the term "forces of destruction," it highlights the increasingly destructive employment of capitalism's rapid scientific and technological advances. In particular, this chapter pays special attention to capitalism's rapid development and regular deployment of increasingly lethal military technologies as well as to the ways in which capital's productive technologies contribute to a deepening ecological crisis.

By advancing a critique of market-oriented strands of the environmental movement, the chapter also initiates this work's analysis of "new social movements" as in part a reaction to capitalism's increasing destructiveness. In this respect, this critique also forms part of a recurring theme in this work, namely that new social movements cannot pursue their objectives effectively without also challenging capital's undemocratic control of the surplus. Last but not least, the chapter argues for the need to analyze social and historical development through a complex three-way interaction between capitalism's (or any other class society's, for that matter) forces of production, forces of destruction, and relations of production. In so doing, it also lays the ground for reformulating the contradiction underlying contemporary capitalism, a task undertaken in the next chapter.

Rethinking the articulation of capitalism's liberatory and destructive moments

Marx's optimism partly stemmed from the liberatory potential implicit in the technological dynamism and growing economic surplus that modern capitalism generates (Marx 1981 [1894]: 958–59; Cohen 2000: 198–99). Marxist thought always recognized that the fulfillment of this potential is not possible within capitalism, however. Although this potential lay in the overcoming of material scarcity, the operation of capitalist society tended, according to many Marxists, to artificially reproduce scarcity, even after scarcity had become historically obsolete (Baran and Sweezy 1966: 352–53; Clarke 1991: 230). As Terry Eagleton (2010: 101–2) observes,

> [t]he Marxist idea of communism involves the development of the productive forces, free from the stymieing and blockages of pre-history or class society, to the point where

they can give birth to a surplus sufficient for the abolition of labour and the fulfilment of the needs of everyone. If this hasn't come about yet, it is among other reasons because the only historical mode of production capable of generating such a surplus – capitalism – is by a supreme irony the one which deploys it to create scarcity.

Capitalism's frustration of this potential for human liberation, along with the human suffering that capitalism's periodic economic crises produced, constituted a systemic contradiction that would make it hard for the system to survive. In this narrative, therefore, it was possible to read even the risks that the operation of capitalism generated as aspects of a contradictory historical process that would ultimately lead to human liberation.

In the course of the twentieth century the mood among Marxist theorists started to darken. Two world wars, the disappointment of the hopes that the Russian Revolution had aroused, the rise of consumerism, the neoliberal counterrevolution's increase of economic inequality after a period of relative (if uneven) social progress, and the deepening ecological crisis are all forcing a shift in the relative weight of the optimistic and pessimistic moments within the Marxist narrative. First of all, these developments have understandably shaken the faith that capitalism will "[subvert] itself" once it fulfills "[t]he mission … [of] carry[ing] humanity to [a] stage of abundance" that would "make it no longer true that most of life and time and energy must be spent joylessly producing means to imperative ends" (Cohen 2000: 198–99).

The scholars most strongly identifying with the classical Marxist tradition may still affirm the necessity of this future. In view of everything that has transpired since Marx's time, however, the sense of this necessity may have to shift. Less than expressing the communist future's inevitability, it may be more plausible to interpret this necessity as a moral imperative to avert the risks that capitalism creates and to realize the potential it suppresses. The weight of events and social developments of the last century or more seem to have uncoupled the former "causal" form of necessity from the latter "conditional" form. Although the belief in the possibility of human liberation may be alive and, indeed, necessary, the faith that this liberation is imminent and inevitable is much harder to come by.

Part of the reason for this shift is undoubtedly the fact that capitalism has proved much more resilient than Marx had expected (Bowles, Edwards, and Roosevelt 2005: 530). This resilience has, to begin with, expressed itself in capitalism's continuing development of the forces of production more than 150 years after Marx and Engels (1978 [1848]) announced the system's inevitable downfall. But, second, it has also expressed itself in capitalism's ability to survive despite the unimaginable catastrophes it has continued to visit upon humanity and the planet.

For some Marxists, capitalism's unexpected resilience in the first regard is only a confirmation of Marx's theses (Cohen 2000: 394–95; Callinicos 1991: 20). In this reading, both the survival of capitalism into the twenty-first century and the rise and fall of the Soviet Union are completely in line with the historical materialist assertion that "[n]o social order is ever destroyed before all the productive forces for which it is sufficient have been developed, and new superior relations of production never replace older ones before the material conditions for their existence have matured within the framework of the old society" (Marx 1970 [1859]: 21). Thus, this reading makes it possible to interpret as understandable the Russian Revolution's failure to signal the beginning of capitalism's demise and its replacement by a superior communist society.

But this failure may also represent a confirmation of capitalism's resilience in the second regard. Being a product not only of the class contradictions of pre-revolutionary Russia but also of World War I (Resnick and Wolff 2002: 146–53; Callinicos 1991: 22–23), the eruption of the Russian Revolution may have for a time suggested that the major catastrophes that capitalism visits on humanity can fatally undermine its conditions of reproduction. The eventual failure of that revolution may suggest, however, that even as major a catastrophe as a world war and as major a response to that catastrophe as the Russian Revolution were no more than temporary setbacks for capitalist development the world over.

Thus, the fate of the Russian Revolution could become the basis for an economistic articulation of the two forms of capitalist resilience, in which the former source of capitalism's resilience would serve as the key to explaining the latter. In such an articulation, therefore, capitalism-induced catastrophes might generate radical anti-capitalist movements, but these movements would not achieve a communist classless society until capitalism ceased to develop the forces of production. In Cohen's (2000: 203, emphases in original) words, before capitalism has reached its limits, what is "possible is *potentially reversible* subversion of the capitalist system, *not* construction of socialism: the anti-capitalist revolution can be premature and can therefore fail of its socialist object. What makes a *successful* revolution possible is sufficiently developed productive forces."

This line of reasoning could, potentially, even preserve faith in the inevitability of capitalism's replacement by communism. After all, the continuing development of the forces of production would mean that capitalism's survival into the twenty-first century has not refuted Marxism's confident prediction of this replacement; it simply signifies the postponement of the moment when this prediction will come true.

This kind of confidence is hard to sustain even for theorists who want to preserve the basic framework of Marx's theory of history. In fact, capitalism's continuing technological dynamism has, understandably, shaken such theorists' confidence that a moment will arrive when capitalism becomes an insuperable obstacle to a further development of the forces of production.

A good illustration of this is Cohen's (2000: 326–40) terminological acrobatics regarding "fettering," a term Marxists have used to theorize the role of the contradiction between the forces and relations of production to transitions from one mode of production to another. Conceding that "[t]here may not even be good reason to think that a persisting capitalism would, in time, display a deceleration in the rate of development of the productive forces," Cohen (2000: 327) attempts to preserve the fettering thesis by modifying the traditional understanding of what it meant for capitalism to become a fetter to the development of the forces of production. Not surprisingly, this attempt is less than successful, with Cohen (2000: 341) coming to admit that "I have come to wonder whether [Marx's theory of history] is true (though not whether … it was affirmed by Karl Marx)."

Cohen's attempt to redefine fettering shows that inventive terminological redefinitions can defend the continuing relevance of Marx's theory of history in the face of capitalism's resilience only by exacting a price in terms of the theory's plausibility. As Cohen (2000: 328) himself admits, if fettering no longer signifies an absolute inability of capitalist relations of production to indefinitely continue developing the forces of production but only the claim that "relations which are better at developing the productive forces are possible," it becomes much harder to assume that this new kind of fettering could bring about the working-class revolution that will replace capitalism with a democratic classless society. In particular, it would be hard to see why workers might be willing to endure the risks and privations that a social revolution might entail in a situation in which capitalism has not reached an impasse but allegedly delivers less than its hypothetical alternative (Cohen 2000: 328–29).

Cohen's conundrum, in this respect, points to the indissoluble connection that exists in Marxism between the unfulfilled potential and the menacing risks that capitalism's operation simultaneously generates. In particular, the great human suffering resulting from recurring economic crises does more than illustrate the maturing contradiction between the developing forces of production and capitalism's productive relations; it also provides the intelligible political mechanism that could turn the abstract possibility of a better society into a matter of survival.

Capitalist economic crises that impose immense suffering on untold numbers of people have certainly not come to an end. And compounding this recurrent source of human suffering are, as noted earlier in this chapter, other catastrophic developments that only add to capitalism's devastating toll on human beings and the planet. These developments serve as a reminder that capitalism's technological dynamism expresses itself as much in the rapid growth of the forces of destruction at the system's disposal as it does in the growth of the forces of production highlighted by most Marxists. In other words, capitalism is as likely to put its ever-advancing technologies and techniques to destructive uses as it is to use them for creating new wealth. This and the next chapter develop this insight into a conception of capitalism's contradictoriness different from that focused on the contradiction between the forces and relations of production.

Capitalism's forces of destruction and the need to rethink capitalism's contradictions

One reason to rethink capitalist contradictions is that, if capitalism has always featured regularly recurring economic crises, the latter may not express that system's gradual transformation into an insuperable obstacle to further productive development. On the contrary, it may be more appropriate to interpret crises as conditions for such development, insofar as they facilitate the capitalist economy to restructure in ways that jump-start productive development once again (Sassoon 1996: 592; Panitch and Miliband 1992: 16).

Such an interpretation of capitalist crises renders problematic any productivist assumption that all such development is by definition good and desirable. Instead, it makes it clear that any benefits that such development might entail for the general population and particular groups within it should not make us forget the simultaneous costs that the mechanisms of capitalist productive development, including economic crises, impose on society, in general, and its most vulnerable groups, in particular.

Another reason to question the desirability of the productive development that capitalism generates is the inseparability of such development from its simultaneous development of the forces of destruction available for use. Just as capitalism's rapid scientific and technological advances have vastly increased labor productivity, so have they led, for example, to the refinement of weapons systems, such as nuclear weapons, and to the empowerment of people controlling them from the comfort and safety of their office to wreak devastation on populations living thousands of miles away.

This kind of development of the forces of destruction is not surprising in view of the role that violence and conflict have historically played in the capitalist development of the part of the world enjoying an economic and military advantage. This advantage made it possible for the countries of the global North to pursue capital accumulation and economic development by subordinating to these goals the resources and populations in other parts of the world (Desai 2013, 32–33, 43–44; Panayotakis 2011a: 78–81; Amin 1996: 3–5; Luxemburg 1968 [1913]: 368–71). This subordination has historically provided easy access to valuable and cheap economic resources, including not only land but also labor power, whether that of African slaves in the past or sweatshop labor in the global South's "free export zones" more recently (Clark and York 2008: 14; McMichael 2006: 175–76; Klein 2000: 202–6; Beaud 2001: 42; Polanyi 2001 [1944]: 217; Wolff and Resnick 1987: 184). Thus, in his discussion of capitalist agriculture, Philip McMichael (2006: 175–76) notes that

> [t]he colonial project established specialized agricultures in the colonies for the export of raw materials and foodstuffs to the metropolitan centers. The tropical sugar plantation was an early prototype of modern, land-depleting monoculture. It was matched during the nineteenth century by the relocation of temperate agriculture (grains and livestock farming) to European settler regions of the world economy, as provisioning the European proletariat required increasingly large volumes of food staples. The relocation of temperate agriculture supplied cheap food to Europe and so cheapened the wage-costs of European capital, but it depended on the intensive exploitation of virgin soils in the New World via mono-cropping with increasingly complex farm machinery.

But in addition to providing economic resources, the subordination of distant lands also secured for the capitalist classes of the leading capitalist countries easier access to the markets of the global South. In fact, a number of scholars have described the links between the intensification of colonial rivalries in the late nineteenth century, World War I (and its continuation, World War II, a short generation later), and the eruption of the international capitalist crisis of the late nineteenth century (Desai 2013: 19, 43, 77–79; Engler 2010: 31; Goldsmith 1996a: 256–57).

The subordination of the global South to the global North did not come to an end with the formal end of colonialism in the decades after World War II. In fact, one of the contributing factors to the great economic boom of the post-war period was the fact that oil and raw material prices were kept low by US military dominance over oil-producing regions and the Third World (Bowles and Edwards 1993: 450–54).

All this points to another aspect of capitalist competition that supporters of capitalism usually gloss over. Such competition does not take only the comparatively benign form of productive investment and innovation by capitalist companies anxious to keep up with or stay ahead of their competitors. This should be clear enough by now, in view of the discussion in Chapter 3, of one not so benign form of capitalist competition, namely the accelerating use of marketing and advertising strategies that undercut human well-being and assault consumer rationality. In view of these effects, the refinement of such strategies is a special case of the phenomenon we are currently discussing, namely capitalist competition's contribution to a development of forces of destruction that is no less rapid and dramatic than capitalism's development of the productive forces.

The manifestation of capitalism's development of the forces of destruction that is at issue here, however, is the spiraling growth of lethal military technology. The dramatic development of this lethal technology has gone far beyond early twentieth-century capitalism's newfound ability to engulf the entire planet in world wars. The invention and spread of nuclear weapons, which the US government had already used against Japan's civilian population in the concluding phase of World War II, have given rise to a destructive potential that is large enough to exterminate humanity many times over.

This reality may rightly seem insane from the point of view of human well-being. This is especially so when one takes into account that a fraction of the military spending of the United States alone would be enough to eradicate extreme poverty by covering the basic survival needs of every human being on the planet. Indeed, Ben Harack (2011) reports that

> annual defense spending in the US is about four times as much money as is needed to begin rapidly ending extreme poverty in the entire world. If some of the US military's monstrous budget could be channelled towards humanitarian goals, then extreme poverty in our world could quickly become a thing of the past.

But, insane as the coexistence of easily removable extreme poverty and the extravagantly wasteful and dangerous military build-up in the United States and elsewhere may be, it is completely in line with capitalist rationality given the historic link between capital accumulation, on one side, and military superiority and violence, on the other. Since the end that capitalist rationality serves is profit maximization, its connection to the rapid growth of the forces of destruction follows (Badiou 2010a: 94). Let us consider why this is indeed the case.

First, financing the growth of military spending requires the diversion of significant portions of the surplus. After all, military spending uses economic resources to enforce (or rearrange) the international geopolitical and economic order through which capital's global pursuit of profit and accumulation takes place.

One agent of such spending is, of course, governments. Another such agent is non-state actors and groups that take part in military conflicts around the world. These actors and groups are often able to conduct these conflicts thanks to economic and military help from governments seeking to reshape world capitalism's geopolitical landscape in their own favor as well as in favor of the economic elites that these governments are usually accountable to (Chengu 2017; Norton 2016; Cockburn 2016; Milne 2015). The cooperation of governments with such actors is not without its risks for the former. As the evolution of the Islamic resistance against the Soviet invasion of Afghanistan and the even more recent evolution of the Islamic State make clear, a stateless actor that seemingly serves a government's geostrategic interests today can easily morph into a major threat for this government and its population tomorrow.

In any event, the contribution to capitalism's rapidly developing forces of destruction that governments throughout the capitalist world continue to make provides yet another reason for a full democratization of the political system of all countries. Although workers in advanced capitalist countries and the trade unions and political forces representing them have at times in the past benefited from and supported their governments' use of violence to subordinate the territories and populations of the global South (Losurdo 2011: 317–18; Sarkar 1999: 236; Mies 1986: 200–1), they are usually not the driving force behind such efforts. In this respect, capitalism's rapid growth of the forces of destruction is inseparable from the tensions that exist between capitalism and democracy. Although we have already touched on these tensions earlier in this work, we will revisit this question in Chapter 7.

For the time being it is enough to point out that governments have a stake in the ability of corporations within their borders to make profits and accumulate capital. Indeed, this ability is a condition for governments' ability to continue raising the tax revenues, since,

> [i]n the context of capitalism, the state relies for its own revenue on the health of the economy. That entails a special dependence on the interests of capital owners and managers. It is above all their reactions and anticipations that represent the 'business climate," which is so often decisive for the success of state policies. And it is their investment decisions that determine future economic growth, stagnation or recession and with that the level of employment and the development of tax revenue. This is the basic dependence constraining state autonomy in capitalist societies.
>
> (Rueschemeyer, Huber Stephens, and Stephens 1992: 65)

This dependence has to do with the effects of economic growth not only on tax revenues but also on government spending. In addition to raising tax revenues, economic growth will also tend to reduce the cost of social policies that support the unemployed and address the various social problems (crime, disease, poverty, and so on) that unemployment and economic insecurity aggravate (Panayotakis 2011a: 22–23). Economic stagnation and crisis, on the other hand, reduce tax revenues just when the need for social spending increases.

In view of all this, it is understandable why governments, even in capitalist "democracies," would be willing to take any step necessary to bolster capital accumulation. So, if military power and, thus, military spending could improve domestic corporations' access to foreign resources and markets (Bowles and Edwards 1993: 453; Desai 2013: 47), governments may have a reason to keep increasing that spending at least as rapidly as other foreign governments do.

Moreover, in periods of economic stagnation and crisis, which have been a recurrent phenomenon throughout the history of capitalist development, military spending can boost employment and production both in the industries receiving military contracts and throughout the economy (from the retail sector, benefiting from increased spending by workers in the military-industrial complex, all the way to corporations in the energy, raw materials, steel, electronic, software and informatics, and all other industries that serve as suppliers for the corporations receiving military contracts) (Desai 2013: 102; Wright and Rogers 2011: 421–22; Garrett-Peltier 2010: 7). A good example of this last point is the contribution of World War II to ending the Great Depression of the 1930s, along with the intense social conflict and legitimization problems this depression had produced throughout the capitalist world (Desai 2013: 87; Thompson 2011: 19). Indeed, as Radhika Desai (2013: 87) has pointed out, "[l]ike the First World War, the Second World War also lifted the United States out of depression. However, this time it was the Great Depression, and the boost it gave the US economy was even greater. Nominal US GDP more than doubled."

Thus, capitalist rationality can easily lead to the kind of arms races that have made nuclear Armageddon and the extinction of the human race a distinct possibility. But, even if we were to avert such a catastrophic scenario, the dynamics that we discussed above can also explain smaller-scale, regional conflicts over resources, which are likely to become even more common in the near future (Klare 2001).

In other words, the use of large portions of the surplus to accelerate the growth of ever deadlier forces of destruction is a predictable result of capitalist rationality. And, just as in the case of capital's real subsumption of consumption, this process also relies on an instrumentalization of science and technology that does not add to human well-being. Instead, when it takes the form of lethal military technologies, this instrumentalization increasingly threatens the very survival of the human species.

The overlap between capitalism's forces of production and its forces of destruction

The size of military spending in the world today, the evolution of military technology, and the role of military conflict in the history of capitalist development are an especially glaring example of capitalism's tendency to develop the forces of destruction threatening us all. But capitalist development also blurs the line between the forces of production and the forces of destruction.

On the one hand, capitalism's historic ability to achieve dramatic increases in labor productivity is in line with the traditional Marxist belief in capitalism's ability to develop the forces of production. On the other hand, however, these dramatic increases have relied on the overconsumption of fossil fuels and, thus, on the generation of climate change and a deepening ecological crisis "[t]he outcome of [which] is … impossible to predict, … because it depends on the interaction, both non-linear and chaotic, of innumerably vast ecosystemic processes" (Kovel 2002: 23–24). In other words, the same technologies often exemplify the advance, under capitalism, of the forces of production and the forces of destruction alike. They exemplify the advance of the latter through the adverse effect they have on human well-being and the ecological integrity of the planet. But they also illustrate the advance of the former insofar as they stem from the refinement of scientific and technological knowledge. This refinement could potentially be a positive development, if we could make it serve humanity and the planet rather than the interests of capital.

Thus, for example, the same technologies that have made the auto industry much more productive and have, through the creation of an auto-industrial complex surrounding it, wrought great damage on the ecological integrity of the planet could instead make possible a vast expansion of mass transportation systems, thus also allowing the replacement of private automobiles as the means of transportation of choice for hundreds of millions of people around the world (Townsend 2010: 115–16; Foster 2002: 98–99; Jackson 1987: 248–49).

In this sense, what is mainly lacking for a solution to the urgent ecological problems facing us is not so much technological know-how. Although ever more elaborate and imaginative technological fixes are more appealing to economic and political elites than the economic redistribution and radical social change that the ecological crisis calls for (Ophuls 1976: 127), the truth is that existing technology could take us a long way towards resolving this crisis, if only we deployed it in a very different way (Townsend 2010: 115; Foster 2002: 98). But this would require a break with capitalist exploitation and the elevation of profit and capital accumulation into the driving forces of our economic system. It is these forces underlying the operation of the capitalist system that account for the seemingly paradoxical coincidence of an advance of the forces of production and the forces of destruction alike.

These dynamics ultimately explain why capitalism's long-standing record of improving productive efficiency has not led to the famed "dematerialization of the economy," in which "[e]ven quite sophisticated economists have a faith … that borders on the religious" (Jackson 2017: 85). The dematerialization thesis rests on the fact that increases in economic output may not require a corresponding increase in the natural resources used up, provided that productive efficiency improvements are sufficiently rapid (Jackson 2017; Trainer 2015: 60–62). As Tim Jackson (2017: 86) explains, "[i]f the rate of increase in efficiency is greater than the rate of economic growth, then typically speaking the overall material throughput will decline. If not, then it won't." For example, if the efficiency with which we use natural resources doubles, thus halving the amount of natural resources used up per unit of output, that output could increase significantly without a corresponding increase in the depletion of our natural environment.

Although the premise of the dematerialization argument is in theory sound, it is an entirely different question whether such dematerialization can arrest, let alone reverse, capital's ecological havoc. As far as the latter question is concerned, the belief in the ability of capitalism to dematerialize the economy stems from the benefits of capitalist competition that supporters of the system have long stressed. To the extent that this competition puts pressure on producers to reduce costs, it provides them with an incentive to economize on all resources, natural resources included. This incentive is hardly new, however. It has been present since the beginning of capitalism and has encouraged the more efficient use of resources, though even these efficiency improvements may not be as extensive as is sometimes assumed (Jackson 2017: 94–96). Such efficiency gains as have been achieved have not prevented the deepening of the ecological crisis confronting humanity and the planet, however (Martinez-Alier 2012: 66). This conclusion becomes especially obvious in view of scholarly findings indicating that, "even in a social welfare capitalist state such as Norway, the increased consumption driven by 'sustainable' economic growth has actually increased carbon dioxide emissions in the two decades since the Brundtland Commission first proposed this strategy" (Schwartzman 2009: 93).

This paradox is not new, and, in fact, it was first identified by one of the forefathers of neoclassical economics, Stanley Jevons. In an argument "that has attracted the admiration of ecological economists … [Jevons] argued that increased efficiency in using a natural

resource, such as coal, only resulted in increased demand for that resource, not a reduction in demand ... because such improvement in efficiency led to a rising scale of production" (Foster 2002: 94). Jevons illustrates this paradox by making reference to "the
whole history of the steam engine" and manufacturing, more generally (Foster 2002: 95).
This was a history of "successive economies" in the use of coal, which were nonetheless
accompanied by "further increases in the scale of production and the demand for coal"
(Foster 2002: 95). As John Bellamy Foster points out, moreover, the case of coal is hardly
an exceptional or idiosyncratic one. It is also not unique to the realities of the nineteenth
century, which inspired Jevons' insight. In fact,

> [t]he introduction of more energy-efficient automobiles in th[e United States] in the
> 1970s did not curtail the demand for fuel because driving increased and the number of
> cars on the road soon doubled. Similarly technological improvements in refrigeration
> simply led to more and larger refrigerators. The same tendencies are in effect within
> industry, independent of individual consumption.
>
> (Foster 2002: 95)

In short, by reducing costs, the more efficient use of natural resources, such as raw
materials, has in the past often boosted demand for the commodities using these natural resources as raw materials. In other words, the growth of the material output
generated by the capitalist economy can easily overwhelm any efficiency gains made.
When this happens, when declines in the natural resources depleted per unit of output
are overwhelmed by the more rapid increase in the number of output units produced,
what results is precisely the paradoxical coincidence between advancing technological
efficiency and escalating ecological devastation that characterizes contemporary capitalism. It is no wonder, then, that Jackson (2017: 164) concludes that "[i]n our kind of
society, in this kind of economy, it is highly unlikely that we will be able to ... remain
within environmental limits."

Ultimately, this paradox is no less surprising than the seemingly paradoxical fact
that labor-saving technologies, which may have drastically reduced the amount of labor
necessary per unit of output, have still not been able to generate a consistent and dramatic reduction in the number of hours people have to work for a living (Schor 1991).
The magnitude of this failure is illustrated by Michael Albert's (2003: 243) calculation
that the productivity increases attained in the 40-year period between 1955 and 1995
could, in theory, have reduced "the workweek ... from 40 hours to about 13 ... with
no loss in fulfillment or in output earmarked to engender socially beneficial progress."
As we saw earlier in this book, the fact that advancing labor productivity can, in principle,
reduce the amount of work people perform even as their material consumption stays
the same, or even increases, does not mean that such an outcome is possible within
capitalism. Whether it is or not depends not on abstract technical possibilities but on
social struggles and/or the compatibility of this outcome with capitalism's compulsive
pursuit of profit.

As we have seen, the result of this pursuit over time has been to undercut the
traditional competitive model underlying mainstream neoclassical economics and to
create a more monopolistic or oligopolistic system, in which competition takes the
much less benign form of strategies that fuel consumerism. Just as this consumerist

culture puts pressure on people to work long hours to keep up with the ever-rising standards of material consumption, so has it ensured the growth of material output at a faster rate than any decline in the natural resources consumed per unit of output. Moreover, the same strategies through which transnational mega-corporations first used to restructure the preferences of consumers in the affluent global North are now deployed across the global South, where the vast majority of the world's population resides (Packard 2011: 213; Panayotakis 2011a: 95; Clarke 1996: 300).

All this is perfectly understandable given how capitalism works. Remarkably, however, the very process of capitalist globalization that makes it less likely that capitalism will now magically reverse its centuries-long record of destroying the planet also serves to disguise the absurdity of this notion. Indeed, one of the effects of capitalist globalization is the establishment of a new international division of labor in which many of the highly polluting industries serving mainly consumers in the global North are increasingly located in countries of the industrializing global South, such as China (Lynch 2016: 90; Naess and Hoyer 2009: 100). Ironically, this new division of labor uncouples the environmental destructiveness of the ecologically unsustainable lifestyles in affluent countries from the amount of pollution generated within the borders of these countries (Lynch 2016: 90; Plumer 2018). As far as climate change is concerned, for example, one manifestation of capitalist globalization is "carbon outsourcing," whereby the carbon emissions from the production of commodities consumed by North Americans or Europeans increasingly take place in countries such as China (Plumer 2018). Indeed, describing the contribution of carbon pollution outsourcing to the appearance that "both the United States and Europe have made major strides in reducing their greenhouse gas emissions," New York Times reporter Brad Plumer (2018) explains that the environmental record of these societies looks

> a lot less impressive once you take trade into account. Many wealthy countries have effectively "outsourced" a big chunk of their carbon pollution overseas, by importing more steel, cement and other goods from factories in China and other places, rather than producing it domestically.
>
> Britain, for instance, slashed domestic emissions within its own borders by one-third between 1990 and 2015. But it has done so as energy-intensive industries have migrated abroad. If you included all the global emissions produced in the course of making things like the imported steel used in London's skyscrapers and cars, then Britain's total carbon footprint has actually increased slightly over that time.

Thus, capitalist globalization creates the appearance of affluent capitalist countries being greener than they really are, even giving rise to the ideological notion of "peak stuff," or a level of capitalist economic development in which consumption of natural resources plateaus or even starts to decline, thus uncoupling economic growth from environmental degradation (Jackson 2017: 92–93). In this sense, the operation of the global capitalist system conveniently generates and nurtures the misleading but reassuring appearance that the worst perpetrators of environmental destruction are really environmental pioneers destined to deliver the world from its ecological woes once the countries of the global South follow their inspiring example.

In any case, capitalism's blurring of the line between the forces of production and the forces of destruction, which the coexistence of ever greater ecological devastation and increasing productive efficiency illustrates, has important implications for classical Marxism's specification of the role of advancing forces of production in the transition from capitalism to a democratic classless society. On the one hand, Marx was aware of the contradictory and paradoxical effects of capitalist technological development. In a powerful speech he delivered more than 160 years ago, Marx (1978b [1856]: 577–78) points out, in a passage worth quoting at some length, that,

> [o]n the one hand, there have started into life industrial and scientific forces, which no epoch of the former human history had ever suspected. On the other hand, there exist symptoms of decay, far surpassing the horrors recorded of the latter times of the Roman empire. In our days everything seems pregnant with its contrary. Machinery, gifted with the wonderful power of shortening and fructifying human labour, we behold starving and overworking it. The new-fangled sources of wealth, by some strange weird spell, are turned into sources of want … At the same pace that mankind masters nature, man seems to become enslaved to other men or to his own infamy … All our invention and progress seem to result in endowing material forces with intellectual life, and in stultifying human life into a material force. This antagonism between modern industry and science on the one hand, modern misery and dissolution on the other hand; this antagonism between the productive powers, and the social relations of our epoch, is a fact, palpable, overwhelming, and not to be controverted … [T]o work well the new-fangled forces of society … only want to be mastered by new-fangled men—and such are the working men.

Note the logic structuring this passage. First, Marx recognizes the technological development and the advancement of the forces of production that capitalism generates. Second, he points out the promising aspects of these developments. Third, he points to the paradoxically negative effects that these developments have on human beings and suggests that the horrors these effects bring about are higher than the horrors of previous historical periods. Fourth, he concludes that these advances cannot work well within capitalism and attributes this to the antagonism between the forces and relations of production.

Part of the force of this passage stems from the fact that, though it does not stand in clear contradiction with Marx's theory of history, it does not attempt to stay within the strict parameters of this theory. The contradiction between the forces and relations of production makes an appearance, but only to explain why the promising new productive forces do not currently serve human development and well-being. And, although Marx's reference to revolution makes clear that a good use of these forces requires social change, there is no assumption that such change is inevitable.

On the other hand, the treatment in this speech of the paradoxical effects of capitalist technological development is, of course, closer to Marx's theory of history than to this work's broader distinction between the productive and the destructive forces that capitalism generates. In other words, the paradoxes Marx identifies follow from the operation and dynamics of the capitalist economies, as Marx analyzed them. They do not therefore encompass the broader forces of destruction that this work analyzes.

In this sense, these paradoxes are consistent with Marx's theory of history as well as his application of this theory to capitalism. In particular, economic crises are for Marx manifestations of the underlying contradiction between the forces and relations of production (Marx and Engels 1978 [1848]: 478). Another manifestation, contributing to these crises, is the tendency of capital accumulation to lead to a rising organic composition of capital that would produce a long-term tendency for the rate of profit to fall (Marx 1977 [1867]: 762, 781; Marx 1981 [1894]: 317–23). Because of this long-term tendency, as well as because of the centralization of wealth and economic polarization it also produced (Marx 1977 [1867]: 799, 929), the dynamics of capitalist development would make it difficult for that system to survive its periodic economic crises indefinitely (Marx 1977 [1867]: 799, 929). Describing the long-term results of this tendency, Marx (1977 [1867]: 929) predicts:

> Along with the constant decrease in the number of capitalist magnates, who usurp and monopolize all the advantages of this process of transformation, the mass of misery, oppression, slavery, degradation, and exploitation grows; but with this there also grows the revolt of the working class, a class constantly increasing in numbers, and trained, united and organized by the very mechanism of the capitalist process of production. The monopoly of capital becomes a fetter upon the mode of production which has flourished alongside and under it. The centralization of the means of production and the socialization of labour reach a point at which they become incompatible with their capitalist integument. This integument is burst asunder. The knell of capitalist private property sounds. The expropriators are expropriated.

So Marx's speech on the simultaneously productive and destructive aspects of capitalist dynamism is not inconsistent with his theory of history or with the economic analysis underlying his anticipation, in the passage from *Capital* just cited, of the end of capitalism.

But Marx's speech also invites another reading of the paradoxical effects of capitalist technological development. This alternative reading does not interpret these paradoxical effects in terms of a conflict between forces and relations of production that develops over time and, in so doing, helps to catalyze revolutionary change. Instead, it views the growth of capitalist forces of destruction as a perennial accompaniment of capitalism's development of the forces of production.

Similarly, this alternative reading does not treat economic crises as simply an instantiation of capitalist relations of production becoming an obstacle to the further development of the forces of production. Instead, it recognizes that such crises can facilitate the development of the forces of production (Sassoon 1996: 592; Panitch and Miliband 1992: 16), since "it is through crises that capitalism historically has tended to recover its dynamism" (Panitch and Miliband 1992: 16). This does not mean, of course, that economic crises are unambiguously beneficial for capital, in view of the political threat they can pose for the capitalist system's survival (Wolff and Resnick 2012: 199).

In addition, in this alternative reading, the growth of capitalism's destructive forces is in constant interaction with both capitalism's development of the productive forces and with the uneven and contradictory way that this development takes place. So, for example, the rapid scientific and technological advances that capitalism makes possible do not just develop the forces of production. They also make it possible both to increase the surplus that capital extracts from the direct producers and to allocate increasing portions of that surplus to the development of capitalism's forces of destruction. Thus, for instance, the contribution of scientific and technological advances to capital accumulation could provide governments with the fiscal resources necessary not only to expand their military arsenal but also to make it more deadly. Similarly, the additional surplus that scientific and technological advances make possible could also increase capitalist producers' ability to pursue marketing and advertising strategies that help build a consumerist culture that is toxic for human well-being and the planet alike.

Just like periods of smooth technological advances and capital accumulation, economic crises can also have an impact on the growth of capitalism's forces of destruction. By heightening the need for markets in a context of stagnant demand, they can, as they did in the late nineteenth century, fuel geopolitical rivalries, which raise the specter of major military conflicts (Desai 2013: 19, 43, 77–79; Engler 2010: 31; Goldsmith 1996a: 256–57). In so doing, economic crises can provide governments with an incentive to increase military spending, especially as "failure to invest adequately in the military … can lead to military defeat and the destruction of a substantial part of an economy's infrastructure" (Block 1994b: 703). Of course, the opposite effect is also conceivable, if economic crisis leads to a fiscal crisis of the state that forces cutbacks across the board, including in military budgets.

But capitalism's development and deployment of the forces of destruction at its disposal can also have an effect on capitalism's productive forces. Thus, for example, World War II affected the productive forces of different capitalist countries in contrasting ways. On the one hand, the devastation that the deployment of capitalism's forces of destruction produced in Europe, Japan, and other parts of the world had a great impact both on the human and material components of the capitalist productive forces. Leading to the deaths of millions of people and the injury, mutilation, and incapacitation of even more, it is clear that World War II took a heavy toll on socially available labor power. Similarly, the carpet bombing of entire cities also destroyed much of the built economic infrastructure and productive plant (Thompson 2011: 107). It is not surprising, therefore, that immediately after the war "impoverishment and immiseration" (Thompson 2011: 106) was the norm throughout the European continent.

As World War II also shows, however, the impact of capitalism's development and deployment of its destructive forces is not uniform but uneven. Thus, while landing devastating blows on the economic infrastructures and productive forces of the European continent and Japan, the war not only spared the United States but helped it to overcome the Great Depression of the 1930s and to modernize its productive plant (Desai 2013: 21, 87; Thompson 2011: 28; Bowles and Edwards 1993: 453).

Another after-effect of the war in the United States was the passage of the GI Bill, which sought both to reintegrate returning veterans and to avert the social unrest that a return to the pre-war state of economic depression and unemployment might have produced (Brodkin 2009: 270–71). By providing veterans, especially white males (Brodkin 2009: 270–72; Jackson 1987: 204, 244), with college education as well as mortgage and small business loans, the GI Bill helped to upgrade the socially available labor power. It also bolstered the auto-industrial complex by facilitating the suburbanization of American society. Suburbanization did more than just encourage growth in the productive forces of the auto industry, as well as all the other industries (steel, rubber, oil, etc.) connected to it. It also spurred, while also benefiting from, the building of infrastructures, such as highways (Jackson 1987: 248–51).

Thus, although the effect of the war and its deployment of capitalism's forces of destruction led to a regression of the productive forces in parts of the capitalist world, the United States emerged from the war as the most powerful capitalist economy (Desai 2013: 71, 87, 266; Thompson 2011: 19; Bowles and Edwards 1993: 453). Accompanying this economic power was the political and military power that enabled the United States to restructure the post-war capitalist world in line with its interests, by supporting, for example, a controlled decolonization process that increased the access of American corporations to markets previously controlled by European colonial powers (Desai 2013: 21–22, 87–89; Thompson 2011: 105; Markoff 2009: 56; Bowles and Edwards 1993: 453–54). At the same time,

> [i]nternational institutions, the Bretton Woods agreement, the International Monetary Fund, the World Bank, the General Agreement on Tariffs and Trade (GATT) were established to keep trade barriers minimal, to iron out fluctuations in the global economy and to stabilize the world monetary system by the US Treasury's guarantee to purchase and sell gold at a fixed rate. The US negotiators ensured that the institutions were set up in such a manner as to work primarily in the American interest and, because they held the advantage, representing as they did the only large, intact and flourishing economy in the world, none could gainsay them.
>
> (Thompson 2011: 105)

The post-war reconstruction effort, which led to a growth in the productive forces of countries ravaged by war, had by the 1960s erased much of the gap between some of them (notably in Western Europe and Japan) and the United States (Desai 2013: 22, 124, 267; Wolfson 1994: 139). As the Vietnam War, by contrast, gave rise to inflationary pressures in the United States while also weakening its economic position in the world, the deployment of capitalist forces of destruction to defend the world capitalist order's territory contributed to the collapse of the Bretton Woods system and the end of the post-war economic boom (Desai 2013: 120; Bowles, Edwards, and Roosevelt 2005: 163; Kotz 1994: 67; Wolfson 1994: 140).

But war is not the only illustration of the impact that capitalism's growth and deployment of the forces of destruction can have on the forces of production. Sometimes military spending can provide an impetus for a country's domestic industries and for scientific and technological breakthroughs that reverberate throughout the economy, a good example being the origins of the microelectronics revolution (Block 1994b: 703; Gorz 1994: 80). It can even sometimes encourage the building of other economic infrastructures, such as highways, as it did in the United States after World War II (Jackson 1987: 249). On the other hand, ballooning military budgets can lead to underinvestment in education, health care, and civilian production, all of which are crucial to the development of labor productivity and the development of capitalism's forces of production (Desai 2013: 102; Garrett-Peltier 2010: 7; Galbraith 1984: xxxiii–iv).

In this respect, for the full appreciation of the paradoxes of capitalist technological development, it is not enough to focus solely on the contradictory relationship between the capitalist forces and relations of production. Equally important is the interaction of capitalism's forces and relations of production with its forces of destruction. In addition to the dimensions of this interaction already discussed, such an analysis needs to examine the possible effect of capitalism's forces of destruction on a society's relations of production.

One historical example of the latter effect would be the connection between World War I and the eruption of the Russian Revolution (Resnick and Wolff 2002: 146–53; Callinicos 1991: 22–23). Whether one chooses to describe the outcome of this revolution as a break with capitalism or, as some scholars (Resnick and Wolff 2002) suggest, as an oscillation from private to state capitalism, there is no doubt that the relations of production defining "the economic ownership of productive forces" (Harris 1991: 204) in the socio-economic system that consolidated under Stalin were significantly different from those in pre-revolutionary Russia. Similarly, one of the effects of World War II and the presence of the alternative social system that had emerged in the Soviet Union was to modify the relations of production underlying both the Western European societies, which remained capitalist, and the Eastern European societies, which joined the Soviet bloc.

Although this is especially obvious in the case of the latter, it is no less true of the former. As Donald Sassoon (1996: 84) has pointed out, by the mid-1940s two world wars and a major economic depression had "shattered ... the ... belief that capitalism, if left to its own devices, would be able to generate the 'good society.'" This reality, along with the existence of the Soviet alternative, made necessary both a break with the traditional model of laissez-faire capitalism and significant material concessions to working classes in Western Europe and beyond. "State-led planning and in some instances state ownership of key sectors (coal, steel, automobiles) were not uncommon (for example, in Britain, France, Italy)" (Harvey 2005: 11), while welfare states spread and expanded, protecting working people from the risks of capitalist markets (Desai 2013: 12, 53; Thompson 2011: 138; Folbre 2009: xxi; Aronowitz 2006: 188; Bagchi 2005: 119; Friedman 2000: 158; Greider 1997: 362; Amin 1996: 34–35; Panitch and Miliband 1992: 4). Moreover, the state assumed a more interventionist role in the economy, while pursuing full employment through Keynesian macroeconomic policies (Steger and Roy 2010: 7–9; Harvey 2005: 10–11).

Similarly, one factor contributing to the eventual economic stagnation and collapse of the Soviet Union's socio-economic system was the high and escalating costs of its arms race with the United States (Resnick and Wolff 2002: 310; Callinicos 1991: 44; Bettelheim 1976: 13–14). In particular, the costs of keeping up with the capitalist bloc's build-up of its forces of destruction helped to run down the portion of the surplus the Soviet Union's ruling political and economic elites could devote to the reproduction of the exploitative socio-economic order they controlled (Resnick and Wolff 2002: 310). Thus, the socio-economic system of the Soviet Union and its satellite states collapsed, giving rise to another great shift in the relations of production prevailing in those countries.

Many of these countries did not just align themselves with the capitalist model prevailing in Western Europe. They adopted the neoliberal version of that model, which was at the time beginning to spread even in Western European societies. The collapse of the capitalist world's Cold War nemesis in turn accelerated the rise of neoliberalism even in the Western European heartlands of social democracy and the welfare state, as it lessened the need of these countries' capitalist classes to continue offering any material concessions to their workers (Thompson 2011: 247; Solomon and Palmieri 2011a: 2; Folbre 2009: xxi; Aronowitz 2006: 188; Stiglitz 2001: xv). As Stanley Aronowitz (2006: 188) accurately describes this process,

> one cannot avoid ascribing the utter triumph of neoliberal ideology in part to the collapse of the Soviet Union. For despite its odious features, it represented a putative alternative to the most callous features of capitalism and stood as a barrier to a frontal assault on the welfare state. For hundreds of millions of people in the developing world, even as the Soviet regime began to disintegrate in the 1970s and 1980s it was the closest approximation of a practical utopia, at least with respect to issues of equality, universal health care, and economic security. After its expiation in 1991, social democracy and its US variant, modern liberalism, all but capitulated to the neoliberals.

Thus, just as World War II helped to move the relations of production in Europe and North America away from the free market variant of capitalism, the collapse of the Soviet Union and the arms race that helped to bring it about were among the factors that have led countries around the world to turn towards a neoliberal model based on mass privatizations of state-owned assets and a general assault on working-class standards.

The new social movements and the inadequacy of market-friendly responses to the development of capitalism's forces of destruction

Recognizing capitalism's forces of destruction as a factor no less central to capitalist dynamics than capitalism's forces and relations of production also implies a renewed emphasis on the problems that these forces of destruction generate. In this respect, anti-war and ecological movements have the potential of becoming no less central to the struggle against capitalism than the labor movement itself. Thus, although it is common to contrast the former movements to the latter by referring to them as "new social movements," in reality anti-war and ecological movements too have every reason to fight against capitalism's use of the surplus it extracts from workers.

To be sure, such movements often do not adopt an anti-capitalist stance (Markovits and Gorski 1993: 12; Cohen 1985: 664), preferring "a self-understanding that abandons revolutionary dreams in favor of the idea of structural reform, along with a defense of civil society that does not seek to abolish the autonomous functioning of political and economic systems—in a phrase, self-limiting radicalism" (Cohen 1985: 664). This is to some extent understandable in view of the historic tendency of segments of the traditional, and even the new, left to subordinate the struggles of new social movements to the supposedly more central struggle of the working class against capitalist exploitation (Sassoon 1996: 688–89; Cohen 1985: 668). On the other hand, however, when it ignores the connection between the struggles against capitalism's growing destructiveness and capitalist exploitation, the new social movements' understandable insistence on their "autonomy of struggle" (Scott 1990: 20, 22) vis-à-vis other movements of the traditional left can lead to deradicalization and co-optation by the existing class order. This is evident in the way significant sections of the environmental movement have sought to address the deepening ecological crisis.

In particular, a notable feature of much ecological thinking, among ecological theorists as well as political parties such as the German Greens, has been its growing receptiveness to the idea that capitalism can, through reform, become sustainable and safeguard the ecological integrity of the planet. Saral Sarkar (1999) has understandably described this line of thinking, so reminiscent of social democracy's evolution from its revolutionary origins to a belief in the possibility of subordinating capital to democracy and the needs of human beings, as "eco-capitalism" (Cruddas and Nahles 2012: 200; Berger 2012: 25; Lafontaine 1998: 74; Sassoon 1996: 722).

One reform that the eco-capitalist stream of thought favors is ecological taxation – that is, the imposition of taxes on environmentally harmful activities so as to reflect "the full cost" that such activities impose on the rest of society (Charkiewicz 2001: 220–21; Tietenberg 1996: 124–26; Costanza 1996: 163). As discussed in Chapter 3, this reform builds on the neoclassical analysis of economic externalities. Such externalities prevent capitalist markets from efficiently serving consumers' needs by leading consumers to underestimate the full social cost (in the case of negative externalities) or the full social benefit (in the case of positive externalities) of their decisions.

Ecological taxation seeks to redress this disconnect through taxes that reinstate the "polluter pays" principle (Roodman 1996: 5). Thus, taxes on activities that lead to pollution and adverse ecological effects on third parties would align the private costs facing consumers and producers with the true social costs their decisions entail. In so doing, ecological taxation seeks to attain an optimum level of production, consumption, and pollution, insofar as it encourages the allocation of resources according to the true costs and benefits of production and consumption alike (Gowdy and O'Hara 1995: 104–6).

There is no doubt that such policies would be an improvement over a status quo that often glosses over such externalities and, at times, even provides ecologically perverse subsidies to environmentally harmful activities (Charkiewicz 2001: 222; Gowdy and O'Hara 1995: 117–18; Roodman 1996: 5–9). Economist Robin Hahnel (2002: 88) provides one illustration of this state of affairs:

> In a 1998 report the Center for Technology Assessment estimated that when external effects are taken into account the true social cost of a gallon of gasoline consumed in the US may be as high as $15. I just paid $1.02 a gallon when I filled my car up today in southern Maryland.

Ecological taxation proposals often incorporate a social justice twist that helps to neutralize the divide-and-rule strategies of corporate polluters, who often depict ecological reforms as an unaffordable luxury in view of their supposedly negative effects on working people's jobs and ability to afford basic necessities (Schnaiberg 2005: 712). In particular, governments could redistribute proceeds from ecological taxes progressively, for example, by "rebating an equal amount to every resident" (Hahnel 2011: 135). Thus, corporate producers and highly consuming affluent individuals would bear most of the burden of the ecological taxes, while gaining little from the redistribution of the tax proceeds to the population at large. The converse would obviously be true for low-consuming, low-income individuals, whose benefit from the redistribution of the tax proceeds would exceed the cost that the taxes imposed on them.

Although in one sense ecological taxation seems to go against the thrust of neo-liberalism, with its emphasis on deregulation, in another sense it is consistent with neoliberalism's belief in the power of market incentives to produce outcomes that are consistent with the general public's welfare. In particular, ecological taxation is more consistent with neoliberalism, and the neoclassical economics that purports to demon-strate capitalist markets' efficiency, than alternative "command-and-control" regulations (Boyes and Melvin 2005: 312–13). Instead of taxing polluting activities, this latter type of regulations are more likely, in the words of one prominent neoclassical economist, to "require[e] equal proportional cutbacks on the part of each firm ... [or] to micro-manage each firm's abatement strategy" (Frank 1999: 209).

According to neoclassical economists, such command-and-control regulations do not promote an economically efficient reduction of pollution. For example, companies below the administratively specified pollution level, which could, through very low-cost modifications, reduce their pollution even further, have no incentive to do so. In this respect, neoclassical economists argue, command-and-control regulations do not minimize pollution reduction's economic cost. Thus, they preclude an optimal mix of material goods and services, on one side, and the protection of environmental goods and services, such as clean air and water, on the other (Boyes and Melvin 2005: 312–13; Frank 1999: 209; Frank 2003: 641–43).

Besides ecological taxation, another way to address this "flaw" of command-and-control regulations is another market-friendly form of environmental regulation, known as "cap-and-trade." The idea here is that, after determining what an acceptable level of pollution is, governments distribute pollution quotas that add up to that acceptable level and then allow "underpolluting" businesses to trade the remainder of their pollution quotas with other, "overpolluting," businesses. This scheme also provides the market incentives that command-and-control regulations do not. Companies that can clean up their production process very cheaply will do so, thus increasing the portion of their pollution quota that they can sell to companies that find it cheaper to buy additional pollution quotas in the market than to incur the high costs that, in their case, pollution reductions might entail (Panayotakis 2011a: 100; Williams 2010: 127; Bowles, Edwards, and Roosevelt 2005: 225; Charkiewicz 2001: 221–22).

Hahnel has articulated a progressive argument in favor of using cap-and-trade, rather than a carbon tax, to address climate change. In view of mainstream economists' tendency to minimize the potential risks of climate change and in view of the urgency of decisive measures to address it (Hahnel 2011: 205; Ackerman 2008), Hahnel argues that it would be better for society to give more say on this matter to natural scientists than to economists. Decisive action would be easier with cap-and-trade schemes because, in the eyes of the general public, natural scientists would be the obvious candidate for deter-mining the acceptable maximum level of carbon emissions. Taxes, on the other hand, belong to the purview of economists, who "are unlikely to recommend a tax that is high enough" (Hahnel 2011: 205). Thus, according to Hahnel (2011: 205), natural scientists' greater appreciation of the risks of climate change means that, "strictly from an emission reduction perspective, we are poised to get a much better deal [with cap-and-trade] than we could ever hope to get with an international carbon tax."

One problem with cap-and-trade, however, is that its implementation has often rewarded, rather than penalized, polluters. In particular, if polluters do not have to bid against each other for their pollution permits but receive for free "the amount [they have] historically emitted" (Charkiewicz 2001: 222), such a policy ends up rewarding polluters for reducing their pollution even a little. Thus, a measure whose ostensible purpose is to control climate change and other ecological problems has often subsidized polluting corporations' profits (Williams 2010: 128; Lohmann 2010: 135; Petermann and Langelle 2010: 188; Tanuro 2010: 255). Corporate polluters can then use a portion of these profits to ensure that government policy continues to promote corporate profits over meaningful environmental protection (Lohmann 2010: 135; Schnaiberg 2005: 711).

Although they may dominate environmentalist discourse, these market-friendly approaches and proposals do not get to the heart of the matter. By pretending that an ecologically sustainable capitalism is possible, such approaches and proposals gloss over the systematic ways in which capitalism itself becomes an overwhelming force of eco-logical destruction. In this respect, the forces of destruction contributing to the deepening ecological crisis, including the institutional apparatus fueling capitalism's toxic consumerist culture, the development of transportation systems around the private automobile, the adoption of economic models of development requiring an accelerating use of fossil fuels, and so on, are only manifestations and products of the capitalist pursuit of profit.

Conceptualizing ecological problems as the product of economic externalities abstracts from this reality. In particular, the concept of economic externalities shares a flaw of the neoclassical paradigm, namely the assumption of exogenous consumer preferences. This assumption, already discussed in Chapter 3, ignores the influence of economic forces on consumer preferences. As we saw, this assumption glosses over the systematic ways in which capitalist competition promotes capital's subsumption of con-sumption, which encourages consumers to equate success, happiness, and the good life with ever-increasing material consumption.

Whereas Chapter 3 discussed this dynamic's disastrous effect on human well-being, this dynamic also has important implications for the ecological crisis we face as well as for attempts to analyze this crisis as a product of economic externalities. By taking con-sumer preferences as exogenous, the concept of economic externalities simply focuses on reasons why capitalist markets may not serve these preferences efficiently.

When a factory, for example, dumps its pollutants into waterways or the atmos-phere, negative externalities come into play, since the factory's activity adversely affects third parties other than the producers and consumers of the factory's goods (Wright and Rogers 2011: 56). Such third parties might include consumers who rely on the waterways for their water supply, local fisher folk and farmers, people in the vicinity who might get asthma or cancer as a result of this pollution, and so on.

By creating a disconnect between the private costs faced by producers and con-sumers in this example and the total social costs resulting from the production and consumption of the factory's goods, consumers are likely to consume "'too much' of the [factory's] good," because, as William Boyes and Michael Melvin (2005: 310) explain, "[w]hen you don't have to pay the full cost of a good or service, you will consume more than you would if you had to pay the full cost." According to this logic, the optimal level of consumption for the factory's goods would reflect the relative costs and benefits of production not just for the producers and consumers of the factory's goods but for everyone the externality-generating production process affects (Hahnel 2011: 58).

The problem with this line of reasoning is that the consumer preferences that form the basis of this "optimal" level are the product of capital's subsumption of consumption. This subsumption increases consumers' valuation of material consumption, even at the expense of their own well-being. Thus, even in the absence of economic externalities, the "optimal" that capitalist markets would generate would not really be the optimal for consumers' well-being. Instead, that optimal would entail both more material production than the production level most conducive to consumers' well-being and, as a consequence, a correspondingly higher level of pollution as well.

Moreover, since a society's consumers obviously overlap with that society's citizens, capital's subsumption of consumption inevitably has an impact on the likelihood and extent of the other government interventions that many mainstream environmentalists favor. Consider cap-and-trade, for example. Notwithstanding Hahnel's argument that cap-and-trade would likely increase the influence over environmental policy of more environmentally sensitive natural scientists while decreasing that of the generally more complacent economists, the fact remains that both the decision to adopt a cap and that regarding this cap's restrictiveness are, ultimately, political ones. Thus, even in a liberal democracy in which political decisions were as much a reflection of citizens' preferences as it is possible for this to be the case under capitalism, capital's subsumption of consumption would make environmental regulation less likely and less restrictive. By distorting people's preferences in a materialistic direction, capital's subsumption of consumption would make any sacrifice of production and consumption that the implementation of a restrictive cap might entail seem much more burdensome.

Ecological thinkers have often, and rightly, pointed out that reducing material consumption enough to address the ecological crisis does not have to reduce human well-being and happiness (Sarkar 1999: 202; Sachs 1999: 88–89). One effect of capital's subsumption of consumption, however, is to make widespread acceptance of this truth much harder to achieve. Thus, even in a liberal democratic capitalist society, securing the environmental regulation that is sufficiently decisive to address the deepening ecological crisis is an uphill struggle.

The tension between capitalism and democracy, which we have already touched on in Chapter 3 and which we will further discuss later on, makes the action necessary to prevent future environmental catastrophes even more difficult. Capital's use of substantial portions of the surplus to obfuscate the issues and deny the reality and urgency of major ecological challenges such as climate change is a case in point (Tanuro 2010: 254; Hoggan 2009: 151–67; Simms 2005: 122). These obfuscations make the crossing of critical ecological "tipping points" more likely, potentially triggering dramatic and irreversible changes that would threaten "the relatively benign climate and environmental conditions that have existed during the last 12,000 years" (Hahnel 2011: 9).

But capitalism does not just contribute to the deepening ecological crisis through its effect on people's preferences and beliefs. In other words, its destructive ecological effects do not just stem from the way it influences people's perception and definition of their interests. They also stem from the undemocratic ability of the capitalist class to pursue its interests at the expense of everyone else. This, for example, explains the widespread externalities that, as mainstream environmentalists recognize, contribute to the ecological crisis.

Indeed, such externalities have long served capital accumulation (Wright and Rogers 2011: 55–56; Engler 2010: 37; Townsend 2010: 116; Angus 2010: 214; Schnaiberg 2005: 708; O'Connor 1998: 272; Hahnel 2002: 93–94). Immanuel Wallerstein (1999: 4) has described this as capitalism's "dirty secret," while Joan Martinez-Alier (2006: 282) has highlighted the systematic nature of environmental externalities by describing them not as "market failures" but as "cost-shifting successes."

Thus, fighting against externalities is not a struggle for technocratic fixes but a political one. Capital's continued ability to impose environmental externalities on others is just one more manifestation of how undemocratic capitalist "democracies" really are (Panayotakis 2011a: 103–9). Thanks to its exploitation of workers, capital can use substantial portions of the surplus to secure governments' toleration or even subsidization of the negative externalities that serve capitalist profitability (Charkiewicz 2001: 222; Gowdy and O'Hara 1995: 117–18; Roodman 1996: 5–9). In this sense, fighting this reality remains an important part of the anti-capitalist agenda (Harvey 2014: 3).

Importantly, this struggle is also a struggle for social justice, since it is the poorest and most vulnerable groups that suffer the most from the ecological devastation of the planet. These groups include indigenous people (Harvey 2014: 2–3) and racialized minorities (Bullard 1994), but also poor women, whom "environmental degradation caused by climate change will affect ... disproportionately" (Spitzner 2009: 223). Indeed, capital's negative externalities especially plague highly unequal and undemocratic societies that reduce the ability of socially vulnerable groups to fight back against capital's ecological havoc on their communities (Boyce 2002; Panayotakis 2011a: 103–7).

It is therefore impossible to disengage ecological struggles from struggles against both the capitalist system and the multiple forms of inequality and oppression that this system helps to reproduce. Indeed, capital uses social inequality and oppression not just to keep workers divided. The extreme deprivation of selected segments of the world's working people also facilitates capital's use of poor communities as "optimal dumping grounds for goods that are dangerous, expired, or illegal" (Eglitis 2009: 226).

For example, scholars have described as environmental racism the disproportionate burden that low-income communities of color bear from polluting industries, incinerators, radioactive waste dumps, hazardous waste, and toxic waste disposal facilities (Wright and Rogers 2011: 78–79; Bullard 1994: 254–57). Similarly, scholars have described as "toxic colonialism" (Bullard 1994: 257–59) and "global environmental apartheid" (Shiva 2001: 112) the way the distribution of environmental burdens from the industrial activities fueling high-consumption lifestyles in the global North have entered the evolving international division of labor (Sachs 1999: 152). As we saw, the polluting production of many items consumed in the global North increasingly occurs in the factories of the global South, thus fueling serious ecological crises in countries such as China and the

Newly Industrializing Countries of Southeastern Asia (Wen and Li 2006; McCormack 1999; You 1995; Goldsmith 1996b: 79–80).

Thus, a variety of social movements struggle against capitalism's relentless development and deployment of its forces of destruction. These movements inevitably have to grapple not just with the different manifestations of capitalist destruction but with the different forms of social inequality and oppression that capitalism helps to reproduce.

Conclusion

Continuing the discussion of capital's destructive uses of the surplus, this chapter highlights capital's increasingly destructive uses of the scientific and technological advances it generates. Placing special emphasis on the increasingly lethal military technologies and on the contribution of the capitalist deployment of technology to the deepening ecological crisis, the chapter also offers a critique of market-oriented environmentalism. In this respect, it adds to this work's interpretation of "new social movements" as in part a response to capitalism's increasing destructiveness. Moreover, its emphasis on the three-way interaction between capitalism's forces of production, its forces of destruction, and its relations of production makes it possible to rethink capitalism's contradictory nature. This rethinking is undertaken in the chapter that follows.

6

Futile growth and mounting destruction: capitalism's cost–benefit contradiction

Building on previous chapters' discussion of capital's destructive uses of the surplus, this chapter reformulates the contradiction underlying contemporary capitalism's operation. This reformulation does not assume that capitalism is becoming an insuperable obstacle to further productive development. Instead, it argues that capitalism's continuing development of the forces of production runs parallel to an equally rapidly development of its forces of destruction. The thrust of this system's cost–benefit contradiction then consists in the coincidence of the long-term tendency of the benefits from productive development to decline even as the threats from the simultaneous development of capitalism's destructive forces escalate.

This contradiction creates the potential for a broad anti-capitalist coalition between all the social groups and social movements fighting against both the various manifestations of capitalist destruction and the various forms of injustice that capitalism helps to reproduce. At the same time, however, the social, economic, and geographic divisions that capitalism's operation imposes on the different segments of the world population obstruct this anti-capitalist convergence. Thus, this chapter does more than just analyze the conditions that make it possible to envisage a democratic classless society capable of overcoming the multidimensional crisis we face. It also illuminates some of the obstacles that an anti-capitalist movement would need to overcome in order to turn such an alternative society into a reality.

From the conception of history as progress to the rethinking of contemporary capitalism's contradictoriness

This work's insistence that the development of capitalism's forces of destruction deserves the same prominence that Marxism has in the past accorded to the forces and relations of production also necessitates a rethinking of Marx's optimistic conception of history. This conception, "which preserves the structure" of its Hegelian counterpart (Cohen 2000: 26), sees history as a process of human progress. Progress in this narrative is not smooth or painless, but it does point towards human liberation (Cohen 1988: vii). It does so through the development of the forces of production it postulates and through the change in the prevailing mode of production that this development eventually triggers.

The capitalist mode of production occupies a special place in this narrative because of its unprecedented technological dynamism (Cohen 2000: 303; Marx and Engels 1978 [1848]: 477). This dynamism is supposed to develop the forces of production to the point at which they come into conflict with capitalism's relations of production. One manifestation of this contradiction between the forces and relations of production within capitalism is the periodic recurrence of economic crises (Marx and Engels 1978 [1848]: 478). Although such crises cause great human suffering, even this suffering fits into the ultimately optimistic narrative by providing a motivation for revolutionary change that is substantial enough to counterbalance the risks that any revolutionary attempt would inevitably entail (Cohen 2000: 244, 328–29; Nove 1990: 230). After all, it is precisely "our brave friend, Robin Goodfellow, the old mole that can work in the earth so fast, that worthy pioneer—the Revolution" which is supposed to resolve "th[e] antagonism between the productive powers, and the social relations of our epoch" (Marx 1978b [1856]: 578).

Introducing capitalism's forces of destruction into the mix challenges this optimistic narrative. The interaction between capitalism's relations of production, its forces of production, and its forces of destruction is certainly not free of contradiction. In particular, capitalism's development of the forces of production, on one side, and its development of the forces of destruction, on the other, do not cancel each other out. Instead, as capitalism progresses the benefits from its continuing development of the forces of production eventually begin to decline, while the risks from its forces of destruction continue to increase.

Illustrating the first part of this contradiction is the fact that, although the advancing forces of production have led, especially in affluent countries, to long-term increases in consumption, they have not correspondingly increased levels of satisfaction. On the contrary, the levels of satisfaction and happiness that people report to researchers have stagnated or declined (Layard 2005: 3; Lane 2000: 4). Meanwhile, capitalism's continuing refinement of the methods and technologies used to increase profits increasingly undercuts people's well-being and the ecological integrity of the planet.

These two developments are linked. As discussed earlier, capitalism's creation of a vast institutional apparatus that builds and propagates a toxic consumerist culture does not only increase capitalism's forces of destruction; it also encourages people to seek satisfaction and happiness in the wrong place, namely in material consumption. And, of course, the immense human suffering from other manifestations of capitalism's growing destructiveness adds to capitalism's inability to translate productive growth into greater human happiness and well-being.

In fact, the same consumerist culture that undercuts human well-being and happiness also contributes to a deepening ecological crisis, which already endangers (and will do so even more in the future) the lives, livelihoods, health, and safety of millions (if not billions) of people around the world (Kasser et al. 2003: 13; Kasser 2002: 95; Cross 2000: 15–16; Guha 1994: 287–88; Durning 1992: 21; Simms 2005: 66–67). Climate change alone will likely aggravate and make more frequent droughts, crop failures, and hunger; make water shortages and wars over water increasingly common; trigger extreme weather events that kill masses of people while displacing even more; generate large numbers of environmental refugees, who may face xenophobia and racism when moving to societies whose high levels of consumption have fueled climate change and the disasters, such as floods and the disappearance of entire countries and cities from the map, that caused them to be refugees in the first place; lead to the spread of disease, as mosquitoes and other vectors of disease begin to thrive in new locations; and so on (Tanuro 2010: 265; Li 2008: 51–52; Simms 2005: 66–67; Bowles, Edwards, and Roosevelt 2005: 21; Foster 2002: 21; Klare 2001: 20; Taylor and Tilford 2000: 481; Nolan and Lenski 1998: 393; Goodland 1996: 210; Ekins and Jacobs 1995: 12–13).

In addition to posing a threat to human (and non-human) life and well-being, such effects will also be destructive of socially available forces of production, such as human labor power, soil fertility, and economic infrastructures. In this respect, they are comparable to other manifestations of capitalism's destructiveness, such as economic crises and wars. In fact, the potential for these different manifestations feeding off of each other is not negligible. As Daniel Tanuro (2010) points out,

> [i]n countries that are most vulnerable to capitalist globalization and structural adjustment, the impacts of climate change increase the probability of crises leading to chaotic situations, such as armed conflicts between warlords. By aggravating shortages in regions that are already under intense water stress, climate change increases the importance of control over water resources and creates the conditions for water wars between states.

Similarly, the possible link between economic and ecological crisis is also not hard to see. Even though the adverse ecological impact of rapid economic growth, with the higher levels of production, pollution, and material resource use that it entails, is serious indeed, this does not mean that periods of economic crisis shield the planet from capitalism's ecological destructiveness (Kovel 2002: xii).

On the contrary, because of the social devastation they produce, such periods can lead to the portrayal of environmental protection as an unnecessary luxury. In a context of economic crisis the goal of resuming economic growth often overrides ecological concerns and the need for environmental regulation (Charkiewicz 2001: 191; Merchant 1992: 26). As if this were not enough, countries forced by economic crisis to turn to international organizations, such as the International Monetary Fund (IMF), are often pushed to accelerate agricultural and raw material exports. This adversely impacts their natural environment, however, as well as the well-being of those, often indigenous people or poor farmers, who depend on it for survival (Sachs 1999: 143; Schaeffer 1999: 200–201; Dickenson 1997: 103; Miller 1995: 31; Altvater 1993: 127, 182–83).

Capitalism's long-term cost–benefit contradiction that this work identifies requires a reassessment of the reasons that make it necessary to replace capitalism with a democratic classless society. Some of the reasons animating Marx's work still obtain. A society in which "the free development of each is the condition for the free development of all" remains necessary (Marx and Engels 1978 [1848]: 491).

But such a society is needed irrespective of whether capitalism can continue advancing the forces of production. Even an affirmative answer to this question cannot detract from capitalism's increasing inability to translate continuing productive development into human well-being and happiness. And at least as important a reason for replacing capitalism with a democratic classless society is the growth in risks that capitalism's rapidly growing forces of destruction impose on human beings and the planet.

The stark choice between socialism and barbarism that Marxist theorists have for the last century presented humanity with is an early anticipation of what this work describes as capitalism's cost–benefit contradiction. The Marxist theorists, such as Karl Kautsky and Rosa Luxemburg, who first formulated this dilemma may not have doubted the inevitability of capitalism's replacement by a communist classless society (Angus 2014). Whatever their subjective intentions, however, the continued relevance of this dilemma stems precisely from the fact that fundamental social change is not inevitable. It is a possible (though urgent) choice that people may (or may not) make.

Whether human beings make this choice will depend on a number of different factors. One factor that increases the likelihood of this choice is the contradiction whereby the pursuit of profit and capital accumulation over time reduces the benefits people derive from the continuing development of the forces of production, while increasing the risks that capitalism's growing forces of destruction also generate.

These two trends will, over time, make capitalism's continued existence harder to justify. But they also make it harder to integrate the suffering that capitalism imposes into a broader narrative of progress. Marxists have in the past seen in the liberatory potential implicit in productive development the historical justification of class exploitation, in general, and capitalism, in particular (Engler 2010: 45–46; Cohen 2000: 199; Cohen 1988: vii). According to Cohen (2000: 198–99), for example,

> [s]ocialism's productivity precondition is massive surplus, large enough to make it no longer true that most of life and time and energy must be spent joylessly producing means to imperative ends. The mission of capitalism is to carry humanity to that stage of abundance, whereupon it subverts itself and gives way to a classless society.

In the early stages of capitalism one could plausibly see the suffering that that system imposes as the necessary price for the productive progress that would eventually trigger human liberation. This is no longer the case, as capitalism has time and again proved its resilience. And yet, capitalism's resilience is itself now becoming the source of a new contradiction. Indeed, this resilience is turning from a sign of power to a potential point of vulnerability, as the futility of capitalism's ongoing productive development becomes more apparent and the costs of capitalist destruction become more menacing.

The uneven perception of capitalism's cost–benefit contradiction as an obstacle to radical social change

Capitalism's cost–benefit contradiction is real. The unevenness with which its various manifestations affect people's everyday lives obstructs the formation of the radical anti-capitalist movement this contradiction calls for, however. First, the great, and still increasing, global inequalities mean that access to capitalism's positive fruits has been and remains very uneven (Milanovic 2005). Thus, despite its ultimate futility, the consumerist lifestyle prevailing in affluent countries remains very appealing to the majority of the world's population, who can only observe this lifestyle from afar. Reporting from Kashmir, Swedish philosopher and activist Helena Norberg-Hodge (1996: 35–36) has, for example, described how, in rural areas all over the South, … millions of young people believe contemporary Western culture to be far superior to their own. This is not surprising: looking as they do from the outside, all they can see is the material side of the modern world—the side in which Western culture excels. They cannot so readily see the social or psychological dimensions: the stress, the loneliness, the fear of growing old. Nor can they see environmental decay, inflation, or unemployment.

This appeal, which Norberg-Hodge describes, interacts with capitalism's destructive powers, both being fueled by them and contributing to their further development. For example, one of the forces spreading consumerism to the global South are the marketing and advertising strategies of transnational corporations, often (though not always) originating from countries of the global North (Kasser *et al.* 2003: 18; Clarke 1996: 300; Robertson 1990: 2). To the extent that countries of the global South pursue the models of development and consumption of the global North, however, they do so by also adopting production and transportation systems relying on fossil fuels, thus adding to capitalism's ecological destructiveness. And, although their per capita contribution to pollution and to the deepening ecological crisis is much lower than that of countries in the global North, this contribution is not negligible, as illustrated by the fact that China's greenhouse emissions have surpassed those of the United States (Li 2008: 63).

If global inequalities often obscure capitalism's declining ability to translate productive development into human well-being and happiness, the aspiration of people in the global South and in the countries of the former Soviet bloc (Cross 2000: 7–8) to join the consumerist bandwagon is understandable. This aspiration is one factor behind the fact, reported by Sam Gindin (2012: 18), that, "since 1980, the number of workers in direct competition with each other has tripled, from approximately one billion to some three billion." In other words, the workers in the less affluent global South are increasingly in competition with working people in the North. By contributing to unemployment and the stagnation of working-class incomes even in the global North, this competition increases economic insecurity everywhere (Hacker 2019; Levine 2015).

This development predictably sidelines capitalism's growing inability to translate productive development into higher levels of human well-being and happiness. Instead, focus shifts to the need for more economic growth, since, as is often pointed out, economic growth after a certain point in capitalist development is more valued for its effects on employment and economic security than for the additional output's contribution to people's well-being (Bergmann 2000: 490; Galbraith 1984: 98–99). At the same time, the frustration of working people in the global North who find themselves under mounting economic pressure often expresses itself as hostility towards workers from the global South. This hostility assumes different forms, including right-wing economic nationalism, racism, and xenophobia against immigrants from the global South.

But it is not just the first prong of the capitalist contradiction discussed in this chapter that different segments of the world's population do not experience in a uniform fashion. The same is true for the second prong, namely the growing risks from capitalism's forces of destruction. On the one hand, many of the risks are, in one sense, genuinely universal. A nuclear war would have devastating effects on countries of the global North and South alike. In addition, even though "[t]he most devastating effects of climate change will be felt by the poor, by those who already live on the edge of starvation" (Angus 2010: 33), it is also true that no country in the world is completely immune to its adverse impact.

On the other hand, the costs from capitalism's development and deployment of its forces of destruction are unevenly distributed. It is people in the global South, for example, who suffer the most from today's high-tech military arsenals. People in the global North, by contrast, are less likely to experience this aspect of capitalism's destructiveness, since their everyday lives are often barely affected when their governments unleash their lethal weapons on faraway lands in the global South. Despite the fact, for example, that the United States seems to jump from one war to the next, less than 1 percent of its population actually fights these wars, making the military "exotic territory to most of the American public" (Fallows 2015).

To be sure, the immunity of people in the North from this aspect of capitalist destructiveness is not absolute. Paradoxically, however, even this lack of absolute immunity can often add fuel to the growth and deployment of capitalism's forces of destruction. For example, one segment of the population in the global North that is not immune to the effects of its governments' wars is the soldiers fighting these wars, and their families. As the experience of the Vietnam War made clear, the more deadly a war in faraway lands becomes for the soldiers from countries of the global North, the more likely it is to meet with intense resistance at home.

One of the ways the US military has "remedied" this vulnerability is by "professionaliz[ing] its army and buil[ding] up military capacity in a 'never again' spirit by spending unimaginable amounts" (Desai 2013: 234). Continuing the long-standing trend of "warfare … becoming more and more a matter of science and technology, less and less a matter of masses of men," (Baran and Sweezy 1966: 214), the US government (just like many other governments around the world) is increasingly able to conduct capital-intensive warfare through expensive high-tech equipment that makes it easier to fight the enemy from afar. Although such technologies may be far more deadly for the civilian populations of enemy nations, they minimize the risks for soldiers from the global North. In so doing, such technologies achieve the remarkable feat of increasing capitalism's destructiveness even as they minimize its visibility to people in the global North.

But even the majority in the global North, with no family members in the military, are not completely immune to the side effects of deadly high-tech wars. This has become increasingly obvious since the September 2001 attacks on the World Trade Center and the US Pentagon. Ever since that date a number of high-profile attacks have taken place in large cities in the global North, especially in Europe. The role that the military and geopolitical entanglements of countries from the global North in various parts of the Middle East and beyond has played in triggering such attacks should, of course, not make us forget that such attacks partly reflect the effect of racism, xenophobia, unemployment, and increasing economic inequality on immigrant populations. This has been especially the case in Europe, where the people responsible for many of the high-profile attacks have often been citizens of the countries they attacked, albeit citizens whose Muslim or immigrant background has often subjected them to abuse and discrimination by their countries' social institutions and the police (Holland 2016; Benton and Nielsen 2013).

In any event, the sense of insecurity that populations in the global North feel as a result of such attacks can further fuel the development and deployment of capitalism's forces of destruction. A prime example of this dynamic was the Bush administration's use of the September 2001 attack to start two wars, one in Iraq and one in Afghanistan. The continuing reverberations of these wars include the rise of ISIS and the war in Syria. Far from being merely a civil war, the war in Syria also bears the stamp of geopolitical competition between major economic and military powers, such as the United States and Russia, seeking to position themselves favorably in a region of great economic and political importance (Bennis 2016).

Meanwhile, the declining immunity of populations in the global North to the fallout from their countries' deployment of capitalism's destructive powers in faraway lands has added to the generation, by neoliberalism's crises and attacks on labor rights and the welfare state, of racist, xenophobic, anti-immigrant, and neo-fascist movements of various kinds (Baier 2016: 50; Van Der Veen 2014; Berezin 2013; Panayotakis 2013: 21; Offe 2013: 215–16; Cox 1997: 66; Rifkin 1996: 121). Thus, despite the movements of solidarity with immigrants and refugees that also develop, the declining immunity of the global North's population to the effects of capitalist destruction does not necessarily bring the populations of North and South closer together. Instead, it often feeds the North's perception of the South as a source of risks and dangers for the North (Sachs 1999: 21–23). This perception, in turn, feeds the backlash in the North against the growing numbers of people from the South who

> only leave their own countries, their families, their languages, their friends, their childhoods in such overwhelming numbers when they have no alternative—particularly knowing, as they do, that they may die in the attempt to reach Europe and that, if they are lucky enough to survive the journey, they will face racism, discrimination, dirty jobs, a clandestine life without papers.
>
> (George 2009: 193)

Another contributing factor to the uneven perception of capitalist destruction is capital's pursuit of profit through the systematic externalization of the environmental costs that its activities entail. Although it is a serious problem everywhere, this externalization is likely to take especially severe forms in the global South, for two reasons. First, the greater incidence in the South of regimes that are not even nominally democratic exerts less pressure on governments to regulate environmentally harmful activities (Boyce 2002: 43; You 1995: 164–65). Second, the more dire economic situation of many countries in the global South and their dependence on global institutions such as the IMF, which push deregulation and the neoliberal policies that form part of the so-called "Washington consensus," often force these countries to compete for capitalist investment that comes with heavy environmental costs (Peet and Hartwick 2009: 84–87, 91–94; George 2001: 14–15).

But capital's externalization of environmental costs does not make these effects more visible only for populations in the global South. As the effects of Hurricane Katrina in New Orleans remind us, the same is true for the global North's low-income communities of working-class people and racialized minorities. Thus, both in the global South and in the global North, it is the most exploited and oppressed populations – that is, those least responsible for the ecological crisis facing us – who suffer the most from capitalism's ecological destructiveness (Harvey 2014: 3; Schnaiberg 2005: 719; Simms 2005: 106). Countries in the global South often accept environmentally harmful activities as a means to economic survival. Similarly, low-income communities in the North often face a form of environmental "job blackmail because of the greater threat of unemployment [workers of color] face compared to whites and because of their concentration in low-paying, unskilled, nonunionized occupations" (Bullard 1994: 260–61).

As we have recently seen, moreover, environmental racism not only takes a toll on the health of racialized populations but also increases their vulnerability to sudden public health catastrophes. For example, one of the long-standing manifestations of environmental racism in the United States has been the higher asthma rates among low-income communities of color (Akinbami et al. 2012). It is not surprising, then, that African Americans, who also suffer from other manifestations of structural racism, such as inadequate access to health care, seem to have been disproportionately hit by the global coronavirus pandemic (Oppel, Searcey, and Eligon 2020). Clearly determined to aggravate this situation, the US federal government, in response to corporate polluters' entreaties, has, amazingly, used a pandemic that kills people by attacking their respiratory system as an opportunity to adopt "a sweeping relaxation of environmental rules," which allows "companies to monitor themselves for an undetermined period of time during the outbreak," while also suspending "fines for violations of certain air, water and hazardous-waste-reporting requirements" (Friedman 2020).

By contrast to low-income people of color in the North, and the majority of the population in the global South, more affluent consumers are not just protected from much of their lifestyle's environmental impact. They also benefit from capital's externalization of environmental costs insofar as this externalization keeps the price of the commodities they consume down (Heilbroner and Galbraith 1990: 478). Thus, the structural inequalities of the world capitalist system lead to contrasting experiences of consumerist culture, which make it harder for working people in the global North and the global South to come together in an anti-capitalist alliance. If for the former the futility of consumerist culture is easier to perceive, this is not the case with its environmental impact. And, if capital's use of the surplus to build this toxic culture is harmful to them, they nonetheless benefit from capital's externalization of environmental costs, which makes the fruits of consumer society more affordable. People in the global South may be more familiar with the consumerist culture's environmental fallout but, being less familiar with its futility, are often no less susceptible to its appeal than people in affluent countries.

Thus, the long-term contradiction underlying contemporary capitalism's operation does not automatically generate an anti-capitalist consciousness. It may generate a common interest in a society more consistent with human well-being and the ecological integrity of the planet. But the way the interaction between capitalism's relations of production, forces of production, and forces of destruction manifests itself in people's day-to-day lives creates numerous social cleavages that prevent people's coalescence into an anti-capitalist opposition.

But this obstacle to the spread of an anti-capitalist consciousness among the world's population is not the only one. Also important are the ideological effects of the identification, in many people's minds, of communism with the undemocratic regime that consolidated in the Soviet Union under Stalin (Tanuro 2010: 278; Resnick and Wolff 2002: 298; Bettelheim 1976: 45). As Tanuro (2010: 278) rightly points out, "[t]he crisis of the socialist movement, including the very negative ecological balance sheet of 'really existing socialism' cannot be ignored; it weighs down the ability of the exploited and oppressed to resist and counterattack." Thus, the ultimate fate of the Russian Revolution has undoubtedly fueled popular cynicism and resignation, while boosting people's receptiveness to capitalism's claim to represent progress, democracy, and material prosperity. For this reason, the relationship between communism, democracy, and the socioeconomic system that emerged under Stalin will be a major focus of the next chapter.

Conclusion

This chapter has reformulated the contradiction underlying capitalism's operation by foregrounding the growing threat to humanity and the planet from capitalism's ongoing development and deployment of its forces of destruction. Identifying the potential for a broad anti-capitalist coalition that this contradiction creates, the chapter has also analyzed the obstacles to the formation of such a coalition that capitalism's operation also generates. In this sense, this chapter has built on our analysis, earlier in the book, of the links between capitalist destruction and the system's undemocratic use of the surplus. The chapter that follows revisits another theme traversing this work: the hollowing out of the democratic ideal that the operation of capitalist society is also responsible for. Consistent with its search for a solution to capitalism's multidimensional crisis in a democratic classless society, the next chapter will also discuss why the ultimate fate of the Russian Revolution did not disprove the communist ideal but merely demonstrated the inability of the new class order that consolidated itself in the Soviet Union to prevail over the capitalist class order it had sought to displace.

7

The crisis of capitalist democracy and the continuing relevance of the communist ideal

Continuing this work's analysis of capitalism's destructiveness, this chapter explores the ongoing erosion of democracy. This erosion is yet another effect of capital's undemocratic control of the surplus it extracts from workers. As we have seen, escape from this predicament requires a classless, non-exploitative society that allows ordinary people to democratically control the surplus they collectively produce. Adding to this argument, this chapter also questions the ideological understanding of communism as antithetical to democracy.

Fueling this ideological understanding is the identification, in many people's minds, of communism with the regimes that consolidated themselves in the Soviet Union and its satellite states. Far from disproving the possibility of a democratic classless society, the failure of these regimes merely signified the inability of the new class order these regimes instituted to compete with the capitalist class order they sought to displace. In advancing a critique of the ideological equation of communism to dictatorship, this chapter does not claim to provide an exhaustive and comprehensive account of all the varieties of socialist or communist regimes that emerged in the twentieth century.[1] Instead, the analysis that follows highlights how the many similarities between contemporary capitalism and the unappealing social model that prevailed in the Soviet Union should make us wary of the ideological treatment of communism as the "other" of democracy. Rather than a threat to democracy, the struggle to achieve the communist ideal is the best chance humanity has to reverse the hollowing out of democracy that results from capital's control over the surplus.

Is capitalism a progressive force?

One central theme in this work has been the connection between the destructive effects of capitalist society and this society's use of the surplus it extracts from direct producers. These effects stem from the fact that capitalism is an exploitative class society. Although it is not the first such society, its distinctive socio-economic logic sets capitalism apart from class societies before it. In particular, we have discussed economic competition's contribution to capitalism's dramatic development of both its productive and its destructive forces. We have also seen how the pursuit of profit reduces the benefits that humanity can expect from capitalism's continuing development of the forces of production, while increasing the risks and dangers from the ongoing growth of capitalism's forces of destruction

It is in light of this last contradiction that one must assess the desirability of capitalism's survival into the future. In their description of how "[t]he bourgeoisie, historically, has played a most revolutionary part," Marx and Engels (1978 [1848]: 475, 477) highlight the progressive role that capitalism has played in creating, within a short period of time, "more massive and more colossal productive forces than have all preceding generations together." This assessment formed part of a theory of history that centered on the contradiction between the forces and relations of production and that expected revolutionary change as soon as the latter became an obstacle to further productive development.

Capitalism enjoyed a special place in that theory of history, however, because of the implications of its dramatic development of the productive forces. This dramatic development made possible and necessary a classless society that would liberate humanity by facilitating the continued growth of productive forces and the subordination of these productive forces to human self-development (Cohen 2000: 197–99, 364–65). If social revolution occurred when a mode of production came to obstruct further productive development, the absence of such a revolution presumably meant that capitalism was still a progressive force.

In practice, of course, the longer capitalism survived, the more likely it became for Marx and his followers to see it as a system in decay (Marx 1978b [1856]: 577; Lenin 1975a [1917]: 150). Thus, only eight years after the *Manifesto*'s celebration of capitalist dynamism, we find Marx (1978b [1856]: 577) rounding out his recognition of this dynamism with a reference to the existence, within the capitalism of his time, of "symptoms of decay, far surpassing the horrors recorded of the latter times of the Roman Empire." In a similar vein, Lenin (1975a [1917]: 150–51) describes the early twentieth-century imperialist stage of capitalism as "growing far more rapidly than before," even as he lists all the "distinctive characteristics of imperialism which compel us to define it as parasitic or decaying capitalism."

Although such references to capitalist decay may have at least in part emerged as a response to capitalism's increasing destructiveness, they coexisted uneasily with Marx's theory of history. This uneasy coexistence of seemingly contradictory elements within Marxist thought reflected a transitional moment in capitalist development. As capitalism's destructiveness has increased and the futility of its productive development increasingly shines through, the view of capitalism as a progressive force becomes ever harder to defend.

By foregrounding the importance of capitalism's forces of destruction and of the ways these forces interact with both capitalism's relations and its forces of production, this work suggests the need to rethink our criteria for assessing capitalism as a progressive or reactionary force. Viewing capitalism as a progressive force may have been plausible as long as the benefits, realized and potential, from its development of the productive forces seemingly outweighed its destructive effects. But this stage is coming to an end, making it impossible to continue viewing capitalism as a progressive force. Despite capitalism's ongoing development of productive forces, the declining benefits from this development are increasingly eclipsed by the risks and dangers from the massive forces of destruction that capitalism's operation tends to unleash.

These parallel and contradictory developments follow from the logic of capital accumulation central to the capitalist relations of production. But the interaction between capitalism's relations of production, its forces of production, and its forces of destruction makes it impossible to identify one of the poles of this three-way interaction as the source of historical progress. In particular, our analysis no longer assumes that the development of the productive forces will force a breakthrough to new relations of production when the old ones eventually become an obstacle to further productive progress.

In fact, there is no *a priori* reason to assume that the forces of production cannot continue to develop long after the dangers and risks from capitalist destructiveness have begun to outweigh any benefits that capitalism's productive development could possibly generate. Once that tipping point is reached, capitalism ceases to be a progressive force. Beyond its implications for the question of whether capitalism is still a progressive social force, however, the three-way interaction between capitalism's relations of production and its productive and destructive forces also has important implications for any attempts to break through that system. In particular, any such attempts have to contend not only with capitalism's prodigious development of the productive forces but also with the equally menacing development of its destructive forces.

The implications of capitalism's cost–benefit contradiction for attempts to go beyond capitalism: the case of the Russian Revolution

The record of the Russian Revolution makes this abundantly clear. This revolution led to foreign intervention by Western capitalist powers and a civil war that compounded World War I's very heavy human and economic toll (Thompson 2011: 71–72; Harman 2008: 446; Lewin 2005: 296–97, 310–11; Nove 1992: 49; Callinicos 1991: 25; Bettelheim 1976: 463, note 11). As Lewin (2005: 296–97) has written,

> [t]he combined events of 1914–21 plunged the Russian population into misery and inflicted colossal losses. Naturally, the economy was also devastated. The output of large-scale industry was only 13 per cent of the 1913 total (iron and steel a mere 4 per cent). Grain output was no more than two-thirds of the 1909–13 level, and that was a miracle which can only be explained by peasant vigour and endurance. Foreign trade had collapsed, and at the beginning of 1921 a disastrous fuel, transport and food crisis supervened.

As if this were not enough, less than a generation later another capitalist power, Nazi Germany, invaded the Soviet Union. By fighting back, the latter "saved the world – and practically ruined itself" (Lovell 2009: 139).

In other words, the historical experiment that most people today identify with the idea of communism unfolded in an environment that was very hostile. After all, the hopes of Bolshevik leaders for a spread of working-class revolution to the West did not materialize, as the working-class revolts attempted in various European countries after World War I ended in defeat (Mandel 2011: 128; Thompson 2011: 73; Lewin 2005: 277, 288; Callinicos 1991: 26–27; Bettelheim 1976: 63, note 4; Lenin 1975b [1923]: 544–45). As various scholars have observed, both the civil war and the state of siege that the

Soviet Union experienced in its formative years contributed to the consolidation of an undemocratic socio-economic system under Stalin (Thompson 2011: 72; Negri 2008: 12, 15; Harman 2008: 446–48; Lewin 2005: 297; Newman 2005: 36–37; Kovel 2002: 200, Bottomore 1992: 618; Bettelheim 1976; Bettelheim 1978; Marcuse 1961: 58–59).

In this sense, one lesson we must draw from twentieth-century history is that capitalism's increasing destructiveness is more than a potential point of vulnerability for that system. Capitalism's awesome destructive powers can also create a very difficult environment for any attempt to build a society that moves beyond the capitalist socio-economic order.

As Hillel Ticktin (1998: 71) has pointed out, it is possible that other attempts to achieve communism in the future will fail. This possibility is partly a result of the fact that capitalism's continuing development of its forces of destruction increases the likelihood that the post-revolutionary product of such an attempt may not be a genuinely classless society. The presence of a hostile and dangerous capitalist environment may instead encourage the emergence of a new type of undemocratic class order that, like the one in the Soviet Union, capitalism's supporters could hold up as "proof" of the incompatibility between communism, on one side, and democracy and freedom, on the other.

Nevertheless, it is not just capitalism's increasing destructiveness that has implications for any future attempts to achieve a democratic classless society. The other prong of the capitalist contradiction this work identifies is also relevant. One peculiarity of the undemocratic class order that eventually emerged in the Soviet Union was that, to measure its success, it compared itself to its capitalist rivals, duplicating their definition of success in terms of the growth of production and consumption alike (Holmes 2009: 124; Lovell 2009: 71–72; Lewin 2005: 385; Resnick and Wolff 2002: 174, 303; Altvater 1993: 17). As Stephen Lovell (2009: 71) notes,

> [b]y the early 1960s, the regime was tying its legitimacy much more concretely to consumer well-being. [Soviet leader Nikita] Khrushchev made a series of specific promises – notably the pledge to surpass the USA in per capita output of meat, milk, and butter within a few years – that turned out to be politically problematic.

In one sense, this quantitative logic was consistent with the privileging, within the Marxist theory of history, of the development of the forces of production. In another sense, however, the traditional emphasis on developing the forces of production could also become an obstacle to a speedy convergence with Western levels of consumption. Indeed, although the development of the forces of production could, as happened in parts of the capitalist world, eventually raise the levels of popular consumption, such development itself presupposed growing levels of investment. This in turn led the rulers of the Soviet Union's new class order to prioritize heavy industry over the agricultural and light industry sectors catering to consumers. Meanwhile, the military threat from advanced capitalist countries provided added justification to economic priorities that did not necessarily reflect the wishes and needs of most workers and ordinary people in the Soviet Union (Holmes 2009: 38; Lewin 2005: 214; Resnick and Wolff 2002: 267; Bettelheim 1978: 207, 320, 419).

Thus, although the Soviet Union managed to industrialize, raising popular consumption standards and banishing the specter of hunger hanging over the population both before and after the 1917 revolution and World War II, it never delivered Western levels of consumption (Lovell 2009: 71–74; Lewin 2005: 154, 366–67; Resnick and Wolff 2002: 267, 314, 321). As pro-capitalist ideologues were only too happy to point out, in the Soviet system high material standards of living were available solely to the ruling political and technocratic elite (Friedman and Friedman 1981: 126).

This elite owed its privileges to its control of the surplus Soviet workers produced and/or the rewards they received for their role in reproducing the Soviet class order's conditions of existence (Resnick and Wolff 2002: 167–69; Ticktin 1998: 73). Thus, its construction of a "robust" – if stratified – welfare state, which provided education, health care, pensions, and family benefits was not enough to secure the long-term survival of the Soviet system. As "[m]any citizens looked to the West, and saw that lifestyles and access to goods were much better there" (Holmes 2009: 133), growing popular discontent helped to bring that system down (Resnick and Wolff 2002: 303, 310, 314, 321; Cross 2000: 8; Szelényi, Beckett, and King 1994: 247).

The Russian Revolution as a temporary replacement of one undemocratic class society by another

So, although the Russian Revolution gave rise to a socio-economic order without some of the trappings of capitalism, it certainly did not abolish exploitation or lead to a classless society. Working people still produced wealth, only a fraction of which returned to them. The fraction that did return to them included their wages as well as the social wage that took the form of the services that the Soviet welfare state provided. In other words, the fact that major industries were state-owned and that the coordination of economic activity and investment was heavily reliant on central planning and direction by the state did not make the Soviet Union a classless society. On the contrary, central planning and state direction of the economy provided the mechanisms of extracting an economic surplus that supported the privileges of the ruling elite, while also reproducing the Soviet class order this elite benefited from (Lewin 2005: 95–96, 368; Resnick and Wolff 2002: 90–91, 166–69).

Being an exploitative class order, the Soviet system, which spread after World War II to other parts of Europe and the world, was more akin to capitalism and other class societies of the past than it was to the communist ideal of a democratic classless society (Thompson 2011: 107; Holmes 2009: 26–27; Ginsborg 2008: 20; Resnick and Wolff 2002: 88; Sassoon 1996: 109–10; Johnstone 1991: 410; Eatwell, Milgate, and Newman 1990: xii; Brus 1990: 167). In fact, even its lack of democracy does not really set it apart from capitalism and other class societies of the past.

It is not just that dictatorships and undemocratic regimes have long been part of the capitalist world, partly thanks to the support of such self-proclaimed beacons of freedom and democracy as the United States, France, and Britain (Markoff 2014: 84–85, 101–102; Mason 2012: 111; Thompson 2011: 123, 233; Oelsner and Bain 2009: 295; Bagchi 2005: 274–75; Goldsmith 1996a: 257–59; Rueschemeyer, Huber Stephens, and Stephens 1992: 221–22). Pointing out that, "[i]n the ex-colonial countries or countries ruled by coteries closely allied with major imperial powers, a fascist regime could be externally imposed or could sustain itself through external support," Amiya Kumar

Bagchi (2005: 274), for example, reminds us of the "support of the United States and its allies" to the racist apartheid regime in South Africa as well as to the murderous regimes of General Suharto in Indonesia and General Pinochet in Chile. But, such repressive regimes aside, even the capitalist societies that fit the usual definition of liberal democracy in terms of free electoral competition, the rule of law, and so on seriously limit the ordinary people's influence on many of the decisions that crucially affect their lives (Wright and Rogers 2011: 25; Rose 2009: 10; Haerpfer 2009: 314).

We have already discussed some of the ways that capitalism undercuts democracy, and we will revisit this issue later in this work. The point for now is that, in view of the tensions between capitalism and democracy, the contrast between capitalism and the Soviet system when it comes to democracy is not as drastic as often assumed. Without denying the existence of real differences, especially when one compares the Soviet bloc's one-party states to most Western liberal democracies (rather than to Germany under the Nazis, Italy under Benito Mussolini, Chile under Augusto Pinochet, and so on), it is still true that the class nature of both capitalist and Soviet-style societies has made them fall short of the democratic ideal.

Moreover, in both cases ideologies emerged to obscure the restrictions on democracy that these societies entailed. In different ways these ideologies presented the respective class systems as faithful servants of the ordinary people they exploited. So, whereas in capitalist democracies the existence of competitive elections and an adherence to the "one person, one vote" principle supposedly guarantees the elected governments' implementation of the sovereign people's wishes, the transformation of the main means of production into "common wealth" supposedly signified the subordination of the Soviet socio-economic system to the needs of ordinary citizens and "the nation" (Lewin 2005: 373). In capitalist democracies these ideological justifications mainly drew on liberal and conservative political thought. In an analogous fashion, in Soviet-style societies justifications of the prevailing class order appealed to socialism (Thompson 2011: 77–78; Lewin 2005: 273; Bettelheim 1978: 535; Marcuse 1961: 75, 122) and to a Marxism that had been transformed from a revolutionary "theory to ideology," an ideology that, in Marcuse's (1961: 122) words, had "enter[ed] the superstructure of an established system of domination."

But, just as ideologies have obscured capitalist and Soviet-style societies' profoundly undemocratic nature, so have they sought to erase the existence of class exploitation. As we have seen, one ideology performing this function within capitalism is neoclassical economics. Through its models of perfect competitive markets rewarding workers and capitalists according to their respective contributions to production, neoclassical economics erases capitalist exploitation (Wolff and Resnick 2012: 90–91; Heilbroner and Galbraith 1990: 587). Thus, it reinforces the appearance that an economic system that involves free contracts between workers and capitalists is not exploitative but mutually beneficial. But, apart from this more technocratic ideology, other ideologies also developed, which overstated the opportunities for social mobility within capitalist society.

Such ideologies build on the fact that class boundaries in capitalism are not as rigid as in previous class systems (Panayotakis 2014a: 139–41; Slater 1997: 29–30; Xenos 1989: 16–17). This peculiarity of capitalist societies makes them seem meritocratic, an illusion that free public education systems reinforce by creating the appearance of an even playing field for everybody, irrespective of social and economic background (Panayotakis 2014a: 141; Baran and Sweezy 1966: 315). Thus, its supporters claim, capitalism simply rewards hard work and talent. Hence the idea, underlying the American dream, that material prosperity is available to anyone willing to work hard.

Part of this ideology is the claim that capitalism delivers "a broad movement toward greater security and prosperity for everyone, even the humblest" (Graeber 2013: 85), so that each generation lives better than its parents. In recent years, of course, this claim's refutation by the realities facing young people around the world has contributed to the wave of social protest ever since the global financial crisis of 2008 (Mason 2012: 38, 66–67; Panayotakis 2011b).

The practice of obscuring class exploitation through optimistic projections of the future was also evident in Soviet-style class societies. Such optimistic projections were necessary as, in its pursuit of industrialization, the Soviet Union had to intensify the exploitation of industrial workers and farmers (Resnick and Wolff 2002: 171–72, 243, 258, 263–64; Callinicos 1991: 32–33, 35). In fact, justifying this exploitation could draw on Marx's theory of history, which identified the development of productive forces as a condition for a future communist society delivering abundance. According to Lovell (2009: 15), "[t]he Soviet Union was a state built on the myth of inexorable historical progress from ... poverty to prosperity." Thus, this promised future of abundance played a similar role in the Soviet Union to the ideology of material progress in capitalist societies. Supplementing the Soviet regime's future-oriented ideology was, of course, nationalism, which provided an obvious prop for a class order surrounded by a hostile capitalist world environment (Lewin 2005: 136–37; Resnick and Wolff 2002: 242, 259, 271).

The ideological constructions justifying Soviet-style class societies did not, of course, eliminate resistance. The record of these societies confirmed the *Manifesto*'s declaration that all class societies generate class struggle (Kowalewski 2011: 194; Lewin 2005: 73–74, 78, 184–85, 189, 322; Resnick and Wolff 2002: 265; Callinicos 1991: 32–33; Bettelheim 1978: 228, 243–44, 314). In fact, the Soviet model consolidated under Stalin only after political and technocratic elites had beaten back efforts by workers to gain control over production (Bettelheim 1978: 233–37). Movements for workers' control also developed in the Eastern European satellite states of the Soviet Union, as workers repeatedly challenged the Soviet-style exploitative class orders that, after World War II, were installed in their countries (Cohen 2011: 51; Kowalewski 2011: 193–94).

And, although the ruling elites in Soviet-style class orders turned Marxism into an ideology justifying class exploitation, Marxism's instrumentalization in this way had its limits. The presence of class struggles throughout the existence of such societies casts doubt on whether workers saw the promises of future abundance as a sufficient justification for the hardships they endured in the present (Lovell 2009: 22–23). And, despite the effort of the Soviet media to legitimize growing inequality (Lovell 2009: 85), the egalitarianism inherent in the "communist revolutionary ... commitments" that Soviet society continued to affirm ended up undermining this society's ability to survive (Resnick and Wolff 2002: 297).

Thus, popular discontent and Soviet-style societies' gradual delegitimization undercut labor productivity and those societies' ability to secure their conditions of existence, while holding their own in a costly arms race with the capitalist world, in general, and the United States, in particular. The fact that, unlike capitalist societies, after the international economic crisis of the 1970s Soviet-style class orders were not able to further increase the exploitation of their workers meant that the surplus necessary to reproduce their ideological, repressive, economic, and administrative conditions of existence was no longer forthcoming (Resnick and Wolff 2002: 167–69, 310). The Cold War therefore ended with capitalist class orders prevailing over their Soviet-style counterparts.

As this quick overview makes clear, Soviet-style class societies failed in part because they could not keep up with the capitalist class orders' rapid development of their productive and destructive forces alike. Indeed, the economic stagnation resulting from the class and other social contradictions of Soviet-style societies contributed to these societies' failure to fulfill the goal of catching up with Western standards of living (Lewin 2005: 340; Resnick and Wolff 2002: 303).

Although it mirrored the criteria of success prevailing in the capitalist world, this goal was to a certain extent understandable given the extreme privations that the Soviet population had endured before and after the 1917 revolution. This period featured a bloody civil war, which only compounded the devastation from World War I (Thompson 2011: 71–72; Harman 2008: 446; Lewin 2005: 296–97, 310; Nove 1992: 49; Callinicos 1991: 25; Bettelheim 1976: 463, note 11); the violent collectivization of agriculture and the famine, which accompanied the "breakneck industrialization" of the 1930s; the political repression and Stalinist terror that this breakneck industrialization also brought with it (Holmes 2009: 21–23; Lovell 2009: 1, 49; Lewin 2005: 48, 52–53, 66, 75–76, 78–79, 93; Callinicos 1991: 30; Bettelheim 1978: 592); and, of course, World War II, which exacted a more brutal toll on the Soviet Union than it did on most other countries (Thompson 2011: 107; Lewin 2005: 125–27; Nove 1992: 291–92). As Lovell (2009: 6–7) observes, "such was the level of social and political conflict in the USSR that one might … think of a 'Soviet Civil War' running from 1918 to 1953 (with perhaps a brief ceasefire in the 1920s, when everyone gathered their breath and regrouped)." It is therefore not surprising that most Soviet citizens would yearn for political and economic stability as well as for a growth of material consumption that would bring the recurrence of famine to an end (Holmes 2009: 12).

Lessons to draw from the Russian Revolution

These considerations are relevant to potential future attempts to break with capitalism. This is especially true if such attempts do not spark a worldwide anti-capitalist revolt but stay, as was the case with the Russian Revolution, within the confines of societies that are neither economically nor militarily powerful. Such a context would be highly unfavorable and make it hard for post-revolutionary societies to withstand both the threat and the lure of capitalism's destructive forces.

The threat refers, of course, to the military capacity of the capitalist world, especially the United States. The lure refers to capitalism's toxic consumerist culture, the ultimate futility of which is most perceptible in capitalist societies that have reached a certain level of material consumption.

In the absence of a worldwide revolution, therefore, the societies with the best chance to withstand the threat and the lure of capitalist destructiveness would be the more economically and militarily powerful ones. Although this conclusion is consistent with

Cohen's claim that "what makes a *successful* revolution possible is sufficiently developed productive forces" (Cohen 2000: 203, emphasis in original), the reasons for my conclusion are different. They have to do not with the need to develop productive forces in order to achieve material abundance but with the need to defend a post-revolutionary society from both the lure and the threat of capitalism's formidable forces of destruction.

Although the threat that capitalism's military forces of destruction would pose for a post-revolutionary society is easy to understand, resisting the lure of capitalist consumerism would require the new society to recognize consumerist culture's ultimate futility. Thus, such a society's goal would not be to catch up and surpass levels of consumption in affluent capitalist countries but to use technologically advanced productive forces in ways that served human well-being and the ecological integrity of the planet.

Liberal supporters of capitalism often shun references to social goals as a dangerous mark of totalitarianism (Hayek 1944: 56–57). Their preferred alternative is a private sphere inviolable by the state, in which people can freely pursue their *individual* goals and priorities (Freeden 2015: 74; Berlin 1969: xxxvii; Hayek 1944: 14, 56). In their view, this more pluralist vision respects the uniqueness and individuality of every human being, treating each of them as "an end in himself" (Friedman and Friedman 1981: 119; Hayek 1944: 14) while recognizing that there are different values and goals, often contradictory to each other, that individuals should be free to choose from (Berlin 1969: lii, 167–71).

As an argument in defense of capitalism and against a democratic classless society, this line of reasoning is disingenuous and unconvincing. The right of individuals to experiment with different ways of life, each of them expressing different individual priorities and different resolutions of the dilemmas stemming from the fact that "all the positive values in which men have believed [may not], in the end, be compatible, and ... entail one another" (Berlin 1969: 167), is completely consistent with Marx's distinction between a communist society's realm of necessity and its realm of freedom.

The realm of freedom would be precisely the arena in which individuals could pursue happiness and meaning as they understand it, while also experimenting with what life has to offer. The realm of necessity, by contrast, would be oriented to the use of available productive forces to promote human well-being and the ecological integrity of the planet. The relation between these two realms, moreover, would be one in which the latter would serve the subordinate function of procuring individuals with the material means necessary to pursue their well-being, happiness, and a meaningful life. This relation would, therefore, reverse the perverse sacrifice of human well-being and culture to the imperatives of capital accumulation.[2]

In this respect, Samuel Bowles and Herbert Gintis are right to point out that the appeal of many liberals to individual freedom is often ideological (Bowles and Gintis 1986: 18). It is not just that liberal appeals to "true liberty" and "an inviolable private sphere" have been in the past used to defend extremely oppressive and brutal practices, such as slavery (Losurdo 2011: 301–2). More than that, the liberal concern with the ability of individuals to enjoy an inviolable private sphere focuses on the state as the only threat to the inviolability of that sphere. In so doing, liberalism glosses over the perverse effect that capital's ever more extensive and sophisticated marketing and advertising apparatuses of destruction have on individuals' ability to autonomously pursue their well-being and articulate their individual philosophy of life.

Similarly, though sometimes recognizing the material conditions for any individual's exercise of her freedom (Freedom 2015: 33; Berlin 1969; liii), liberals miss the full implications of this insight. If "freedom does not exist when there are no alternatives; and freedom can be measured only by the range of choices that are available" (Nolan and Lenski 1998: 383), respecting every individual's right to freedom requires maximizing the range of choices open to all individuals. Such a goal is not compatible with the exploit-ation central to capitalism, Soviet-style societies, or any other class order that has existed in the past and may exist in the future.

One reason that questions surrounding the production and control of the surplus within a society are important is precisely because of their implications for individual freedom and democracy. As we have seen, capital's use of the surplus contributes to the growth of awesome destructive forces, with grave implications for individual freedom and democracy. Conversely, the appeal of a classless communist society consists in its potential contribution to freedom and democracy. In particular, such a society would institute a democratic use of the surplus that empowered all individuals to pursue the kind of life they found most fulfilling and meaningful. In this respect, democracy is a *sine qua non* for this work's understanding of communism.

This work's insistence on this point differs from other conceptualizations of com-munism in terms of the social processes regulating the production, distribution, and dis-posal of the surplus. Resnick and Wolff (2002: 10), for example, have argued that one can think of "countless forms of communism corresponding to all the possible ways in which nonclass structures can affect a communist class structure with which they interact." Although in all of them the direct producers of the surplus would receive, appropriate, and distribute the surplus, these varieties of communism would differ from each other in terms of the way they coordinated economic activity and political life. Thus, in Resnick and Wolff's conception, communism could conceivably involve the use of markets or the use of central planning, just as it could coexist with democratic or undemocratic decision making over the surplus, and with a democratic, oligarchical, or even despotic political system (Resnick and Wolff 2002: 46, note 9, 60–61, 69–70). The various forms of eco-nomic coordination that a communist society might employ relate to the long-standing debate between democratic planning and cooperative-based market socialism (Mulder 2015; Wolff 2012; Albert and Schweickart 2008; Albert 2003; Sarkar 1999; Ollman 1998; Wright 1996; Roosevelt and Belkin 1994; Roemer 1994; Schweickart 1996; Le Grand and Estrin 1989; Nove 1983; Nove 1990). Having discussed this debate elsewhere (Panayotakis 2011a), I focus here on communism's relationship to political democracy.

Resnick and Wolff illustrate the possible coexistence of communist class structures with a non-democratic political system in their discussion of the Soviet collectivization of agriculture under Stalin (Resnick and Wolff 2002: 69–70, 244–47). Although they argue that the Soviet Union never instituted communist class structures throughout its economy, promoting instead an exploitative state capitalist model, they also suggest that, for a time, producers in agricultural collectives did receive, appropriate, and distribute the surplus they produced (Resnick and Wolff 2002: x, 19, 244–47).

As their analysis also shows, however, one reason these communist experiments fizzled out was the undemocratic Stalinist state's use of force and a variety of other mechanisms, including "mandatory procurements, price manipulations, tractor rents, and taxes," to extract much of the surplus from the agricultural workers who produced it (Resnick and Wolff 2002: 247). This not only "undermined the communist class structures on the collective farms" but also undercut the appeal of the communist ideal (Resnick and Wolff 2002: 256). The ruling elites' transformation of that ideal into an ideology obscured the extent to which the central state's attack on these collectives was an attack by an exploitative class order on a communist class experiment. Facing a "state and party [which] called this [situation] socialism …, many collective farmers found little in such a socialism to celebrate" (Resnick and Wolff 2002: 247). Instead, they probably experienced themselves as under attack by an undemocratic communist regime, thus anticipating the ideological association between communism and dictatorship that largely persists to this day.

This historical example highlights the incompatibility between a communist classless society and an undemocratic political system. Lack of democracy in a society emerging from an anti-capitalist revolution will likely lead to the return, possibly in a new form, of class exploitation. As Lewin's analysis of the "emancipation of bureaucracy" in the Soviet Union makes clear (Lewin 2005: 217, 343, 347–48, 369, 383), a new exploiting class could emerge from a political and technocratic elite that used an undemocratic state's administrative, coercive, and ideological instrumentalities to extract a surplus from the workers producing it.

Depending on the specific characteristics of the class order emerging from this process, the surplus extracted from the producers could take the form of taxes or of public enterprise profits. In this sense, one lesson from the Russian Revolution is that even an apparently successful overthrow of capitalism does not guarantee the emergence of a genuinely classless society. As Charles Bettelheim (1976: 18) has observed, "[t]he Soviet experience confirms that what is hardest is not the overthrow of the former dominant classes: the hardest task is, first, to destroy the former social relations—upon which a system of exploitation similar to the one supposed to have been overthrown for good can be reconstituted." This is why the sustainability of a truly classless society requires political democracy.

In other words, analyzing, as Baran (1957: xxxvi) has done, the transition from the capitalist present to a future democratic classless society in terms of "a more or less acute conflict between socialism and democracy, between people's long-run needs and their short-run wants," is very risky. Baran's (1957: xxxv) reasoning is to some extent understandable, especially for those of "the world's underdeveloped countries," which, at the time Baran was writing, hoped to break with capitalism and make a successful transition to socialism. In view of the privations that the revolutionary effort imposed on the masses, Baran (1957: xxxv) argues, the latter "[sought] and [felt] entitled to immediate improvements in the daily lives of their cities and villages." As immediate improvements were not economically feasible, growing popular discontent and hostility to the revolution could result. To the extent this occurred, it was a manifestation of the failure of

> [b]road strata of the population … [to] grasp that the suffering under the ancient regime was suffering for the benefit of their domestic overlords and their imperialist exploiters, that the misery which they had to endure in the past was misery without

hope and prospect—while the privations accompanying the revolutions are the birth-pangs of a new and better society.

(Baran 1957: xxxvi)

If this is, indeed, the case, Baran concludes, "the socialist government's unwavering and uncompromising commitment to the overriding interests of society as a whole ... creates the need for political repression, for curtailment of civil liberties, for limitation of individual freedom" (Baran 1957: xxxvi). Only after "the most burning economic problems are at least approximately solved" would it be possible for this suspension of democracy to end (Baran 1957: xxxvi).

One can see how suspending democracy might help a socialist government survive "against [its] foreign and domestic enemies" (Baran 1957: xxxvi). It is much less clear how, having come at the cost of democracy, this survival might reflect the government's "unwavering and uncompromising commitment to the overriding interests of society as a whole." In fact, it is not even clear what the latter proposition might mean. In the absence of democratic deliberation, how could "the overriding interests of society as a whole" be defined? After all, one crucial function of democracy is precisely to produce a defensible definition of these interests.

Indeed, once democracy is suspended, the overriding interests of society will tauto-logically become whatever the socialist government says they are. This obviously facilitates the transformation of society's overriding interest in socialism into an ideology that jus-tifies the establishment of a new class society subjecting the masses to the socialist government's functionaries. In other words, the socialist government's monopolization of the right to define what is in the interest of society as a whole can promote its mon-opolization of the surplus produced by the masses, from whom the socialist govern-ment "must demand 'blood, sweat, and toil,' without being able to offer commensurable rewards *hic et nunc*" (Baran 1957: xxxv).

The problem Baran poses is a real one. The radical restructuring of society that a transition to a democratic classless society requires will be a difficult and protracted process. This means, however, that it can be easily derailed. To minimize the likelihood of such an adverse development, and thus to minimize the chance that the sacrifices of a popular revolution come to naught, democracy must be an integral and inviol-able element of that revolution. The extent, moreover, to which a society struggling to become classless adheres to democracy must function as one of the criteria for judging whether the likely endpoint of the transition process is indeed the attainment of a democratic classless society or the institutionalization of a new exploitative class order.

Admittedly, this section's comparison between capitalism and Soviet-style communism, as well as its discussion of the conditions for fundamental social change, may seem hope-lessly optimistic or delusional, given that, as Slavoj Žižek (2010: 211, emphasis in original) observes, "most people *are* Fukuyamean: liberal-democratic capitalism is accepted as the finally found formula of the best possible society, all one can do is try to make it more just, tolerant, etc." Nonetheless, Fukuyama's (1992) interpretation of the end of the Cold War as the end of history is, its ideological effectiveness notwithstanding, little more than a catchy oxymoron. Capitalism may have triumphed over its Soviet nemesis. But it is this very triumph, and the dynamism of the capitalist order underlying it, that makes the "end of history" thesis seem so premature – and, indeed, foolish. After all, there is nothing in capitalism's history to suggest that its own operation cannot lead to the development of revolutionary anti-capitalist challenges. What this history does suggest is that, if there is one thing we can be sure about, it is the constant and dizzyingly rapid change that has always accompanied the capitalist system's operation (Stacey 2002: 94; Schumpeter 2000 [1943]: 154). It may be hard to imagine overcoming capitalism, when even intellectuals sympathetic to that prospect, such as Žižek, concede that most people today accept Fukuyama's diagnosis. And this sense of pessimism is not allayed by the invocation, by other similarly inclined intellectuals, such as Frederic Jameson (2003), of the notion that "it is easier to imagine the end of the world than the end of capitalism."

On the other hand, Teresa Amott and Julie Matthaei (1991: 353) are certainly correct to point out that "[e]conomic injustice, endemic in our system since its inception, continues. However, in the face of such continual injustice, we can take heart in the constancy of social change." Indeed, it is capitalism's constant, dizzyingly rapid change that can explain why communism's current demonization was preceded, not so long ago, by the opposite situation (Badiou 2016: 22). Less than 100 years ago, at the end of World War II, it was capitalism that had lost all credibility in most people's eyes (Sassoon 1996: 84), leading even prominent pro-capitalist intellectuals, such as Joseph Schumpeter (1942), to conclude that socialism's triumph over capitalism was a foregone conclusion. Needless to say, there is no way for even the most committed and astute pro-capitalist ideologue to prove that another swing of the pendulum may not occur in the next 100 years. In fact, none of these ideologues even came close to foreseeing the major global capitalist crisis that occurred less than 20 years after the "end of history," or the fact that a self-proclaimed "socialist" would a few years thereafter be a credible contender for the Democratic Party's presidential nomination in the United States, the heart of the "free world."

As we have seen, the never-ending and rapid social and economic changes that have in the past confounded and will, in the future, continue to confound all confident pronouncements by capitalism's foes and supporters alike are intimately connected to the way that system channels the surplus extracted from workers. Equally, this use of the surplus accounts both for the contradiction traversing contemporary capitalism, in general, and for that system's growing destructiveness, in particular. At the root of capitalism's destructiveness lies the undemocratic control of the surplus by a small capitalist elite. As we have also seen, the use of this surplus crucially shapes not only economic life and ordinary people's ability to meet basic needs but also our culture, our democracy, and the future of the planet on which our survival depends. In this sense, reversing capitalism's growing threat to humanity and the planet requires the democratic control of the surplus that only a classless society can achieve. This democratic control of the surplus is inseparable from political democracy. The economistic notion, by contrast, that a post-revolutionary society may have to suspend democracy until urgent economic needs are addressed (Baran 1957: xxxvi), is dangerous because it can pave the way for the re-establishment of class exploitation and political oppression by a political and technocratic elite in control of the state's economic, repressive, and ideological apparatuses.

We have already seen, and I will amplify this discussion later in this work, that capital's undemocratic use of the surplus seriously compromises the democratic character of the political systems prevailing even in stable liberal regimes, such as the ones in the

United States and Western Europe. In not challenging capital's control of the surplus, these regimes also do not challenge its control over the economy. Capital's control over economic life, as we will see, fatally undermines democratically elected governments' ability to prioritize the wishes and needs of ordinary citizens over the interests of capital.

In this sense, the totalitarianism of capitalist democracies is much more subtle than that prevailing in Soviet-style class societies. Unlike the latter, the former can tolerate genuine political competition between different political parties swearing allegiance to very different ideologies. If the occasional presence of multiple parties could not legitimize the transparently undemocratic Soviet-style class orders, this is less so in their capitalist counterparts. In the latter, self-proclaimed anti-systemic socialist and even communist parties can run for – and, at times, even gain – political power. But the political constraints that result from capital's control over the surplus and economic life often guarantee that, for example, even governing parties of the "radical left" in Greece or communist parties in control of provincial governments in India find themselves presiding over brutal neoliberal policies, which are imposed, if necessary, through the use of institutionalized violence and repression (Lapavitsas and Kouvelakis 2018; Sen 2016). The function of such examples is to reinforce the neoliberal notion that there is no alternative. If ordinary citizens can vote for parties of the communist or radical left and still get the same destructive and inegalitarian neoliberal policies, is it surprising that they would, as Žižek suggests, embrace the Fukuyamean diagnosis? In this sense, it is not surprising that, in his historical overview of the long-term decline of the labor movement in advanced capitalist countries, Friedman (2008: 23, emphases in original) reaches the seemingly paradoxical conclusion that,

> [r]ather than enhancing the capacity of the working-class to act, political power has undermined labor movements because it has been exercised by socialist politicians *against* the working class. Contrary to the fundamental ideals of the Labor Movement, socialist political power is used to *repress* political democracy.

As noted earlier in this work, some theoreticians of horizontal politics attribute this predicament to the failings of political representation and conclude that it is possible for people to struggle for fundamental social change by "circumventing" the state (Solnit 2009). We have instead insisted on the need to democratize the state. Such democratization is not an easy task, in view of the political power that capital derives from its control of the economy and the state (Held 1996: 215; Wright and Rogers 2011: 343–45). But, as we also saw, paths to such a democratization can already be glimpsed in innovative political practices such as participatory budgeting. To the extent that such practices increase the influence of oppressed, disenfranchised, and underprivileged social groups over political outcomes, thus also boosting these groups' political participation, such practices can interact with democratized economic institutions, such as worker-controlled businesses, to generate a virtuous circle of economic and political democratization (Avritzer 2005: 393–94; Sader 2005: 464; Menser and Robinson 2008).

Only by establishing such a virtuous circle is the transition to a democratic classless society conceivable. The struggle to establish such a virtuous circle avoids the pitfalls of fetishizing state power or assuming that a "socialist" government can be trusted to temporarily suspend democracy until more economically pressing issues are addressed

(Baran 1957: xxxvi). It also recognizes, however, how democratizing, rather than merely sidestepping, the state can provide support for popular initiatives and worker-controlled businesses that cultivate ordinary people's democratic skills (Hahnel 2008: 255).

Last but not least, it is only by establishing this virtuous circle of democratization that we can achieve a genuinely pluralistic political democracy. Wolff (2012: 171) has pointed out that recognizing workers' right to choose whether they want to work in a democratic or capitalist workplace would, in effect, enhance "their freedom of choice between alternative work experiences." Wolff's observation suggests that it is only by leveling the playing field between these two different ways of organizing production that we will be able to judge their relative merits. One can amplify this point by arguing that only by leveling the playing field between different political and ideological orientations will we be able to achieve a genuinely democratic political system. A democratic classless society need not be devoid of a multiplicity of political parties, some of which might support capitalism. But such a society would not confer capitalist interests a structural advantage of such magnitude as to virtually guarantee that even supposedly anti-capitalist parties have, when they come to power, to adopt the selfsame pro-capitalist policies they were elected to challenge. In capitalist democracies, it is precisely this state of affairs that diminishes political pluralism by domesticating left-wing political forces. In generating this outcome, however, this state of affairs also breeds political cynicism and disengagement, fueling the view of politics as a game for crooks, and allowing the xenophobic, racist, and sexist far right to channel popular discontent with growing material insecurity into a challenge to political democracy (Markoff 2014: 119; Schaefer and Streeck 2013: 13; Baier 2016: 51; Payiatsos 2017).

Capitalism as an obstacle to democracy

We have discussed the links between a truly classless society and the preservation and deepening of political democracy. We have also begun to examine why the substantive content of political democracy is not reducible to civil and political rights and multi-party competition but requires democratic control over the economic surplus. In Chapter 4 we examined some of the ways that capitalism undermines democracy. Unfortunately, however, there is much more to be said on this issue. As many scholars recognize, capitalist and business interests have historically not been reliable advocates of democracy (Bernhagen 2009: 119–21; Rueschemeyer, Huber Stephens, and Stephens 1992: 8, 61, 98). In fact, the comparative study of liberal democratic regimes suggests that ordinary people and the working class have historically been much more consistent supporters of democratization (Markoff 2014: 100; Rossi and della Porta 2009: 178; Oelsner and Bain 2009: 298–300; Tilly 2007: 39–40; Rueschemeyer, Huber Stephens, and Stephens 1992: 8, 97–98). If there is a connection between capitalism and democracy, this is because of the structural changes, such as urbanization and industrialization, that capitalism brings about and that facilitate the organization of popular interests (Rueschemeyer, Huber Stephens, and Stephens 1992: vii, 6–7, 66, 76–77, 143, 152).

The prevailing liberal democratic political system cannot effectively challenge the power of the capitalist class, however. To begin with, history shows that the capitalist class in different parts of the world has repeatedly used its resources and power to instigate and bolster authoritarian dictatorships, notably when it experienced democrat-ically elected governments' responsiveness to popular needs and aspirations as a threat to its interests (Thompson 2011: 54–55; Losurdo 2011: 251; Bernhagen 2009: 119; Rueschemeyer, Huber Stephens, and Stephens 1992: 10–11; Baran and Sweezy 1966: 155–56). As Domenico Losurdo (2011: 251) has explained,

> [t]he status of the popular classes, whom the dominant elite often tended to assimilate to "savages," long remained uncertain. The assimilation became a veritable identification on the occasion of rebellions and revolutions. And as in the case of external barbarism [arising in the colonies], the remedy for the internal variety was dictatorship.

In addition to the ambivalence of the capitalist class towards political democracy, another factor undermining democracy is the serious economic crises that periodically result from capitalism's economic contradictions. Capitalists' effort to increase profit by keeping wage costs down can undermine their sales (Desai 2013: 37; Albo and Evans 2010: 288; Bowles, Edwards, and Roosevelt 2005: 252). Conversely, high wages may boost demand for capitalist commodities but also increase the costs capitalists face, thus potentially undercutting profits (Bowles and Gintis 1986: 6).

Therefore, wages that are too low and wages that are too high can both spark capit-alist crises. In the first case, the inability of capitalist enterprises to sell their commodities would likely reduce investment, "since spending on investment or growth ma[kes] no sense in a depressed, declining economy" (Wolff 2012: 58). Such a development would trigger worker layoffs and lower capacity utilization (Bowles, Edwards, and Roosevelt 2005: 252). This, in turn, could produce a downward spiral, as increasing layoffs and declining investment would further reduce demand, further reducing investment and augmenting worker layoffs.

The second case could also lead to investment declines and rising layoffs (Bowles and Gintis 1986: 6), but the reason would not be insufficient demand but capitalists' inability to get what they deemed an adequate return on new productive investment. In this second case as well, the capitalists' decision to reduce productive investment and increase worker layoffs could spark a negative economic spiral similar to the one just discussed. Bowles and Gintis (1986: 6) describe a capitalist crisis that results from low wages as the product of a capitalist class that is too strong (and, thus, able to impose on workers wages that are so low they end up undercutting demand). Similarly, they char-acterize a crisis that results from high wages as the product of a capitalist class that is too weak (and, thus, forced to concede wages that are high enough to reduce its profits).

In either case, however, capitalist crises do not just undermine capitalist profits; they also impose great suffering on ordinary people, while also generating acute social problems of various kinds (Wolff 2012: 53; Panayotakis 2011a: 22–3; Stiglitz 2003: 8). As we can see in capitalism's recurrent economic crises in the last two decades, in such circumstances people are more likely to face unemployment, poverty, hunger, homeless-ness, and so on. And, as the global coronavirus pandemic makes clear, these problems are no less painful in cases when economic crises are not sparked by capitalism's endogenous economic dynamics but by "external" shocks from seemingly non-economic geopolit-ical, ecological, or public health events. As explained in this work's prefatory remarks on the pandemic, even a seemingly external shock may be more or less directly related to the capitalist system's operation. Even were one to treat the eruption of the global covid pandemic as a purely public health accident that could not possibly be blamed on capitalism, however, the fact would remain that the economic inequality and insecurity intrinsic to an economic system based on wage labor cannot but compound the suffering of those struck by disease with that of the many more people struck by the social misery that results when a pandemic strikes a *capitalist* society. In any event, whatever the specific precipitating cause of different capitalist economic crises may be, the immense human suffering these crises always inflict often leads to intense social strife and political turmoil, as disaffection grows and people look for a way out.

Although this disaffection may sometimes lead to a challenge of capitalism and its undemocratic nature, it can also take much more ominous forms. For example, economic crises have often strengthened xenophobic and racist political forces, which scapegoat immigrants or racial and ethnic minorities for the problems resulting from capitalism's operation (Baier 2016: 50; Van Der Veen 2014; Berezin 2013; Panayotakis 2013: 21; Offe 2013: 215–16; Cox 1997: 66; Rifkin 1996: 121). In an overview of the forms this phenomenon has taken in recent decades, Claus Offe (2013: 215–16) writes,

> Key elements of the formula that has been used with remarkable success by rightist populist movements and parties are the strengthening of borders (against foreign goods, foreign migrants and foreign political influence, e.g., from the EU) as a means to protect the "weak"; the intolerant and often aggressive denial of difference (from ethnic difference to differences of political views and opinion) in the name of ethno-national homogeneity; and the strong reliance on charismatic leaders and successful political entrepreneurs. These parties and movements have become successful by organizing a game of losers against other (namely "foreign") losers.

Even more reactionary examples of this phenomenon of course include the rise of the Nazis to power during the economic depression of the 1930s and the growth of neo-fascist political forces in Europe and the United States in recent years (Rueschemeyer, Huber Stephens, and Stephens 1992: 111).

Capitalism encourages the channeling of popular disaffection in an anti-democratic direction in two ways. First, for reasons already discussed in Chapter 4, capitalist media have an incentive to frame capitalist crises in ways that do not challenge the interests of their corporate advertisers and of the affluent audience these advertisers primarily target. Thus, movements and politicians trying to channel popular discontent in an anti-democratic direction receive more attention and positive coverage than movements seeking to organize this discontent in an anti-capitalist direction[3].

This is especially true given the ambivalent feelings towards democracy that the capitalist class has long harbored. This ambivalence therefore represents the second way that capitalism encourages the channeling of popular disaffection in an anti-democratic direction. So, for example, capitalists and other segments of the social elite in Germany and Italy supported the political rise of the Nazis and fascists, whom they viewed as the most effective counterweight to communists and the threat of "red revolution" (Thompson 2011: 22, 54; Rueschemeyer, Huber Stephens, and Stephens 1992: 109–11). In his description of how "[t]he role played by conservative elites in Italy in 1920–22 was a remarkable anticipation of what was to happen in Germany in 1932–33," Willie

Thompson (2011: 54), for example, has traced Mussolini's rise to power to the fact that "after 1920 Italian capital and Italian elites generally had lost confidence in the ability of the liberal parliamentary regime to keep the masses in their place."

The exploitative nature of capitalist society also encourages both the corruption of the democratic political process and the popular political cynicism and apathy that this corruption engenders (Graeber 2013: 114–15; Cunningham 2002: 146; Dowd 2000: 208). Indeed, the capitalist class regularly diverts part of the economic surplus to political campaign contributions, lobbying expenses, and the like (Crouch 2012: 80–81; Dowd 2000: 208). Through such political "investments," capitalists can effectively push for policies that serve their interests (Nichols 2011b: 274; Engler 2010: 21; Block 1994a: 375). In so doing, they compound the exploitation that ordinary people face in their capacity as workers with their, at least partial, disenfranchisement as citizens.

As government policies increasingly prioritize capitalist interests, they add to economic inequality as well as to the increase in capital's share of the output, thus bolstering the resources that capital can invest in politics (Markoff 2014: 170; Genschel and Schwarz 2013: 70, 74; Schaefer 2013: 181; Crouch 2013: 233; Wolff 2012: 37; Wright and Rogers 2011: 232; Albo and Evans 2010: 291–92; Oelsner and Bain 2009: 298; Bagchi 2005: 302–3; Milios 2005: 209; Sackrey and Schneider 2002: 114). What results, therefore, is a vicious (from the point of view of ordinary citizens, albeit virtuous from the point of view of capitalist interests) cycle of ever-growing exploitation, inequality, and capitalist control of our ostensibly democratic political system (Crouch 2013: 80–81; Graeber 2013: 39; Chomsky 2011: 153; Sackrey and Schneider 2002). As David Graeber (2013: 39) explains, over the last few decades

> [t]he [wealthiest] 1 percent ... made the overwhelming majority of campaign contributions. In other words, they were exactly that proportion of the population that was able to turn their wealth into political power—and use that political power to accumulate even more wealth.

But, as the political system's bias in favor of capital and the wealthy has become increasingly transparent (Markoff 2014: 170), it has fueled the wave of protests that followed the global financial crisis of the late 2000s (Sitrin and Azzellini 2014; Markoff 2014: 1; Graeber 2013).

Lavish campaign contributions and lobbying expenses are only one way that capital keeps liberal "democracy" contained, however. Even more important is the structural dependence, within capitalism, of all governments, irrespective of ideological complexion, on the smooth accumulation of capital. Indeed, capital's control of the surplus also implies a control over productive investment, and, as the earlier discussion of capitalist crises suggests, this control makes the overall health of the economy dependent on capitalist investment (Wright and Rogers 2011: 13–14).

If significant numbers of capitalists and capitalist corporations, for whatever reason, decide not to reinvest the surplus they extract from workers, this decision will affect not just workers but also governments. After all, no government wants to preside over the economic crisis and growing unemployment, poverty, and homelessness that a collapse of capitalist investment can trigger. In such circumstances the opposition in capitalist democracies predictably accuses the governing party of mismanaging the economy, gaining an advantage in the next election. The outcomes, since the eruption of the global economic crisis in the late 2000s, of successive elections in liberal democratic countries around the world confirm a truth that politicians are keenly aware of.[4]

Moreover, since "a decline in jobs, income, and production ... [leads to] a decline in tax revenues available to the state" (Wright and Rogers 2011: 344), governments find it easier to finance their operations during periods of smooth capital accumulation than during economic crises. As the coronavirus pandemic demonstrates, furthermore, economic crises can quickly take a toll on public finances by simultaneously increasing government expenses and reducing government revenues (Riley 2020; Wolff 2012: 53). Partly the result of corporate bailouts, government spending increases also reflect the fact that economic crises generate unemployment, poverty, and a series of social problems, which inevitably also increase ordinary citizens' claim on public resources (Desai 2013: 260).

National security has been used as one justification for the covid-pandemic-induced corporate bailout (Slotnick 2020), but another justification used in the past has been the need to support industries that the government views as "too big to fail." Although this justification of bailouts gained notoriety in the global financial crisis of the late 2000s, this problem is not new. Instead, it reflects capitalism's long-term evolution from the more competitive model of the nineteenth century to the more monopolistic model prevalent today. When a handful of giant corporations dominate an economy's major industries, the prospect of any of them failing becomes harder to countenance, since a failure's negative consequences on the larger economy are hard to predict. Thus,

> it becomes necessary for the state to take a hand by way of loans of public funds, subsidies, and even in some cases government ownership of the no-longer profitable enterprises. In this fashion capitalist states are forced to go in for an ever greater degree of "socialism." What is socialized is almost invariably the losses of the capitalists involved.
>
> (Sweezy 1942: 318–19)

The fact that capitalist economic crises often increase public spending, even as they reduce government resources, means that, under capitalism, governments cannot challenge but only manage capital accumulation. This is evident in the history of European social democracy, which, having evolved from a political force wanting to replace capitalism to one seeking to reform it (Bottomore 1991: 498; Sassoon 1996: 733–34), has found that, since progressive reform is costly, the only way to achieve it is by safeguarding the conditions for capital accumulation (Sassoon 1996: xxii, 247, 353, 684–85). Needless to say, the felt need to protect capital accumulation is not unique to social democratic governments.

Interestingly, the paramount political importance of protecting capital accumulation also accounts for the fact that government intervention and regulation of all kinds characterize even countries, such as the United States, that stay closer to a laissez-faire model of capitalism (Desai 2013: 2; Wright and Rogers 2011: 18–20; Folbre 2009: xxvi; Stiglitz 2001: xiii-xiv; Piven and Cloward 1987: 93–94). Although liberal and neo-liberal theorists have sometimes lambasted them as creeping socialism and a threat to economic growth and human freedom (Friedman and Friedman 1981: 55–56; Hayek 1944: x, 13), these interventions respond to the instability and social problems that result from capitalism's contradictory and uneven development (Desai 2015: 4, Desai 2013: 11; Olson 1971: 172). Since capitalist economic crises, for example, potentially call into question not only the government of the day but the capitalist system as a whole, governments have long "manag[ed] capitalism's contradictions and legitimacy deficits" (Desai 2015: 4) through interventions that attempt to make capital accumulation more orderly, less socially destructive, and thus less vulnerable to popular contestation (Desai 2015: 4; Bowles, Edwards, and Roosevelt 2005: 506–13).

In fact, governments in capitalist societies have to walk on a tightrope, since interventions that capital perceives as "too onerous" can lead to investment strikes and economic crises, which can in turn trigger social and economic problems worse than the ones that the interventions sought to avert. In this respect, even democratically elected governments have to accept the power to define reality that capital derives from its control of the surplus.

Indeed, capital's ability to engage in investment strikes can easily turn its perception of government intervention and social programs as too onerous into a self-fulfilling prophecy. Capital's control of investment means that the burden of proof is not on itself to show that such interventions irreparably harm the economy. Its ability to respond to government interventions it objects to with an investment strike means that capital can trigger economic crises that seemingly confirm its dire predictions (Block 1994a: 375; Bowles and Edwards 1993: 431–37). In this respect, capitalism "holds a kind of blackmail over democratically elected political leaders" (Bowles and Edwards 1993: 433), thus keeping society hostage to capital's self-serving assessment of which economic policies and interventions are too onerous and which serve "national security" or serve to avert "systemic risk" in the economy.

Given all this, it is not surprising, for example, that, "[r]esearch comparing the policy preferences of US citizens to the legislation actually enacted by Congress clearly demonstrates that those with higher incomes may not always get what they want but that they are far more likely to than those of more modest means" (Markoff 2014: 135). Neither is it surprising that levels of inequality in countries such as the United States are higher than those most citizens prefer (Domhoff 2017). Thus, political democracies' capitalist framework makes for a system that is only selectively representative.

This selective representation, which privileges the interests, views, and preferences of the economically powerful, predictably leads to political participation variations that tend to feed on themselves (Offe 2013: 198–99). In particular, voting participation rates are higher among the more affluent strata of capitalist society and lower among low-income groups (Markoff 2014: 119; Schaefer and Streeck 2013: 13). Although, for the former group, participation in political processes responsive to their preferences seems meaningful, the opposite is the case for the segments of the population that experience the political system as not responsive to their views and needs.

Amplifying the lower political participation rates of working people and ordinary citizens is the veto power that capital can derive from its ability to ignite investment strikes. The negative effects that such strikes can impose on ordinary citizens and their elected governments often take off the table progressive economic policies in areas such as employment, education, health care, and social policy, which could make a difference in people's lives (Offe 2013: 202). Thus, by restricting the range of interests the political system can represent as well as the range of policies that elected governments can select (Wright and Rogers 2011: 343–45; Held 1996: 215), capitalism encourages the popular strata to look upon electoral politics with a sense of futility and disinterest (Offe 2013: 202; Cox 1992: 33).

Not only does such a development make political democracy "safe for capitalism," mitigating the fear with which the capitalist classes of past centuries had viewed the prospect of universal suffrage and majority rule (Streeck 2013: 263); it can also naturalize the "restricted version of democracy" that capitalist business prefers (Bernhagen 2009: 120–21). By glossing over both the extent to which lack of popular participation in politics is a result of capitalism's fundamentally undemocratic nature and the fact that "[w]hen there is a chance of having a real influence over the allocation of resources, … and when people are … at least half convinced that it could make a difference, then they engage" (Wainwright 2003: 109), one can easily interpret the apparent political apathy of many ordinary citizens as proof that the common affairs of society are best left to small economic and political elites who understand and show interest in the complex public issues that contemporary societies face.

Reinforcing this ideological effect is capitalism's hierarchical division of labor. Integral to capital's real subsumption of labor, this division of labor has often deskilled workers, consigning many of them to jobs that neither engage their critical faculties nor develop the skills central to democratic participation (Braverman 1974). The opposite, meanwhile, is true for capitalist elites, who decide how to organize production and manage the surplus. So, as low-wage, low-skill jobs proliferate even in affluent capitalist societies, such as the United States (Wright and Rogers 2011: 167), capitalism divides the population into a ruling elite fully equipped with the skills necessary for effective political intervention and a majority for which this is not the case. As the recent rise of the far right demonstrates, however, even on the occasions when the majority abandons its apparent disinterest in politics and seeks to find ways to express its discontent, the disempowering effects of the capitalist division of labor make many citizens vulnerable to demagogic manipulation, thus seemingly confirming the fundamental inability of ordinary people to make constructive contributions to political life.

In any event, the consolidation of a class gap in voting participation tends to produce a vicious cycle (Offe 2013: 198–99). Politicians competing for votes "will tend to form rational strategies that are biased in favour of those social categories known to participate and that ignore or downgrade those less likely to do so" (Offe 2013: 198). Although this increases the relevance of political participation for the more affluent groups that are already more likely to vote, it also further undercuts the interest of working and low-income people in a political process that speaks less and less to their needs. As the majority of the population disengages from the political process, what results is a paradox. Democracy becomes hollowed out even as the trappings of liberal democracy are adopted in more parts of the world than ever (Santos 2005a; Markoff 2009: 69; Brown 2010: 44; della Porta 2013: 185; Ginsborg 2008: 26; Fung and Wright 2003: 39–40).

The prospects for democratization in
contemporary capitalist societies

This last paradox illustrates the limits that capitalism places on processes of democratization around the world. In fact, the two contrasting ways that the term "democratization" is used in the literature capture the two sides of this paradox.

On the one hand, the term refers to the diffusion of liberal democratic institutions to parts of the world where such institutions have either been absent in the past or have proved fragile and short-lived (Welzel 2009: 74). Using the term in this sense, political scientists and sociologists have identified waves of democratization, during which the spread of liberal democratic institutions around the world accelerates (Markoff 2014: x; Markoff 2009; Berg-Schlosser 2009; Welzel 2009: 81; Tilly 2007: 40–44). In this view, the most recent democratization wave began with the fall of military dictatorships in Greece, Portugal, and Spain in the 1970s. The trend continued with the fall of the one-party states in Eastern Europe, of the racist apartheid regime in South Africa, and of military dictatorships in a number of countries of Latin America and Southeast Asia since the 1980s (Markoff 2009: 62–69). Thanks to this trend, democratization seems to have reached more parts of the world than ever.

Positive as this trend may be, things look different once we examine the other meaning of the term "democratization." This other meaning focuses on "the deepening of the democratic qualities of given democracies" (Welzel 2009: 74). This alternative meaning is, therefore, more cognizant of the limitations that capitalism places on the ability of liberal democratic institutions to truly represent the will and interests of ordinary citizens. From the point of view of this second meaning, contemporary capitalism is, for all the reasons reviewed in this work, an obstacle to democratization.

This has become painfully obvious in a number of countries in the world, which have time and again seen capitalism's incompatibility with democratization in the second sense of the word negate the gains from their recent democratization in the first sense of the word. For example, a number of the countries that benefited from the most recent wave of democratization have often had to surrender their sovereignty over economic and social matters to international organizations, such as the International Monetary Fund and the European Union.

As a result of successive capitalist crises since the 1970s, people both in European countries (such as Greece and Portugal) and throughout the global South have found that their ability to elect their governments does not always translate into a meaningful choice over the economic and social policies that crucially affect their lives. Contributing to this state of affairs has been the inability of many of these countries to continue servicing debts that accumulated over time. Although these debts partly reflect the long-standing unevenness of global capitalist development, their accumulation was also the product of

> deep-seated patterns of social domination left behind by colonialism; misguided development strategies often devised by First World aid agencies; the dramatic oil price hikes of the 1970s; the rise of global interest rates in the early 1980s; waning global demand for Third World products; decreasing importance of domestic markets; ill-considered

and wasteful mega-construction projects; and widespread corruption among domestic governing elites.

(Steger and Roy 2010: 98)

Especially interesting, in view of the last chapter's discussion, is the contribution, in some countries, such as Greece, of military contracts to this debt. On the one hand, the Greek example illustrates the contribution that, even in liberal democratic regimes, corruption makes to the accumulation of public debt, since the industries of affluent capitalist countries such as the United States and Germany that received those contracts did so after bribing some of the highest officials in the Greek state (Smith 2012). On the other hand, this example also illustrates how inter-state competition for capitalism's ever-growing forces of destruction can sabotage the democratization efforts of countries around the world.

In any event, looming debt crises have forced many new democracies to turn to the IMF and (in the case of Greece and Portugal) to the European Union and its member countries for loans to keep them afloat. In return for these loans, these countries have had to adopt punishing "structural adjustment" and austerity programs that

included putting more emphasis on production for export rather than on meeting the needs of national and local markets; severe spending cuts – especially for social programmes; sweeping privatization measures; reduced regulation on the activities of transnational corporations; and, in a number of cases, significant currency devaluations.

(Steger and Roy 2010: 98)

To be sure, the governments implementing these programs are often democratically elected. This does not make these policies any more democratic. On the contrary, the policies in the neoliberal toolkit invariably undercut democracy by increasing inequalities and magnifying the hold of financial markets and the financial sector over government policy. The fact, moreover, that the democratic rulers implementing them often ascend to power by opposing neoliberal austerity and promising a different course highlights the fundamentally undemocratic nature of capitalist democracy.

In other words, democratization in the first sense of the word does not subordinate capitalism to democracy. It simply reflects capitalism's ability to thrive in the midst of political systems that are nominally democratic but that also grant ordinary citizens a limited say over many of the decisions that crucially affect their lives.

There was a time during capitalism's golden age, after World War II, when the idea of a capitalism with a human face did not seem to many as a contradiction in terms (Thompson 2011: 126–27; Sassoon 1996: 210). This idea derived its plausibility from a number of features of the post-war model of capitalist development. These included increasing government intervention in the economy, the active pursuit of full employment through Keynesian macroeconomic policies, and the building of welfare states protecting people from the ups and downs of capitalist markets (Steger and Roy 2010: 7–9; Harvey 2005: 9–12; Garrett 2000: 306). The widespread acceptance of these features reflected a consensus between social democracy and liberal forces of the political center and right, which since the late nineteenth century had become more cognizant of the dependence of freedom on a modicum of equality and social justice (Freeden 2015. 46–47, 81; Berger 2012: 22; Thompson 2011: 30, 40, 126; Steger and Roy 2010: 5–9; Sassoon 1996: 199, 322, 675).

Integral to the ideological notion of a capitalism with a human face was the suggestion that the convergence of socialism with liberalism had brought traditional laissez-faire capitalism, with its cut-throat competition and periodic generation of economic depressions, to an end (Thompson 2011: 126–27; Sassoon 1996: 247; Scott 1990: 56). According to this narrative, "capitalists had become socially conscious and responsible and if they were tempted to act otherwise the countervailing powers of government and trade unions were available to keep them in line" (Thompson 2011: 127). In other words, political democracy had humanized capitalism, making democratic capitalism a superior alternative to the undemocratic "communist" systems of the Soviet Union and its satellite states (Sassoon 1996: 210). Although this narrative may have contributed to the gradual discrediting and eventual unraveling of Soviet-style class societies, what has transpired since then suggests a different reading of the relationship between capitalism, communism, and democracy. It is with the articulation of this alternative reading that the conclusion of this work will begin.

Notes

1 For an attempt to provide such an account, which is useful in its comprehensiveness even though informed by a different theoretical and political perspective from mine, see Archie Brown (2009).

2 This formulation does not preclude the possibility of people finding happiness and meaning in material production. On the contrary, for people who do find happiness and meaning in work that would normally form part of the realm of necessity, such work would form part of their individual realm of freedom. In this respect, it is impossible to draw the line between the two realms in a clear-cut and rigid fashion. Thus, strictly speaking, individual experimentation with different ways of life might also include experimentation with different ways of drawing the line between the two realms. Beyond an individual affair, of course, such an experimentation could become a political issue, as in a society that debated the merits of making the experience of working in the realm of material production as meaningful and satisfying as possible, even at the cost of reducing the free time that people could spend in the realm of freedom.

3 The coverage of Donald Trump's 2016 presidential campaign exemplifies the attention that media are willing to extend to the far right's channeling of people's discontent with the growing economic insecurity prevailing today. Eric Alterman (2016) offers a brief but useful overview of Trump's favorable coverage, even though his piece prematurely celebrates the Trump campaign's "implosion," thus demonstrating the liberal intelligentsia's blissful insulation from the popular mood.

4 It is, of course, not only the governments in capitalist "democracies" that are dependent on the smoothness of capital accumulation. Both the Arab Spring uprisings and the literature on democratization confirm that economic crises can bring down even authoritarian regimes in parts of the capitalist world that are not even nominally democratic (Teorell 2010: 70–76; Oelsner and Bain 2009: 298).

Conclusion: Rethinking the relationship between capitalism, communism, and democracy

The speedy and complete abandonment of the post-war consensus after the end of the Cold War is instructive. It suggests that the momentary humanization of capitalism in parts of the capitalist world after World War II was, at least in part, a product of the pressure that capitalist elites felt as a result of the Russian Revolution and the possibility that other parts of the world could follow its example (Desai 2013: 12, 53; Thompson 2011: 138; Folbre 2009: xxi; Aronowitz 2006: 188; Bagchi 2005: 119; Friedman 2000: 158; Greider 1997: 362; Amin 1996: 34–35; Panitch and Miliband 1992: 4). After all, even though that revolution never led to a classless society, it did lead to the expropriation of capitalists, thus raising the anxiety of capitalist elites in the rest of the world to a level sufficient to produce the less inegalitarian model of capitalism that prevailed immediately after World War II.

The more recent return to a more brutal and inegalitarian model of capitalism is a reminder of the precariousness of all social gains under capitalism and of the utopianism of the social democratic hope to subordinate capital to democracy and the needs of humanity (Wolff 2012: 10, 33–37; Cruddas and Nahles 2012: 200; Berger 2012: 25; Hahnel 2008: 239; Aronowitz 2006: 174–75; Lafontaine 1998: 74; Sassoon 1996: 722; Mandel 1995: 443; Sweezy 1942: 352). Describing the end of the New Deal era of progressive reforms, Wolff (2012: 10) has this to say:

> The New Deal-era taxes on business and the rich and regulations of enterprise behavior proved vulnerable and unsustainable. The enemies of the New Deal had the incentives (profit maximization) and the resources (their returns on investments) to undo many of its reforms after World War II, with ever-greater effect in the period since the 1970s. They systematically evaded, then weakened, the taxes and regulations of the New Deal, and eventually, when politically possible, eliminated them altogether.

The picture that Wolff paints is a reminder that the ambition of social democrats and left liberals to subordinate capitalism to democracy has not been any more successful than the Soviet Union's attempt to build a viable and desirable alternative to capitalism. This is because, being a class society, capitalism allows a small exploiting minority to use the surplus it receives in ways that undercut not only human well-being and the ecological integrity of the planet but democracy itself.

Thus, far from demonstrating the superiority of capitalism over communism, the collapse of Soviet-style class societies has a very different meaning. The identification of Soviet-style societies with the communist ideal may have been a convenient ideological prop for both Cold War competitors. The exploiting elites in Soviet-style societies sought through their appeals to the communist ideal to legitimize their class rule over the direct producers whose surplus they extracted (Resnick and Wolff 2002: 259, 263–64). The exploiting elites in the capitalist world, on the other hand, could equate the communist ideal with brutal dictatorship and personal unfreedom. Nevertheless, the fact that in the competition between two different class orders one of them prevailed is hardly a proof that a classless social order would not be preferable to the class orders of various kinds that have lorded over humanity for the last few thousands of years.

The frequent support in the past of capitalist powers, such as the United States, for brutal military dictatorships in the name of defending democracy against the communist threat is not a reason to discard the democratic ideal. Similarly, the ideological abuse of the communist ideal by a repressive and undemocratic class order is not a reason to discard the ideal of a society in which ordinary people collectively decide on the size of the surplus they produce and on the best ways to make this surplus serve human well-being, the ecological integrity of the planet, and the ability of all human beings to pursue a meaningful and fulfilling life.

The paradox of political democracy spreading to new regions at the same time as its hollowing out proceeds even in countries that have long enjoyed stable liberal democratic institutions dramatizes the political impasse we have reached. The coexistence between capitalism and political democracy is not leading towards the felicitous outcome of democracy taming capitalism and rendering it more humane. It is, rather, leading to the subordination of democracy to the requirements of capital accumulation. Thus, many of the processes, such as neoliberal globalization, that increase the power of capital and transnational corporations at the expense of working people, ordinary citizens, and their democratically elected governments stem, at least in part, from the decisions, agreements, and policies of governments that are supposedly elected to represent the interests of the many, not the few (della Porta 2013: 28–29; Panitch 2000: 374–75; Dowd 2000: 170; Helleiner 1999: 141; Helleiner 1996: 193; Strange 1996: 44; Bienefeld 1996: 422). As Donatella della Porta (2013: 28) rightly insists,

> [m]arket deregulation and the privatization of public services are not "natural" effects of technological development, but a strategy adopted and defended by international financial institutions and by the governments of the most powerful nations (in particular through the G7 and the G8) to the advantage of multinational corporations … Neoliberal globalization, therefore, is a matter not only of new technologies and modes of production, but also of the political tools set in place to regulate and reproduce this social structure.

Through neoliberal globalization, capital further augments the formidable political power that it already derives from its campaign contributions, its lobbying campaigns, and its ability to veto business-unfriendly policies through investment strikes. For example, transnational corporations are increasingly using international agreements to gain the right to sue democratically elected governments for laws or decisions that may reduce their profits. Making the success of such lawsuits more likely is the fact that hearing such cases are special private courts in which business-friendly arbitrators can force governments to pay hefty fines (Warren 2015; Sorscher 2013).

As US senator Elizabeth Warren (2015) has pointed out, corporations producing a toxic chemical could potentially use such provisions to sue governments that ban this chemical because of its environmental and health risks. Not only does this example fit into the broader use of free trade agreements and supra-national institutions, such as the European Union, to "constitutionalize" neoliberalism and/or balanced budgets and economic austerity (Schaefer and Streeck 2013: 23; Milios 2005: 211–12; Panitch 1994: 74). It is also a reminder of the sobering implications that capitalism's fundamentally undemocratic nature has for humanity's ability to reverse that system's relentless development and deployment of its forces of destruction.

Indeed, as Warren's example and the discussion earlier in this work make clear, governments are often complicit in capitalism's growing destructiveness, both directly and indirectly. Their direct contribution to this growing destructiveness is evident in their accumulation of weapons sufficient to exterminate humanity many times over, while their indirect contribution takes the form of decisions that facilitate capitalist corporations' profit-driven development of the forces of destruction. Thus, the evolution of contemporary capitalism points to the inextricable connection between the class nature of capitalist society, on one side, and its increasing destructiveness and incompatibility with democracy, on the other. This is why a commitment to democracy today is inconceivable without a simultaneous commitment to a classless socio-economic order that allows people to democratically control the surplus they produce. Alain Badiou (2010b: 15) is, therefore, right to proclaim that "we will only ever be true democrats … when we become communists again."

In other words, the recent record of capitalist society forces us to rethink the lessons that supporters of capitalism draw from the end of the Cold War. Far from signifying the bankruptcy of communism and "the triumph of liberalism and free-market capitalism as the most effective way to organize a society" (Friedman 2000: xxi), the end of the Cold War simply confirmed the impossibility of pursuing human liberation and the ecological integrity of the planet within the framework of a class society. Nothing that has occurred since the end of the Cold War contradicts this conclusion. And, since this conclusion points to the democratic control of the surplus as an indispensable moment of the further democratization that today's societies so urgently need, the vision of a classless society has itself become indissolubly connected with the future of the democratic ideal.

Communism and the struggle against racial and gender oppression

But, if it is also a struggle for democracy and against capitalism's growing destructiveness, the struggle for communism cannot afford to privilege workers as the one group that "[t]o abolish … their own exploitation and alienation [has to] do away with all forms of oppression" (Ollman 1998: 98). This work's reconceptualization of the surplus and its insistence that households and the public sector are no less important sites of surplus production than capitalist workplaces mean that struggles against exploitation are inseparable from struggles against austerity and patriarchy alike. The centrality, moreover, of the racial and gender dimensions of struggles over austerity also demonstrates that it is impossible to fight austerity and exploitation without, at the same time, challenging racial and gender oppression.

As we have seen, the struggle for the democratization of the social processes determining the size and use of the surplus is inseparable from the challenge of seemingly non-class forms of oppression. Thus, implicit in this work's analysis of the socioeconomic processes through which the production of the surplus takes place is also a reconceptualization of the communist ideal.

Central to this work's conception of this ideal has been the vision of a democratic classless society. Such a society would not just end the social division of the population into a class of surplus producers not fully enjoying or controlling the fruits of their labor and an exploiting class channeling the surplus they extract from producers to their consumption and to the reproduction of the exploitative class order they benefit from. It would also allow all people to make a contribution to the production of the surplus as well as to participate in the democratic determination of its size and use.

Both these aspects of a classless society presuppose a struggle against and an overcoming of racial and gender inequalities. The abolition of capitalism is inconceivable as long as capital can successfully use racial and gender inequalities to keep working people and ordinary citizens divided. Thus, the struggle against capitalism can be successful only if it is simultaneously a struggle for a society that has overcome gender and racial inequalities as well as the social constructs of gender and race.

At the same time, the condition for the desirability of any post-capitalist order, namely the democratic control of the surplus, also presupposes the challenge of racism and patriarchy. Debra Satz (1996: 85) has rightly insisted on the adverse effect that racial and gender inequalities can have on "people's ... ability to freely participate in deliberations about the public good." What Satz's insight means for our purposes is that the process of determining the size and use of the surplus cannot be truly democratic unless the overcoming of racial and gender inequalities ensures that people's views, priorities, and needs receive equal consideration irrespective of whether they are male or female, "white" or "non-white," and so on.

In this respect, any past tendency in segments of the political left to privilege the struggle against capital over the struggles against patriarchy and racism is counterproductive, because it obscures the mutual interconnectedness of all these struggles (Sassoon 1996: 419; Cohen 1985: 668). Without challenging patriarchy and racism, no movement hoping to replace capitalism with a classless society will be successful. But the reverse is also true. Without challenging capitalism, feminist and anti-racist movements will find that capital's ongoing use of such inequalities to divide workers will inevitably hobble struggles against racial and gender injustice.

Communism, the new social movements, and the prospects for an anti-capitalist alliance

The inseparability of the struggle for a democratic classless society from those against racial and patriarchal oppression provides one example of how the former struggle, which scholars often identify as the terrain of "old left" politics, is inseparable from the "new left" politics of the "new social movements" (Markovits and Gorski 1993: 10–13). Insisting on the inseparability of "old" and "new" left politics is important, because paying "lip service" to the struggles against gender and racial inequality, while in practice subordinating these struggles to the struggle of labor against capital (Sassoon 1996: 688–89), does not only have an alienating effect on feminist and anti-racist movements.

By implying that the struggles against patriarchy and racism have to take back seat to that against capital, this political practice also suggests that it is possible to separate the former struggles from the latter. In so doing, it inadvertently also invites new social movements to conclude that it is possible for them to pursue their objectives without struggling, at the same time, against capitalism. As this work makes clear, this assumption is untenable, and not just for the feminist and anti-racist movements. It is also untenable for those new social movements, such as the ecological and peace movements, that fight the various manifestations of capitalism's growing destructiveness. These movements are an expression of the cost–benefit contradiction within contemporary capitalism that this work identifies.

In particular, capitalism is increasingly unable to translate its ongoing productive development into greater human well-being, even as its simultaneously growing forces of destruction not only undermine human well-being but, indeed, threaten the future of humanity and the planet. This contradiction means that the anti-capitalist struggle for a classless (and, thus, raceless and genderless) society is also a struggle against the growing threats to humanity and the planet that result from capital's undemocratic use of the surplus.

In this sense, the new social movements are not a manifestation of new "post-materialist" concerns, which, according to some scholars, stand in contrast to the values of the old left (Markovits and Gorski 1993: 10; Scott 1990: 69–70). After all, spiraling military expenditures, bloody military conflicts, and environmental catastrophes that lead to hundreds of thousands of deaths a year,[1] while making wars over resources such as water more likely and creating the prospect of millions of environmental refugees in the near future,[2] have no less impact on people's material lives than "conventional 'bread and butter' concerns" (Markovits and Gorski 1993: 10). On the contrary, the need of new social movements to struggle against such phenomena demonstrate that the threats to people's material interests have over time become more numerous and more grave as a result of capitalism's cost–benefit contradiction. Moreover, this work's demonstration of the close link between capitalism's growing destructiveness and its mode of extracting and distributing the surplus that the direct producers generate makes clear how misleading it is to contrast the concerns of new social movements to what Andrei Markovits and Philip Gorski (1993: 11) describe as "the old politics of material distribution."

As this work has also pointed out, however, the coming together of all these different movements fighting against different manifestations of the cost–benefit contradiction traversing capitalist development is by no means inevitable. The unevenness of capitalist development implies that different segments of the world's population do not experience this contradiction uniformly.

People in the global North, for example, are more likely to have experienced the futility of using capitalism's growing productive forces to sustain a consumerist way of life, while people in the global South, as well as the poor in the global North, are more likely to experience the effects of capitalism's growing forces of destruction. Thus, in addition to manifesting itself in many different ways and giving rise to a variety of social movements, capitalism's cost–benefit contradiction also produces variation in how different people perceive it and react to it.

It may be tempting to postulate that the logic of capitalist development will somehow lead to a convergence of the conditions underlying these differing standpoints and, thus, to a convergence of the standpoints themselves. The habit of succumbing to this temptation has a long pedigree within Marxism. In fact, we can trace it back to the prediction, by Marx and Engels (1978 [1848]: 474, 483), that the logic of capitalist development and the social struggles it triggered would, over time, produce a class polarization that would "simplif[y] the class antagonisms" and "[replace] the isolation of the labourers, due to competition, by their revolutionary combination, due to association." Because of the tendency of capitalist contradictions to express themselves in painful economic crises, it was plausible to assume that the increasingly organized and class-conscious working class would sooner or later intervene to overthrow an obsolete capitalist class order that had come to obstruct the further development of the forces of production (Marx and Engels 1978 [1848]: 478).

This work makes no such assumptions. In fact, even when forces of convergence are present in contemporary capitalism, they are as likely to lead to divisions between the populations hurt by capitalism's contradictory development as they are to lead to a broadening anti-capitalist alliance. We saw in Chapter 6, for example, that, as a result of their declining insulation from the effects of their governments' deployment of capitalism's military forces of destruction in the global South, ordinary people in the global North often turn to racism, xenophobia, and a hostility towards refugees from the war-torn regions of the global South.

Similarly, we saw that the increasing exploitation and economic insecurity that neoliberal globalization foists upon working people in the global North often leads, with the help of the corporate media, not to alliances between working people in the global North and South alike but, rather, to ultra-conservative or even neo-fascist economic nationalism. Fueled by the toll that the decline of welfare capitalism is taking on working people in the global North, these reactionary movements turn against immigrants from the global South who flee the devastating effects on their countries of international organizations such as the International Monetary Fund and the North Atlantic Treaty Organization, which "are 'accountable' only to their sponsors who are often the few militarily and economically powerful nation-states" (Sheth 2005: 13).

In fact, far from being a hypothetical concomitant of capitalism's cost–benefit contradiction, such reactionary movements may already be gaining enough strength to partially reverse the spread of liberal democratic values and institutions discussed earlier in this book. Even before the global coronavirus pandemic, Arjun Appadurai (2017: 1) had warned that

> [t]he central question of our times is whether we are witnessing the worldwide rejection of liberal democracy and its replacement by ... populist authoritarianism. Strong signs of this trend are to be found in Trump's America, Putin's Russia, Modi's India and Erdogan's Turkey. In addition, we have numerous examples of already existing authoritarian

governments (Orban in Hungary, Duda in Poland) and major aspirants to authoritarian right-wing rule in France, Austria and other European Union countries. The total population of these countries is almost a third of the total population of the world.

It should be clear that the fear and restrictions on social life that the covid pandemic has brought can only add fuel to this pre-existing trend. The signs are there: "Hungary's parliament has voted to allow Prime Minister Viktor Orban to rule by decree indefinitely, in order to combat the coronavirus pandemic" (Picheta and Halasz 2020); not to be outdone, "Philippine President Rodrigo Duterte orders police and military to kill citizens who defy coronavirus lockdown" (Capatides 2020); and the governments of the United States and Greece are using the pandemic as an opportunity and excuse to suspend refugees' internationally recognized right to apply for asylum (Refugees International 2020). As examples such as these proliferate, moreover, so do warnings that, "[a]cross Europe, the Middle East, Asia, Africa and the Americas, governments have introduced states of emergency to combat the spread of the new coronavirus, imposing some of the most stringent restrictions on civil liberties since the attacks of Sept. 11, 2001" (Baker, Tostevin, and Ghoshal 2020). In view of all this, there is clearly no guarantee that capitalism's cost–benefit contradiction will find its felicitous resolution in an alternative social order. An alternative classless (but also genderless and raceless) order is necessary, but this necessity is normative rather than causal. In other words, this alternative order is necessary, if one wants the technological advances capitalist dynamism generates to serve human well-being and the ecological integrity of the planet rather than to fuel the capitalist forces of destruction, which currently cast a menacing shadow over humanity and the planet.

This normative necessity may increase the likelihood that the numerous movements fighting against the different manifestations of capitalism's cost–benefit contradiction will in the future recognize the need for an anti-capitalist coalition and act accordingly. This is especially likely if capitalism's translation of productive development into human well-being continues to stall while the threats for humanity and the planet from capitalism's destructive forces continue to mount.

Capitalist dynamics will not automatically trigger a radical anti-capitalist consciousness, however. The formation of such a consciousness, as well as of a robust and majoritarian anti-capitalist coalition capable of bringing about fundamental social change, is a political task. And this task presupposes the transcendence of the false dichotomy between an "old" left fighting against capital and a "new" left having moved to new, supposedly post-materialist, concerns.

To the extent that the dichotomy between the "old" and the "new" left has any basis in reality, it does so not because the concerns of the former are more material than those of the latter. If this dichotomy is at all plausible, it is because, in the historical trajectory of capitalist societies, the threat from capitalism's forces of destruction, which animates some of the new social movements, has become especially menacing in recent decades.

At the same time, however, the international capitalist crisis of the 1970s, along with the collapse of the Soviet-style class orders in the late 1980s, set the stage for the neoliberal restructuring of capitalist societies around the world (Thompson 2011: 247; Solomon and Palmieri 2011a: 2; Folbre 2009: xxi; Aronowitz 2006: 188; Stiglitz 2001: xv). As this restructuring gave rise to a range of social and economic problems, from "famines, epidemics, and ensuing political instability" (Steger and Roy 2010: 110) to growing inequalities, stagnating wages, and the rise of personal debt, as well as the marginaliza-tion of growing segments of the population (Wolff and Resnick 2012: 23; Thompson 2011: 190; Milios 2005: 208), old-fashioned economic insecurity has returned with a vengeance, even as the materiality of the concerns of many new social movements is becoming more and more obvious. In short, any suggestion that new left post-materialist concerns are displacing old left materialist ones is deeply misleading and counterpro-ductive. And, as Donald Trump's election has proved, when progressive political forces ignore this reality they make it possible for far right political forces to channel popular discontent with the status quo in a reactionary direction.

This is not the only lesson that the left and humanity have to draw from recent his-tory. The rise of neoliberalism has laid to rest the illusion, stemming from capitalism's brief golden age immediately after World War II, that it is possible to humanize capitalism by subjecting it to democratic controls. The Cold War context of that period contributed to this illusion in a number of ways. On the one hand, it put pressure on capitalist elites to make concessions to working classes, especially in the global North, so as "to buy off … workers so they wouldn't go communist" (Friedman 2000: 158). These concessions included the introduction by democratically elected governments of significant reforms. Growing levels of government intervention in and regulation of the capitalist economy, the growth of welfare states, and the use of Keynesian macroeconomic policies to attain full employment all seemed to confirm the ability of political democracy to control, reshape, and tame the capitalist beast (Steger and Roy 2010: 7–9; Harvey 2005: 9–12; Garrett 2000: 306). At the same time, the blatantly undemocratic nature of Soviet-style class orders predictably made the political systems of affluent capitalist countries look much more democratic and attractive by comparison (Sassoon 1996: 210).

Although supporters of capitalism rushed to interpret the end of the Cold War as the definitive proof of the economic and political superiority of capitalist democracy to any conceivable alternatives, this euphoria has proved to be premature (Friedman 2000: xxi). Capitalist crises have returned and increasing inequality is corrupting the political system, thus leading to growing discontent with the kind of democracy as well as with the kind of future that ordinary people, and especially young people, can look forward to. This turn of events is a reminder of how fragile any social and democratic gains will always be in the face of capital's use of the surplus to defend and reproduce the privileges of the few against the needs, aspirations, and well-being of the many.

Thus, one of the main lessons from recent history is the inseparability of continuing democratization from the fight for a classless, raceless, and genderless society capable of turning the communist ideal into a reality. The urgency of moving towards such a future is all the greater in view of the fact that the longer capitalism survives the more its destruc-tiveness is likely to increase.

To prevent the ecological, military, social, and public health catastrophes that capit-alism likely has in store for us, the movements fighting against the different manifestations of capitalism's cost–benefit contradiction will have to converge towards a democratic anti-capitalist alliance. By fighting for a society that allows direct producers and ordinary people to control the surplus they produce, such an alliance could put an end to capitalism's use of the surplus not to promote human well-being but to develop the forces of destruction that increasingly threaten the future of humanity and the planet.

The current crises of capitalism and democracy make the formation of this alliance necessary; but the fragmented ways in which people experience the contradiction traversing contemporary capitalism make the formation of this alliance difficult. In this sense, this contradiction does not represent for the left, or for humanity, a mechanism that guarantees the eventual advent of human liberation. Instead, it represents a challenge that the social movements fighting against capitalism's injustices and destructiveness will have to take up, if the dystopian future staring us in the face is to give its place to a future worthy of our dreams.

Notes

1 Andrew Simms (2005: 67) points out, for example, that "[r]esearch from a group of UN organizations estimated conservatively that global warming was responsible for 150,000 extra deaths in the year 2000."
2 See Tanuro 2010: 265; Li 2008: 51–52; Bowles, Edwards, and Roosevelt 2005: 21; Simms 2005: 66–67; Kasser et al. 2003: 13; Kasser 2002: 95; Cross 2000: 15–16; Guha 1994: 287–88; Durning 1992: 21; Foster 2002: 21; Klare 2001: 20; Taylor and Tilford 2000: 481; Nolan and Lenski 1998: 393; Goodland 1996: 210; Ekins and Jacobs 1995: 12–13.

References

Abramovitz, Mimi. 2002. "Still under Attack: Women and Welfare Reform," in Nancy Holmstrom (ed.), *The Socialist Feminist Project: A Contemporary Reader in Theory and Politics.* New York: Monthly Review Press, 216–27.

———— 2012. "The Feminization of Austerity." *New Labor Forum*, 21(1): 30–39.

Acker, Joan. 2003. "Revisiting Class: Thinking from Gender, Race, and Organizations," in Ellen Mutari and Deborah M. Figart (eds), *Women and the Economy: A Reader.* Armonk, NY: M. E. Sharpe, 13–24.

Ackerman, Frank. 2008. "Climate Economics in Four Easy Pieces." *Dollars and Sense: Real World Economics*, 279: 22–26.

Aglietta, Michel. 1987. *A Theory of Capitalist Regulation: The US Experience.* London: Verso.

Ahrne, Göran. 1988. "A Labor Theory of Consumption," in Per Otnes (ed.), *The Sociology of Consumption: An Anthology.* Oslo: Solum Forlag, 49–64.

Akinbami, Lara J., Jeanne E. Moorman, Cathy Bailey, Hatice S. Zaran, Michael King, Carol A. Johnson, and Xiang Liu. 2012. "Trends in Asthma Prevalence, Health Care Use, and Mortality in the United States, 2001–2010," NCHS Data Brief 94. Atlanta: Centers for Disease Control and Prevention, www.cdc.gov/nchs/products/databriefs/db94.htm.

Albert, Michael. 2003. *Parecon: Life after Capitalism.* London: Verso.

Albert, Michael, and David Schweickart. 2008. "There Is an Alternative: Economic Democracy and Participatory Economics, a Debate," in Jenna Allard, Carl Davidson, and Julie Matthaei (eds), *Solidarity Economy: Building Alternatives for People and Planet: Papers and Reports from the US Social Forum 2007.* Chicago: ChangeMaker Publications, 47–82.

Albo, Greg, and Bryan Evans. 2010. "From Rescue Strategies to Exit Strategies: The Struggle over Public Sector Austerity," in Leo Panitch, Greg Albo, and Vivek Chibber (eds), *Socialist Register 2011: The Crisis This Time.* London: Merlin Press, 283–308.

Almasy, Steve, and Raja Razek. 2020. "Colorado Meat Packing Plant with Thousands of Employees Closed after Coronavirus Outbreak." CNN, April 11, www.cnn.com/2020/04/10/us/colorado-meat-packing-plant-coronavirus/index.html.

Alperovitz, Gar. 2011. *America beyond Capitalism: Reclaiming Our Wealth, Our Liberty, and Our Democracy.* Takoma Park, MD: Democracy Collaborative Press.

Alterman, Eric. 2016. "How Trump's Media Cheerleaders Turned Campaign Coverage into a Total Disaster." *The Nation*, October 28, www.thenation.com/article/how-trumps-media-cheerleaders-turned-campaign-coverage-into-a-total-disaster.

Altvater, Elmar. 1993. *The Future of the Market: An Essay on the Regulation of Money and Nature after the Collapse of "Actually Existing Socialism."* London: Verso.

Amin, Samir. 1996. *Capitalism in the Age of Globalization: The Management of Contemporary Society.* London: Zed Books.

Amott, Teresa L., and Julie A. Matthaei. 1991. *Race, Gender, and Work: A Multicultural Economic History of Women in the United States*. Boston: South End Press.

Angus, Ian. 2010. "For a Society of Good Ancestors!," in Ian Angus (ed.), *The Global Fight for Climate Justice: Anticapitalist Responses to Global Warming and Environmental Destruction*. Black Point, NS: Fernwood Publishing, 210–20.

———— 2014. "The Origin of Rosa Luxemburg's Slogan 'Socialism or Barbarism.'" WordPress, October 21, https://johnriddell.wordpress.com/2014/10/21/the-origin-of-rosa- luxemburgs-slogan-socialism-or-barbarism.

Appadurai, Arjun. 2017. "Democracy Fatigue," in Heinrich Geiselberger (ed.), *The Great Regression*. Cambridge: Polity Press, 1–12.

Appelbaum, Binyamin, and Jim Tankersley. 2018. "What Could Kill Booming US Economy? 'Socialists,' White House Warns." *New York Times*, October 23, www.nytimes.com/2018/10/23/us/politics/socialist-democrats-trump-elections.html.

Aronowitz, Stanley. 1992. *False Promises: The Shaping of American Working Class Consciousness*. Durham, NC: Duke University Press.

———— 2006. *Left Turn: Forging a New Political Future*. Boulder, CO: Paradigm Publishers.

Avritzer, Leonardo. 2005. "Modes of Democratic Deliberation: Participatory Budgeting in Brazil," in Boaventura de Sousa Santos (ed.), *Democratizing Democracy: Beyond the Liberal Democratic Canon*. London: Verso, 377–404.

Badger, Emily. 2018. "The Outsize Hold of the Word 'Welfare' on the Public Imagination." *New York Times*, August 6, www.nytimes.com/2018/08/06/upshot/welfare-and-the-public-imagination.html.

Badiou, Alain. 2010a. *The Communist Hypothesis*. London: Verso.

———— 2010b. "The Democratic Emblem," in Giorgio Agamben, Alain Badiou, Daniel Bensaid, Wendy Brown, Jean-Luc Nancy, Jacques Ranciere, Kristin Ross, and Slavoj Žižek (eds), *Democracy in What State?* New York: Columbia University Press, 6–15.

———— 2016. *Our Wound Is Not So Recent*. Cambridge: Polity Press.

Bagchi, Amiya Kumar. 2005. *Perilous Passage: Mankind and the Global Ascendancy of Capital*. Lanham: Rowman & Littlefield.

Baier, Walter. 2016. "Europe on the Precipice: The Crisis of the Neoliberal Order and the Ascent of Right-Wing Populism." *New Labor Forum*, 25(3): 48–55.

Bakalar, Nicholas. 2018. "More Americans Are Dying of Cirrhosis and Liver Cancer." *New York Times*, July 18, www.nytimes.com/2018/07/18/health/cirrhosis-liver-cancer.html?action=click&pgtype=Homepage&version=Moth-Visible&moduleDetail=inside-nyt-region-2&module=inside-nyt-region&region=inside-nyt-region&WT.nav=inside-nyt-region.

Baker, Luke, Matthew Tostevin, and Devjyot Ghoshal. "In Global War on Coronavirus, Some Fear Civil Rights Are Collateral Damage." Reuters, April 10, www.reuters.com/article/us-health-coronavirus-rights/in-global-war-on-coronavirus-some-fear-civil-rights-are-collateral-damage-idUSKCN21S1CZ.

Baran, Paul A. 1957. *The Political Economy of Growth*. New York: Monthly Review Press.

Baran, Paul A., and Paul M. Sweezy. 1966. *Monopoly Capital: An Essay on the American Economic and Social Order*. New York: Monthly Review Press.

Barber, Benjamin R. 2007. *Consumed: How Markets Corrupt Children, Infantilize Adults, and Swallow Citizens Whole*. New York: Norton.

Basso, Pietro. 2003. *Modern Times, Ancient Hours: Working Hours in the Twenty-First Century*. London: Verso.

Beaud, Michel. 2001. *A History of Capitalism, 1500–2000*. New York: Monthly Review Press.

Behagg, Clive. 1988. "Controlling the Product: Work, Time, and the Early Industrial Workforce in Britain, 1800–1850," in Gary Cross (ed.), *Worktime and Industrialization: An International History*. Philadelphia: Temple University Press, 41–58.

Benería, Lourdes. 2003. "Globalization, Gender, and the Davos Man," in Ellen Mutari and Deborah M. Figart (eds), *Women and the Economy: A Reader*. Armonk, NY: M. E. Sharpe, 312–25.

————— 2011. "Accounting for Women's Work: The Progress of Two Decades," in Nalini Visvanathan, Lynn Duggan, Nan Wiegersma, and Laurie Nisonoff (eds), *The Women, Gender and Development Reader*, 2nd edn. London: Zed Books, 114–20.

Bennholdt-Thomsen, Veronika. 2001. "What Really Keeps Our Cities Alive, Money or Subsistence?," in Veronika Bennholdt-Thomsen, Nicholas Faraclas, and Claudia von Werlhof (eds), *There Is an Alternative: Subsistence and Worldwide Resistance to Corporate Globalization*. London: Zed Books, 217–31.

Bennis, Phyllis. 2016. "The War in Syria Cannot Be Won. But It Can Be Ended." *The Nation*, 303(22): 12–15, www.thenation.com/article/the-war-in-syria-cannot-be-won-but-it-can-be-ended.

Benton, Meghan, and Anne Nielsen. 2013. "Integrating Europe's Muslim Minorities: Public Anxieties, Policy Responses." Migration Policy Institute, May 10, www.migrationpolicy.org/print/4206#. WUAIIMaIvIU.

Berezin, Mabel. 2013. "The Normalization of the Right in Post-Security Europe," in Armin Schaefer and Wolfgang Streeck (eds), *Politics in the Age of Austerity*. Cambridge: Polity Press, 239–61.

Berg-Schlosser, Dirk. 2009. "Long Waves and Conjunctures of Democratization," in Christian W. Haerpfer, Patrick Bernhagen, Ronald F. Inglehart, and Christian Welzel (eds), *Democratization*. Oxford: Oxford University Press, 41–54.

Berger, Stefan. 2012. "Social Democratic Trajectories in Modern Europe: One or Many Families?," in Henning Meyer and Jonathan Rutherford (eds), *The Future of European Social Democracy: Building the Good Society*. Basingstoke: Palgrave Macmillan, 13–26.

Bergmann, Barbara R. 2003. "The Economic Risks of Being a Housewife," in Ellen Mutari and Deborah M. Figart (eds), *Women and the Economy: A Reader*. Armonk, NY: M. E. Sharpe, 101–7.

Bergmann, Frithjof. 2000. "Ecology and New Work: Excess Consumption and the Job System," in Juliet B. Schor and Douglas B. Holt (eds), *The Consumer Society Reader*. New York: New Press, 488–502.

Berlin, Isaiah. 1969. *Four Essays on Liberty*. Oxford: Oxford University Press.

Bernhagen, Patrick. 2009. "Democracy, Business, and the Economy," in Christian W. Haerpfer, Patrick Bernhagen, Ronald F. Inglehart, and Christian Welzel (eds), *Democratization*. Oxford: Oxford University Press, 107–25.

Berry, Joe, and Helena Worthen. 2012. "Higher Education as a Workplace." *Dollars and Sense: Real World Economics*, 303: 19–23.

Bettelheim, Charles. 1976. *Class Struggles in the USSR: First Period, 1917–1923*. New York: Monthly Review Press.

————— 1978. *Class Struggles in the USSR: Second Period, 1923–1930*. Brighton: Harvester Press.

Bienefeld, Manfred. 1996. "Is a Strong National Economy a Utopian Goal at the End of the Twentieth Century?," in Robert Boyer and Daniel Drache (eds), *States against Markets: The Limits of Globalization*. London: Routledge, 415–40.

Biggart, Nicole Woolsey. 1994. "Labor and Leisure," in Neil J. Smelser and Richard Swedberg (eds), *The Handbook of Economic Sociology*. Princeton, NJ: Princeton University Press, 672–90.

Bittner, Jochen. 2018. "How the Far Right Conquered Sweden." *New York Times*, September 6, www.nytimes.com/2018/09/06/opinion/how-the-far-right-conquered-sweden.html.

Block, Fred. 1994a. "Remaking Our Economy: New Strategies for Structural Reform," in Frank Roosevelt and David Belkin (eds), *Why Market Socialism? Voices from Dissent*. Armonk, NY: M. E. Sharpe, 371–81.

————— 1994b. "The Roles of the State in the Economy," in Neil J. Smelser and Richard Swedberg (eds), *The Handbook of Economic Sociology*. Princeton, NJ: Princeton University Press, 691–710.

Blumenfeld, Emily, and Susan Mann. 1980. "Domestic Labour and the Reproduction of Labour Power: Towards an Analysis of Women, the Family and Class," in Bonnie Fox (ed.), *Hidden in the Household: Women's Domestic Labour under Capitalism*. Toronto: Women's Press, 267–307.

Bonaiuti, M. 2012. "Degrowth: Tools for a Complex Analysis of the Multidimensional Crisis." *Capitalism Nature Socialism*, 23(1): 30–50.

Bookchin, Murray. 1986. *Post-Scarcity Anarchism*, 2nd edn. Montreal: Black Rose Books.

Bordwell, Marilyn. 2002. "Jamming Culture: Adbusters' Hip Media Campaign against Consumerism," in Thomas Princen, Michael Maniates, and Ken Conca (eds), *Confronting Consumption*. Cambridge, MA: MIT Press, 237–53.

Borosage, Robert L. 2017. "A Taxing Debate." *The Nation*, 305(5): 3.

Bottomore, Tom. 1991. "Social Democracy," in Tom Bottomore (ed.), *A Dictionary of Marxist Thought*, 2nd edn. Malden, MA: Blackwell, 497–500.

——— 1992. "Socialism," in William Outhwaite and Tom Bottomore (eds), *The Blackwell Dictionary of Twentieth-Century Social Thought*. Oxford: Blackwell, 617–19.

Bowles, Samuel. 1991. "What Markets Can—and Cannot—Do." *Challenge*, 34(4): 11–16.

Bowles, Samuel, and Richard Edwards. 1993. *Understanding Capitalism: Competition, Command, and Change in the US Economy*, 2nd edn. New York: HarperCollins.

Bowles, Samuel, Richard Edwards, and Frank Roosevelt. 2005. *Understanding Capitalism: Competition, Command, and Change*, 3rd edn. New York: Oxford University Press.

Bowles, Samuel, and Herbert Gintis. 1986. *Democracy and Capitalism: Property, Community, and the Contradictions of Modern Social Thought*. New York: Basic Books.

Boyce, James K. 2002. *The Political Economy of the Environment*. Cheltenham: Edward Elgar.

Boyer, Robert, and Daniel Drache. 1996. "Introduction," in Robert Boyer and Daniel Drache (eds), *States against Markets: The Limits of Globalization*. London: Routledge, 1–27.

Boyes, William, and Michael Melvin. 2005. *Microeconomics*, 6th edn. Boston: Houghton Mifflin.

Braverman, Harry. 1974. *Labor and Monopoly Capital: The Degradation of Work in the Twentieth Century*. New York: Monthly Review Press.

Brenner, Johanna. 2002. "Intersections, Locations, and Capitalist Class Relations: Intersectionality from a Marxist Perspective," in Nancy Holmstrom (ed.), *The Socialist Feminist Project: A Contemporary Reader in Theory and Politics*. New York: Monthly Review Press, 336–48.

Brenner, Robert. 2016. "The Dynamics of Retreat." *Jacobin*, 20: 11–21.

Briskin, Linda. 1980. "Domestic Labour: A Methodological Discussion," in Bonnie Fox (ed.), *Hidden in the Household: Women's Domestic Labour under Capitalism*. Toronto: Women's Press, 135–72.

Brodkin, Karen B. 2009. "How Did Jews Become White Folks?," in John J. Macionis and Nijole V. Benokraitis (eds), *Seeing Ourselves: Classic, Contemporary, and Cross-Cultural Readings in Sociology*, 8th edn. Boston: Prentice Hall, 266–75.

Brown, Archie. 2009. *The Rise and Fall of Communism*. New York: Ecco.

Brown, Wendy. 2010. "We Are All Democrats Now … ," in Giorgio Agamben, Alain Badiou, Daniel Bensaid, Wendy Brown, Jean-Luc Nancy, Jacques Ranciere, Kristin Ross, and Slavoj Žižek (eds), *Democracy in What State?* New York: Columbia University Press, 44–57.

Brown, Lester R. 2001. *Eco-Economy: Building an Economy for the Earth*. New York: Norton.

Brus, W. 1990. "Market Socialism," in John Eatwell, Murray Milgate, and Peter Newman (eds), *The New Palgrave: Problems of the Planned Economy*. New York: Norton, 164–77.

Bullard, Robert. 1994. "Environmental Racism and the Environmental Justice Movement," in Carolyn Merchant (ed.), *Ecology*. Amherst, NY: Humanity Books, 254–65.

Callinicos, Alex. 1991. *The Revenge of History: Marxism and the East European Revolutions*. University Park, PA: Pennsylvania State University Press.

Capatides, Christina. 2020. "'Shoot Them Dead': Philippine President Rodrigo Duterte Orders Police and Military to Kill Citizens Who Defy Coronavirus Lockdown." CBS, April 2, www.cbsnews.com/news/rodrigo-duterte-philippines-president-coronavirus-lockdown-shoot-people-dead.

Casselman, Ben, Patricia Cohen, and Tiffany Hsu. 2020. "'It's a Wreck': 3.3 Million File Unemployment Claims as Economy Comes Apart." *New York Times*, March 26, www.nytimes.com/2020/03/26/business/economy/coronavirus-unemployment-claims.html?searchResultPosition=1.

Charkiewicz, Eva (with Sander van Bennekom and Alex Young). 2001. *Transitions to Sustainable Production and Consumption: Concepts, Policies and Actions*. The Hague: Tools for Transition.

Chengu, Garikai. 2017. "America Created Al-Qaeda and the ISIS Terror Group." Global Research, May 23, www.globalresearch.ca/america-created-al-qaeda-and-the-isis-terror-group/5402881.

Chomsky, Noam. 2011. "The Cairo–Madison Connection," in Erica Sagrans (ed.), We are Wisconsin: The Wisconsin Uprising in the Words of the Activists, Writers, and Everyday Wisconsinites Who Made It Happen. Minneapolis: Tasora, 151–55.

Clark, Brett, and Richard York. 2008. "Rifts and Shifts: Getting to the Root of Environmental Catastrophe." Monthly Review, 60(6): 13–24.

Clarke, Simon. 1991. Marx, Marginalism and Modern Sociology: From Adam Smith to Max Weber, 2nd edn. Basingstoke: Macmillan Academic and Professional.

Clarke, Tony. 1996. "Mechanisms of Corporate Rule," in Jerry Mander and Edward Goldsmith (eds), The Case against the Global Economy and for a Turn toward the Local. San Francisco: Sierra Club Books, 299–308.

Cockburn, Patrick. 2016. "We Finally Know What Hillary Clinton Knew All Along: US Allies Saudi Arabia and Qatar Are Funding Isis." Independent, October 14, www.independent.co.uk/voices/hillary-clinton-wikileaks-email-isis-saudi-arabia-qatar-us-allies-funding-barack-obama-knew-all-a7362071.html.

Cohen, G. A. 1988. History, Labour, and Freedom: Themes from Marx. Oxford: Clarendon Press.

———— 2000. Karl Marx's Theory of History: A Defense, expanded edn. Princeton, NJ: Princeton University Press.

Cohen, Jean L. 1985. "Strategy or Identity: New Theoretical Paradigms and Contemporary Social Movements." Social Research: An International Quarterly of the Social Sciences, 52(4): 663–716.

Cohen, Sheila. 2011. "The Red Mole: Workers' Councils as a Means of Revolutionary Transformation," in Immanuel Ness and Dario Azzellini (eds), Ours to Master and to Own: Workers' Control from the Commune to the Present. Chicago: Haymarket Books, 48–65.

Collins, Randall. 1985. Three Sociological Traditions. New York: Oxford University Press.

Consumer Reports. 2000. "Reading, Writing, and … Buying?," in Jerome H. Skolnick and Elliott Currie (eds), Crisis in American Institutions, 11th edn. Boston: Allyn and Bacon, 382–86.

Costanza, Robert. 1996. "Ecological Economics: Creating a Transdisciplinary Science," in Peter H. May and Ronaldo Serôa da Motta (eds), Pricing the Planet: Economic Analysis for Sustainable Development. New York: Columbia University Press, 139–69.

Costanza, Robert, John Cumberland, Herman Daly, Robert Goodland, and Richard Norgaard. 1997. An Introduction to Ecological Economics. Boca Raton, FL: St. Lucie Press.

Cox, Robert W. 1992. "Global Perestroika," in Ralph Miliband and Leo Panitch (eds), New World Order? Socialist Register 1992. London: Merlin Press, 26–43.

———— 1997. "Democracy in Hard Times: Economic Globalization and the Limits to Liberal Democracy," in Anthony McGrew (ed.), The Transformation of Democracy? Globalization and Territorial Democracy. Cambridge: Polity Press, 49–72.

Cross, Gary. 1988. "Worktime and Industrialization: An Introduction," in Gary Cross (ed.), Worktime and Industrialization: An International History. Philadelphia: Temple University Press, 3–19.

———— 2000. An All-Consuming Century: Why Commercialism Won in Modern America. New York: Columbia University Press.

Crouch, Colin. 2012. "As Much Market as Possible; as Much State as Necessary," in Henning Meyer and Jonathan Rutherford (eds), The Future of European Social Democracy: Building the Good Society. Basingstoke: Palgrave Macmillan, 74–89.

———— 2013. "From Markets versus States to Corporations versus Civil Society?," in Armin Schaefer and Wolfgang Streeck (eds), Politics in the Age of Austerity. Cambridge: Polity Press, 219–39.

Cruddas, Jon, and Andrea Nahles. 2012. "Building the Good Society: The Project of the Democratic Left." London: Compass.

Cunningham, Frank. 2002. Theories of Democracy: A Critical Introduction. London: Routledge.

Curtis, Bruce. 1980. "Capital, the State and the Origins of the Working-Class Household," in Bonnie Fox (ed.), Hidden in the Household: Women's Domestic Labour under Capitalism. Toronto: Women's Press, 101–34.

Dahl, Robert A. 1989. *Democracy and Its Critics*. New Haven, CT: Yale University Press.

Davis, Angela Y. 1998. "JoAnne Little: The Dialectics of Rape," in Joy James (ed.), *The Angela Y. Davis Reader*. Malden, MA: Blackwell, 149–60.

De Jong, Alex. 2013. "The Netherlands: Neoliberal Dreams in Times of Austerity." *New Politics*, 14(2): 22–29.

Della Porta, Donatella. 2013. *Can Democracy Be Saved? Participation, Deliberation and Social Movements*. Cambridge: Polity Press.

Desai, Meghnad. 1994. "Neoclassical Economics," in William Outhwaite and Tom Bottomore (eds), *The Blackwell Dictionary of Twentieth-Century Social Thought*. Oxford: Blackwell, 415–17.

Desai, Radhika. 2013. *Geopolitical Economy: After US Hegemony, Globalization and Empire*. London: Pluto Press.

——— 2015. "Geopolitical Economy: The Discipline of Multipolarity," Valdai Paper 24. Moscow: Valdai Discussion Club. http://valdaiclub.com/files/10943.

Dickenson, Donna. 1997. "Counting Women In: Globalization, Democratization and the Women's Movement," in Anthony McGrew (ed.), *The Transformation of Democracy? Globalization and Territorial Democracy*. Cambridge: Polity Press, 97–120.

DiMaggio, Paul. 1994. "Culture and Economy," in Neil J. Smelser and Richard Swedberg (eds), *The Handbook of Economic Sociology*. Princeton, NJ: Princeton University Press, 27–57.

Dobb, Maurice. 1975. *Theories of Value and Distribution since Adam Smith: Ideology and Economic Theory*. Cambridge: Cambridge University Press.

Dominick, Brian. 2008. "From Here to Parecon: Thoughts on Strategy for Economic Revolution," in Chris Spannos (ed.), *Real Utopia: Participatory Society for the 21st Century*. Edinburgh: AK Press, 380–95.

Domhoff, William G. 2017. "Who Rules America? Wealth, Income, and Power." University of California at Santa Cruz, April, www2.ucsc.edu/whorulesamerica/power/wealth.html.

Dowd, Douglas. 2000. *Capitalism and Its Economics: A Critical History*. London: Pluto Press.

Dugger, William M., and James T. Peach. 2009. *Economic Abundance: An Introduction*. Armonk, NY: M. E. Sharpe.

Dullien, Sebastian, Hansjörg Herr, and Christian Kellermann. 2012. "A Decent Capitalism for a Good Society," in Henning Meyer and Jonathan Rutherford (eds), *The Future of European Social Democracy: Building the Good Society*. Basingstoke: Palgrave Macmillan, 57–73.

Duménil, Gérard and Dominique Lévy. 2005. "The Neoliberal (Counter-)Revolution," in Alfredo Saad-Filho and Deborah Johnston. (eds), *Neoliberalism: A Critical Reader*. London: Pluto Press, 9–19.

Durning, Alan Thein. 1992. *How Much Is Enough? The Consumer Society and the Future of the Earth*. New York: Norton.

Eagleton, Terry. 2010. "Communism: Lear or Gonzalo?," in C. Douzinas and S. Žižek (eds), *The Idea of Communism*. London: Verso, 101–10.

Eatwell, John, Murray Milgate, and Peter Newman (eds). 1990. *The New Palgrave: Problems of the Planned Economy*. New York: Norton.

Eglitis, Daina Stukuls. 2009. "The Uses of Global Poverty: How Economic Inequality Benefits the West," in John J. Macionis and Nijole V. Benokraitis (eds), *Seeing Ourselves: Classic, Contemporary, and Cross-Cultural Readings in Sociology*, 8th edn. Boston: Prentice Hall, 222–29.

Ehrenreich, Barbara, and Arlie R. Hochschild. 2011. "Global Women," in Nalini Visvanathan, Lynn Duggan, Nan Wiegersma, and Laurie Nisonoff (eds), *The Women, Gender and Development Reader*, 2nd edn. London: Zed Books, 237–44.

Eisenstein, Zillah R. 1979. "Patriarchy in Revolutionary Society," in Zillah R. Eisenstein (ed.), *Capitalist Patriarchy and the Case for Socialist Feminism*. New York: Monthly Review Press, 267–69.

Ekins, Paul, and Michael Jacobs. 1995. "Environmental Sustainability and the Growth of GDP: Conditions for Compatibility," in V. Bhaskar and Andrew Glyn (eds), *The North, the South and the Environment: Ecological Constraints and the Global Economy*. New York: Saint Martin's Press, 9–46.

Elson, Diane. 2011. "International Financial Architecture: A View from the Kitchen," in Nalini Visvanathan, Lynn Duggan, Nan Wiegersma, and Laurie Nisonoff (eds), *The Women, Gender and Development Reader*, 2nd edn. London: Zed Books, 295–305.

————— 2017. "Recognize, Reduce, and Redistribute Unpaid Care Work: How to Close the Gender Gap." *New Labor Forum*, 26(2): 52–61

Elson, Diane, and Ruth Pearson. 2011. "The Subordination of Women and the Internationalization of Factory Production," in Nalini Visvanathan, Lynn Duggan, Nan Wiegersma, and Laurie Nisonoff (eds), *The Women, Gender and Development Reader*, 2nd ed. London: Zed Books, 212–24.

Engels, Frederick. 1844. "Outlines of a Critique of Political Economy." Available at www.marxists.org/archive/marx/works/1844/df-jahrbucher/outlines.htm.

————— 1972 [1884]. *The Origin of the Family, Private Property and the State*. New York: International Publishers.

Engler, Allan. 2010. *Economic Democracy: The Working Class Alternative to Capitalism*. Black Point, NS: Fernwood Publishing.

Ewen, Stuart. 1977. *Captains of Consciousness: Advertising and the Social Roots of the Consumer Culture*. New York: McGraw-Hill.

Fabricant, Michael. 2011. "Reimagining Labor: The Lessons of Wisconsin." *WorkingUSA: The Journal of Labor and Society*, 14(2): 235–41.

Fallows, James. 2015. "The Tragedy of the American Military." *The Atlantic*, January 15, www.theatlantic.com/magazine/archive/2015/01/the-tragedy-of-the-american-military/383516.

Federici, Silvia. 2012. *Revolution at Point Zero: Housework, Reproduction, and Feminist Struggle*. Oakland, CA: PM Press.

Fisher, Max, and Amanda Taub. 2018. "Trump Wants to Make it Hard to Get Asylum. Other Countries Feel the Same." *New York Times*, November 2, www.nytimes.com/2018/11/02/world/europe/trump-asylum.html.

Folbre, Nancy. 2008. *Valuing Children: Rethinking the Economics of the Family*. Cambridge, MA: Harvard University Press.

————— 2009. *Greed, Lust and Gender: A History of Economic Ideas*. Oxford: Oxford University Press.

————— 2011. "The Invisible Heart: Care and the Global Economy," in Nalini Visvanathan, Lynn Duggan, Nan Wiegersma and Laurie Nisonoff (eds), *The Women, Gender and Development Reader*, 2nd edn. London: Zed Books, 41–42.

Foster, John Bellamy. 2002. *Ecology against Capitalism*. New York: Monthly Review Press.

Fox, Bonnie (ed.). 1980. *Hidden in the Household: Women's Domestic Labour under Capitalism*. Toronto: Women's Press.

Fraad, Harriet. 2008. "Post Bush America: A Site of Family Disintegration and Revolutionary Personal Change." *Transform! European Journal for Alternative Thinking and Political Dialogue*, 3: 25–34.

Frank, Robert H. 1999. *Luxury Fever: Why Money Fails to Satisfy in an Era of Excess*. New York: Free Press.

————— 2003. *Microeconomics and Behavior*, 5th edn. Boston: McGraw-Hill Irwin.

Frank, Thomas C. 2000. "Advertising as Cultural Criticism: Bill Bernbach versus the Mass Society," in Juliet B. Schor and Douglas B. Holt (eds), *The Consumer Society Reader*. New York: New Press, 375–94.

Fraser, Nancy. 2016. "Contradictions of Capital and Care." *New Left Review*, 100: 99–117.

Freeden, Michael. 2015. *Liberalism: A Very Short Introduction*. Oxford: Oxford University Press.

Frenzen, Jonathan, Paul M. Hirsch, and Philip C. Zerrillo. 1994. "Consumption, Preferences, and Changing Lifestyles," in Neil J. Smelser and Richard Swedberg (eds), *The Handbook of Economic Sociology*. Princeton, NJ: Princeton University Press, 403–25.

Friedman, Gerald. 2008. *Reigniting the Labor Movement: Restoring Means to Ends in a Democratic Labor Movement*. London: Routledge.

Friedman, Lisa. 2020. "E.P.A., Citing Coronavirus, Drastically Relaxes Rules for Polluters." *New York Times*, March 26, www.nytimes.com/2020/03/26/climate/epa-coronavirus-pollution-rules.html.

Friedman, Milton, and Rose Friedman. 1981. *Free to Choose: A Personal Statement*. New York: Avon Books.

Friedman, Thomas L. 2000. *The Lexus and the Olive Tree*. New York: Anchor Books.

Fukuyama, Francis. 1992. *The End of History and the Last Man*. New York: Avon Books.

Fung, Archon, and Erik Olin Wright. 2003. "Thinking about Empowered Participatory Governance," in Archon Fung and Erik Olin Wright (eds), *Deepening Democracy: Institutional Innovations in Empowered Participatory Governance*. London: Verso, 3–42.

Galbraith, John Kenneth. 1984. *The Affluent Society*, 4th edn. Boston: Houghton Mifflin.

——— 1985. *The New Industrial State*, 4th edn. New York: New American Library.

Gardiner, Jean. 1979. "Women's Domestic Labor," in Zillah R. Eisenstein (ed.), *Capitalist Patriarchy and the Case for Socialist Feminism*. New York: Monthly Review Press, 173–89.

Garrett, Geoffrey. 2000. "Global Markets and National Politics," in David Held and Anthony McGrew (eds), *The Global Transformations Reader: An Introduction to the Globalization Debate*. Cambridge: Polity Press, 301–18.

Garrett-Peltier, Heidi. 2010. "Is Military Keynesianism the Solution? Why War Is Not a Sustainable Strategy for Economic Recovery," *Dollars and Sense: Real World Economics*, 287: 21–25.

Gebeloff, Robert. 2018. "The Numbers that Explain Why Teachers Are in Revolt." *New York Times*, June 4, www.nytimes.com/2018/06/04/upshot/school-funding-still-lags-after-recession-ended.html.

Genschel, Philipp, and Peter Schwarz. 2013. "Tax Competition and Fiscal Democracy," in Armin Schaefer and Wolfgang Streeck (eds), *Politics in the Age of Austerity*. Cambridge: Polity Press, 59–83.

George, Susan. 2001. "Corporate Globalisation," in Emma Bircham and John Charlton (eds), *Anti-Capitalism: A Guide to the Movement*. London: Bookmarks Publications, 11–24.

——— 2009. "The Common Good: Towards an Alternative Europe," in Heather Gautney, Omar Dahbour, Ashley Dawson, and Neil Smith (eds), *Democracy, States, and the Struggle for Global Justice*. New York: Routledge, 171–91.

Germanos, Andrea. 2020. "Fueled by US Under Trump, Global Military Spending in 2019 Had Biggest Increase in a Decade." Common Dreams, February 4, www.commondreams.org/news/2020/02/14/fueled-us-under-trump-global-military-spending-2019-had-biggest-increase-decade.

Ghosh, Jayati. 2011. "Financial Crises and the Impact on Women: A Historical Note," in Nalini Visvanathan, Lynn Duggan, Nan Wiegersma, and Laurie Nisonoff (eds), *The Women, Gender and Development Reader*, 2nd edn. London: Zed Books, 22–27.

Gindin, Sam. 2012. "Marx's Proletariat: What Can Today's Labor Movement Learn from Marx?" *New Labor Forum*, 21(2): 15–23.

Ginsborg, Paul. 2008. *Democracy: Crisis and Renewal*. London: Profile Books.

Gladwell, Malcolm. 2000. "The Coolhunt," in Juliet B. Schor and Douglas B. Holt (eds), *The Consumer Society Reader*. New York: New Press, 360–74.

Goldberg, Michelle. 2018. "The Millenial Socialists Are Coming." *New York Times*, June 30, www.nytimes.com/2018/06/30/opinion/democratic-socialists-progressive-democratic-party-trump.html?searchResultPosition=5.

Goldman, Robert, and Stephen Papson. "Advertising in the Age of Accelerated Meaning," in Juliet B. Schor and Douglas B. Holt (eds), *The Consumer Society Reader*. New York: New Press, 81–98.

Goldsmith, Edward. 1996a. "Development as Colonialism," in Jerry Mander and Edward Goldsmith (eds), *The Case against the Global Economy and for a Turn toward the Local*. San Francisco: Sierra Club Books, 253–66.

——— 1996b. "Global Trade and the Environment," in Jerry Mander and Edward Goldsmith (eds), *The Case against the Global Economy and for a Turn toward the Local*. San Francisco: Sierra Club Books, 78–91.

Goodland, Robert. 1996. "Growth Has Reached Its Limit," in Jerry Mander and Edward Goldsmith (eds), *The Case against the Global Economy and for a Turn toward the Local*. San Francisco: Sierra Club Books, 207–17.

Gornick, Janet C., and Marcia K. Meyers. 2005. "Supporting a Dual-Earner/Dual-Carer Society," in Jody Heymann and Christopher Beem (eds), *Unfinished Work: Building Equality and Democracy in an Era of Working Families*. New York: New Press, 371–408.

Gorz, André. 1994. "Which Way Is Left? Social Change in the Post-Industrial Age," in *Capitalism, Socialism, Ecology*, trans. Chris Turner. London: Verso, 78–101.

Gowdy, John, and Sabine O'Hara. 1995. *Economic Theory for Environmentalists*. Delray Beach, FL: St. Lucie Press.

Graeber, David. 2013. *The Democracy Project: A History, a Crisis, a Movement*. New York: Spiegel & Grau.

Greider, William. 1997. *One World, Ready or Not: The Manic Logic of Global Capitalism*. New York: Simon & Schuster.

Gude, Shawn. 2016. "The Business Veto." *Jacobin*, 20: 63–69.

Guha, Ramachandra. 1994. "Radical Environmentalism: A Third-World Critique," in Carolyn Merchant (ed.), *Ecology*. Amherst, NY: Humanity Books, 281–89.

Gunawardana, Samanthi. 2011. "Struggle, Perseverance, and Organization in Sri Lanka's Export Processing Zones," in Nalini Visvanathan, Lynn Duggan, Nan Wiegersma, and Laurie Nisonoff (eds), *The Women, Gender and Development Reader*, 2nd edn. London: Zed Books, 432–38.

Habermas, Jürgen. 1984. *The Theory of Communicative Action: Lifeworld and System – A Critique of Functionalist Reason*. Boston: Beacon Press.

Hacker, J. S. 2019. *The Great Risk Shift: The New Economic Insecurity and the Decline of the American Dream*, 2nd edn. New York: Oxford University Press.

Haerpfer, Christian W. 2009. "Post-Communist Europe and Post-Soviet Russia," in Christian W. Haerpfer, Patrick Bernhagen, Ronald F. Inglehart, and Christian Welzel (eds), *Democratization*. Oxford: Oxford University Press, 309–20.

Hahnel, Robin. 2002. *The ABCs of Political Economy: A Modern Approach*. London: Pluto Press.

———— 2005. *Economic Justice and Democracy: From Competition to Cooperation*. New York: Routledge.

———— 2008. "Winnowing Wheat from Chaff: Social Democracy and Libertarian Socialism in the 20th Century," in Chris Spannos (ed.), *Real Utopia: Participatory Society for the 21st Century*. Edinburgh: AK Press, 204–62.

———— 2011. *Green Economics: Confronting the Ecological Crisis*. Armonk, NY: M. E. Sharpe.

Harack, Ben. 2011. "How Much Would it Cost to End Extreme Poverty in the World?." Vision of Earth, August 26, www.visionofearth.org/economics/ending-poverty/how-much-would-it-cost-to-end-extreme-poverty-in-the-world.

Harman, Chris. 2008. *A People's History of the World: From the Stone Age to the New Millennium*. London: Verso.

Harris, Laurence. 1991. "Forces and Relations of Production," in Tom Bottomore (ed.), *A Dictionary of Marxist Thought*, 2nd edn. Malden, MA: Blackwell, 204–6.

Hartmann, Heidi. 1979. "Capitalism, Patriarchy, and Job Segregation by Sex," in Zillah R. Eisenstein (ed.), *Capitalist Patriarchy and the Case for Socialist Feminism*. New York: Monthly Review Press, 206–47.

Harvey, David. 2005. *A Brief History of Neoliberalism*. Oxford: Oxford University Press.

———— 2014. "Foreword," in Marina Sitrin and Dario Azzellini (eds), *They Can't Represent Us! Reinventing Democracy from Greece to Occupy*. London: Verso, 1–4.

Hayek, Friedrich A. 1944. *The Road to Serfdom*. Chicago: University of Chicago Press.

Heilbroner, Robert L. 1986. *The Worldly Philosophers: The Lives, Times and Ideas of the Great Economic Thinkers*. New York: Simon & Schuster.

Heilbroner, Robert L., and James K. Galbraith. 1990. *The Economic Problem*, 9th edn. Boston: Pearson.

Held, David. 1996. *Models of Democracy*, 2nd edn. Stanford, CA: Stanford University Press.

Helleiner, Eric. 1996. "Post-Globalization: Is the Financial Liberalization Trend Likely to Be Reversed?," in Robert Boyer and Daniel Drache (eds), *States against Markets: The Limits of Globalization*. London: Routledge, 193–210.

———— 1999. "Sovereignty, Territoriality and the Globalization of Finance," in David A. Smith, Dorothy J. Solinger, and Steven C. Topik (eds), *States and Sovereignty in the Global Economy*. London: Routledge, 158–67.

Heller, Agnes. 1976. *The Theory of Need in Marx*. London: Saint Martin's Press.

Higgins, Eoin. 2020. "'Far More to Do,' Say Progressives after House Approves and Trump Signs Corporate-Friendly Coronavirus Relief Act." Common Dreams, March 28, www.commondreams.org/news/2020/03/28/far-more-do-say-progressives-after-house-approves-and-trump-signs-corporate-friendly.

Hildebrandt, Cornelia. 2015. "The Left Party in Germany." *New Politics*, 14(2): 31–36.

Hochschild, Arlie (with Anne Machung). 1989. *The Second Shift: Working Parents and the Revolution at Home*. New York: Avon Books.

Hoggan, James (with Richard Littlemore). 2009. *Climate Cover-Up: The Crusade to Deny Global Warming*. Vancouver: Greystone Books.

Holland, Joshua. 2016. "Islamic Extremism Is Not the Root Cause of Europe's Terror Problem." *The Nation*, March 30, www.thenation.com/article/islamic-extremism-is-not-the-cause-of-europes-terror-problem.

Holmes, Leslie. 2009. *Communism: A Very Short Introduction*. Oxford: Oxford University Press.

Horowitz, Jason. 2018. "Salvini Seizes on 2nd Italian Teenager's Death to Push Immigration Issue." *New York Times*, October 27, www.nytimes.com/2018/10/27/world/europe/italy-salvini-immigration.html?rref=collection%2Fissuecollection%2Ftodays-new-york-times&action=click&contentCollection=todayspaper&region=rank&module=package&version=highlights&contentPlacement=9&pgtype=collection.

Hunnicutt, Benjamin Kline. 1988. *Work without End: Abandoning Shorter Hours for the Right to Work*. Philadelphia: Temple University Press.

Jackson, Kenneth T. 1987. *Crabgrass Frontier: The Suburbanization of the United States*. New York: Oxford University Press.

Jackson, Tim. 2017. *Prosperity without Growth: Foundations for the Economy of Tomorrow*, 2nd edn. Abingdon: Routledge.

Jacobs, Jerry A., and Kathleen Gerson. 2004. "Understanding Changes in American Working Time: A Synthesis," in Cynthia Fuchs Epstein and Anne L. Kalleberg (eds), *Fighting for Time: Shifting Boundaries of Work and Social Life*. New York: Sage, 25–45.

Jameson, Frederic. 2003. "Future City." *New Left Review*, 21: 65–79. https://newleftreview.org/issues/II21/articles/fredric-jameson-future-city.

Johnstone, Monty. 1991. "Party," in Tom Bottomore (ed.), *A Dictionary of Marxist Thought*, 2nd edn. Malden, MA: Blackwell, 408–11.

Kanner, Allen D., and Renée G. Soule. 2003. "Globalization, Corporate Culture, and Freedom," in Tim Kasser and Allen D. Kanner (eds), *Psychology and Consumer Culture: The Struggle for a Good Life in a Materialistic World*. Washington, DC: APA Press, 49–67.

Kasser, Tim. 2002. *The High Price of Materialism*. Cambridge, MA: MIT Press.

Kasser, Tim, and Allen D. Kanner. 2003. "Where Is the Psychology of Consumer Culture?," in Tim Kasser and Allen D. Kanner (eds), *Psychology and Consumer Culture: The Struggle for a Good Life in a Materialistic World*. Washington, DC: APA Press, 3–7.

Kasser, Tim, Richard M. Ryan, Charles E. Couchman, and Kennon M. Sheldon. 2003. "Materialistic Values: Their Causes and Consequences," in Tim Kasser and Allen D. Kanner (eds), *Psychology and Consumer Culture: The Struggle for a Good Life in a Materialistic World*. Washington, DC: APA Press, 11–28.

Keen, Steve. 2001. *Debunking Economics: The Naked Emperor of the Social Sciences*. London: Zed Books.

Keynes, John Maynard. 1963 [1930]. "Economic Possibilities for Our Grandchildren," in *Essays in Persuasion*, introd. Donald Moggridge. New York: Norton, 358–73.

Khalil, Y. 2015. "Neoliberalism and the Failure of the Arab Spring." *New Politics*, 15(3): 77–82.

Kilbourne, Jean. 2003. "'The More You Subtract, the More You Add': Cutting Girls Down to Size," in Tim Kasser and Allen D. Kanner (eds), *Psychology and Consumer Culture: The Struggle for a Good Life in a Materialistic World*. Washington, DC: APA Press, 251–70.

Kim, Soo. 2020. "More Than 200 Doctors and Nurses Have Died Combating Coronavirus across the Globe." Newsweek, April 10, www.newsweek.com/more-200-doctors-nurses-died-combating-coronavirus-1497181.

King, Mary C. 2003. "Black Women's Breakthrough into Clerical Work: An Occupational Tipping Model," In Ellen Mutari and Deborah M Figart (eds), *Women and the Economy: A Reader.* Armonk, NY: M. E. Sharpe, 221–33.

Kingsley, Patrick. 2018. "'Better to Drown': A Greek Refugee Camp's Epidemic of Misery." *New York Times,* October 2, www.nytimes.com/2018/10/02/world/europe/greece-lesbos-moria-refugees.html.

Klare, Michael T. 2001. *Resource Wars: The New Landscape of Global Conflict.* New York: Metropolitan Books.

Klein, Naomi. 2000. *No Logo.* New York: Picador.

Kolko, Joyce. 1999. "Restructuring and the Working Class," in Harry F. Dahms (ed.), *Transformations of Capitalism: Economy, Society, and the State in Modern Times.* New York: New York University Press, 274–95.

Kotz, David M. 1994. "Interpreting the Social Structure of Accumulation Theory," in David M. Kotz, Terrence McDonough, and Michael Reich (eds), *Social Structures of Accumulation: The Political Economy of Growth and Crisis.* Cambridge: Cambridge University Press, 50–71.

——— 2008. "Crisis and Neoliberal Capitalism." *Dollars and Sense: Real World Economics,* 279: 13–15.

Kovel, Joel. 2002. *The Enemy of Nature: The End of Capitalism or the End of the World?* Black Point, NS: Fernwood Publishing.

Kowalewski, Zbigniew Marcin. 2011. "Give Us Back Our Factories! Between Resisting Exploitation and the Struggle for Workers' Power in Poland, 1944–1981," in Immanuel Ness and Dario Azzellini (eds), *Ours to Master and to Own: Workers' Control from the Commune to the Present.* Chicago: Haymarket Books, 191–207.

Lafontaine, Oskar. 1998. "The Future of German Social Democracy." *New Left Review,* 227: 72–87.

Laidler, David, and Saul Estrin. 1989. *Introduction to Microeconomics,* 3rd edn. New York: Philip Allan.

Lane, Robert E. 2000. *The Loss of Happiness in Market Democracies.* New Haven, CT: Yale University Press.

Lapavitsas, Costas, and Stathis Kouvelakis. 2018. "Syriza's Repressive Turn." Verso, October 8, www. versobooks.com/blogs/4067-syriza-s-repressive-turn.

LaPoint, Velma D., and Priscilla J. Hambrick-Dixon. 2003. "Commercialism's Influence on Black Youth: The Case of Dress-Related Challenges," in Tim Kasser and Allen D. Kanner (eds), *Psychology and Consumer Culture: The Struggle for a Good Life in a Materialistic World.* Washington, DC: APA Press, 233–50.

Lav, I. 2014. "Curbing the Consequences: Achieving Better Outcomes for Workers in Municipal Bankruptcies." *New Labor Forum,* 23(3): 48–56.

Layard, Richard. 2005. *Happiness: Lessons from a New Science.* New York: Penguin Books.

Le Grand, Julian, and Saul Estrin (eds). 1998. *Market Socialism.* Oxford: Clarendon Press.

Lenin, V. I. 1975a [1917]. *Imperialism, the Highest Stage of Capitalism: A Popular Outline.* Peking: Foreign Languages Press.

——— 1975b [1923]. "Report on War and Peace," in Robert C. Tucker (ed.), *The Lenin Anthology.* New York: Norton, 542–49.

Levin, Diane E., and Susan Linn. 2003. "The Commercialization of Childhood: Understanding the Problem and Finding Solutions," in Tim Kasser and Allen D. Kanner (eds), *Psychology and Consumer Culture: The Struggle for a Good Life in a Materialistic World.* Washington, DC: APA Press, 213–32.

Levine, A. S. 2015. *American Insecurity: Why Our Economic Fears Lead to Political Inaction.* Princeton, NJ: Princeton University Press.

Lewin, Moshe. 2005. *The Soviet Century.* London: Verso.

Lewis, Rebecca C. 2020. "Medicaid Cuts Make the State Budget, with Some Tweaks." City and State, April 3, www.cityandstateny.com/articles/policy/budget/medicaid-cuts-make-state-budget-some-tweaks.html.

Li, Minqi. 2008. "Climate Change, Limits to Growth, and the Imperative for Socialism." *Monthly Review,* 60(3): 51–67.

Lichtenstein, Nelson. 2012. "Class Unconsciousness: Stop Using 'Middle Class' to Depict the Labor Movement." *New Labor Forum,* 21(2): 10–13.

Lichtman, Richard. 2009. "Myths of the Marketplace: The Terrible Violence of Abstraction." *Capitalism Nature Socialism*, 20(2): 14–21.

Lohmann, Larry. 2010. "Six Arguments against Carbon Trading," in Ian Angus (ed.), *The Global Fight for Climate Justice: Anticapitalist Responses to Global Warming and Environmental Destruction*. Black Point, NS: Fernwood Publishing, 134–39.

Losurdo, Domenico. 2011. *Liberalism: A Counter-History*. London: Verso.

Lovell, Stephen. 2009. *The Soviet Union: A Very Short Introduction*. Oxford: Oxford University Press.

Luxemburg, Rosa. 1968 [1913]. *The Accumulation of Capital*. New York: Modern Reader Paperbacks.

Lynch, Michael J. 2016. "A Marxian Interpretation of the Environmental Kuznets Curve: Global Capitalism and the Rise and Fall (and Rise) of Pollution." *Capitalism Nature Socialism*, 27(4): 77–95.

McAllister, Ian, and Stephen White. 2009. "Conventional Citizen Participation," in Christian W. Haerpfer, Patrick Bernhagen, Ronald F. Inglehart, and Christian Welzel (eds), *Democratization*. Oxford: Oxford University Press, 186–200.

McChesney, Robert W., John Bellamy Foster, Inger L. Stole, and Hannah Holleman. 2009. "The Sales Effort and Monopoly Capital." *Monthly Review*, 60(11): 1–23.

McCormack, Gowan. 1999. "Modernism, Water, and Affluence: The Japanese Way in East Asia," in Walter L. Goldfrank, David Goodman, and Andrew Szasz (eds), *Ecology and the World-System*. Westport, CT: Greenwood Press, 147–63.

McCracken, Grant. 1988. *Culture and Consumption: New Approaches to the Symbolic Character of Consumer Goods and Activities*. Bloomington, IN: Indiana University Press.

MacDonald, Martha. 2003. "Feminist Economics: From Theory to Research," in Ellen Mutari and Deborah M. Figart (eds), *Women and the Economy: A Reader*. Armonk, NY: M. E. Sharpe: 25–34.

McKeever, Vicky. 2020. "Nearly 25 Million Jobs Could Be Lost Globally due to the Coronavirus, UN Labor Organization Estimates." CNBC, March 19, www.cnbc.com/2020/03/19/nearly-25-million-jobs-could-be-lost-globally-due-to-the-coronavirus.html.

McLellan, David. 1979. *Marxism after Marx: An Introduction*. New York: Harper & Row.

McMichael, Philip. 2006. "Feeding the World: Agriculture, Development and Ecology," in Leo Panitch and Colin Leys (eds), *Coming to Terms with Nature: Socialist Register 2007*. London: Merlin Press, 170–94.

Magnani, Esteban. 2009. *The Silent Change: Recovered Businesses in Argentina*. Buenos Aires: Teseo.

Mandel, David. 2011. "The Factory Committee Movement in the Russian Revolution," in Immanuel Ness and Dario Azzellini (eds), *Ours to Master and to Own: Workers' Control from the Commune to the Present*. Chicago: Haymarket Books, 104–29.

Mandel, Ernest. 1971. *Marxist Economic Theory*, vol. 1. New York: Monthly Review Press.

———— 1973. *An Introduction to Marxist Economic Theory*. New York: Pathfinder Press.

———— 1977. "Introduction" [to "Results of the Immediate Process of Production"], in Karl Marx, *Capital: A Critique of Political Economy*, vol. 1. New York: Vintage Books, 943–47.

———— 1995. "The Relevance of Marxist Theory for Understanding the Present World Crisis," in *Marxism in the Postmodern Age: Confronting the New World Order*. New York: Guilford Press, 438–47.

Marcuse, Herbert. 1961. *Soviet Marxism: A Critical Analysis*. New York: Vintage Books.

———— 1969. *An Essay on Liberation*. Boston: Beacon Press. Available at www.marxists.org/reference/archive/marcuse/works/1969/essay-liberation.pdf.

Marglin, Stephen A., and Juliet B. Schor (eds). 1990. *The Golden Age of Capitalism: Reinterpreting the Postwar Experience*. Oxford: Clarendon Press.

Markoff, John (with Amy White). 2009. "The Global Wave of Democratization," in Christian W. Haerpfer, Patrick Bernhagen, Ronald F. Inglehart, and Christian Welzel (eds), *Democratization*. Oxford: Oxford University Press, 55–73.

Markoff, John. 2014. *Waves of Democracy: Social Movements and Political Change*, 2nd edn. Boulder, CO: Paradigm Publishers.

Markovic, Mihailo. 1991. "Self-Management," in Tom Bottomore (ed.), *A Dictionary of Marxist Thought*, 2nd edn. Malden, MA: Blackwell, 493–94

Markovits, Andrei S., and Philip S. Gorski. 1993. *The German Left: Red, Green and Beyond*. New York: Oxford University Press.

Martinez-Alier, Joan. 2006. "Social Metabolism and Environmental Conflicts," in Leo Panitch and Colin Leys (eds), *Coming to Terms with Nature: Socialist Register 2007*. London: Merlin Press, 273–93.

———— 2012. Environmental Justice and Economic Degrowth: An Alliance between Two Movements." *Capitalism Nature Socialism*, 23(1): 51–73.

Marx, Karl. 1963 [1847]. *The Poverty of Philosophy*. New York: International Publishers.

———— 1964 [1844]. *The Economic and Philosophic Manuscripts of 1844*, ed. Dirk J. Struik. New York: International Publishers.

———— 1970 [1859]. *A Contribution to the Critique of Political Economy*, ed. Maurice Dobb. New York: International Publishers.

———— 1973 [1861]. *Grundrisse: Foundations of the Critique of Political Economy*. New York: Vintage Books.

———— 1977 [1867]. *Capital: A Critique of Political Economy*, vol. 1. New York: Vintage Books.

———— 1978b [1856]. "Speech at the Anniversary of the *People's Paper*," in Robert C. Tucker (ed.), *The Marx–Engels Reader*, 2nd edn. New York: Norton, 577–78.

———— 1978c [1849]. "Wage Labour and Capital," in Robert C. Tucker (ed.), *The Marx–Engels Reader*, 2nd edn. New York: Norton, 203–17.

———— 1981 [1894]. *Capital: A Critique of Political Economy*, vol. 3. London: Penguin Books.

Marx, Karl, and Friedrich Engels. 1971 [1846]. *The German Ideology*. New York: International Publishers.

———— 1978 [1848]. "Manifesto of the Communist Party," in Robert C. Tucker (ed.), *The Marx–Engels Reader*, 2nd edn. New York: Norton, 469–500.

Mason, Paul. 2012. *Why It's Kicking Off Everywhere: The New Global Revolutions*. London: Verso.

Menser, Michael, and Juscha Robinson. 2008. "Participatory Budgeting: From Porto Alegre, Brazil to the US," in Jenna Allard, Carl Davidson, and Julie Matthaei (eds), *Solidarity Economy: Building Alternatives for People and Planet: Papers and Reports from the US Social Forum 2007*. Chicago: ChangeMaker Publications, 291–303.

Merchant, Carolyn. 1992. *Radical Ecology: The Search for a Livable World*. New York: Routledge.

Mies, Maria. 1986. *Patriarchy and Accumulation on a World Scale: Women in the International Division of Labor*. London: Zed Books.

Milanovic, Branko. 2005. *Worlds Apart: Measuring International and Global Inequality*. Princeton, NJ: Princeton University Press.

Milios, John. 2005. "European Integration as a Vehicle of Neoliberal Hegemony," in Alfredo Saad-Filho and Deborah Johnston (eds), *Neoliberalism: A Critical Reader*. London: Pluto Press, 208–14.

Miller, John. 2015. "Slow Growth and No Growth: Why the US Economy Is Outperforming Europe and Japan." *New Labor Forum*, 24(3): 44–51.

Miller, Marian A. L. 1995. *The Third World in Global Environmental Politics*. Boulder, CO: Lynne Rienner Publishers.

Milne, Seumas. 2015. "Now the Truth Emerges: How the US Fuelled the Rise of Isis in Syria and Iraq." *Guardian*, June 3, www.theguardian.com/commentisfree/2015/jun/03/us-isis-syria-iraq.

Mishel, Lawrence, John Schmitt, and Heidi Shierholz. 2014. "Wage Inequality: A Story of Policy Choices." *New Labor Forum*, 23(3): 26–31.

Mishra, Ramesh. 1996. "The Welfare of Nations," in Robert Boyer and Daniel Drache (eds), *States against Markets: The Limits of Globalization*. London: Routledge, 316–33.

Moody, Kim. 2011. "Wisconsin and Beyond," in Erica Sagrans (ed.), *We Are Wisconsin: The Wisconsin Uprising in the Words of the Activists, Writers, and Everyday Wisconsinites Who Made It Happen*. Minneapolis: Tasora, 219–27.

Mulder, Catherine P. 2015. *Transcending Capitalism through Cooperative Practices*. Basingstoke: Palgrave Macmillan.

Munck, Ronaldo. 2005. "Neoliberalism and Politics, and the Politics of Neoliberalism," in Alfredo Saad-Filho and Deborah Johnston (eds), *Neoliberalism: A Critical Reader*. London: Pluto Press, 60–69.

Naess, Petter, and Karl Georg Hoyer. 2009. "Shadows in Schwartzmann's Sunny Society." *Capitalism Nature Socialism*, 20(4): 98–102.

Negri, Antonio (in conversation with Raf Valvola Scelsi). 2008. *Goodbye Mr. Socialism: Radical Politics in the 21st Century*. New York: Seven Stories Press.

Ness, Immanuel, and Dario Azzellini. 2011. "Introduction," in Immanuel Ness and Dario Azzellini (eds), *Ours to Master and to Own: Workers' Control from the Commune to the Present*. Chicago: Haymarket Books, 1–7.

Newman, Michael. 2005. *Socialism: A Very Short Introduction*. Oxford: Oxford University Press.

Newport, Frank. 2018. "Democrats More Positive about Socialism than Capitalism." Gallup, August 13, https://news.gallup.com/poll/240725/democrats-positive-socialism-capitalism.aspx.

Nichols, John. 2011a. "Introduction: Why Wisconsin?," in Mari Jo Buhle and Paul Buhle (eds), *It Started in Wisconsin: Dispatches from the Front Lines of the New Labor Protest*. London: Verso, 3–8.

——— 2011b. "Epilogue: The Spirit of Wisconsin," in Erica Sagrans (ed.), *We are Wisconsin: The Wisconsin Uprising in the Words of the Activists, Writers, and Everyday Wisconsinites Who Made It Happen*. Minneapolis: Tasora, 270–79.

Nolan, Patrick, and Gerhard Lenski. 1998. *Human Societies: An Introduction to Macrosociology*, 8th edn. New York: McGraw-Hill College.

Norberg-Hodge, Helena. 1996. "The Pressure to Modernize and Globalize," in Jerry Mander and Edward Goldsmith (eds), *The Case against the Global Economy and for a Turn toward the Local*. San Francisco: Sierra Club Books, 33–46.

Norton, Ben. 2016. "Turkey's 'Double Game' on ISIS and Support for Extremist Groups Highlighted after Horrific Istanbul Attack." Salon, June 30, www.salon.com/2016/06/30/turkeys_double_game_on_isis_and_support_for_extremist_groups_highlighted_after_horrific_istanbul_attack.

Nove, Alec. 1983. *The Economics of Feasible Socialism*. London: HarperCollins.

——— 1990. "Socialism," in John Eatwell, Murray Milgate, and Peter Newman (eds), *The New Palgrave: Problems of the Planned Economy*. New York: Norton, 227–49.

——— 1992. *An Economic History of the USSR, 1917–1991*. London: Penguin Books.

O'Brien, Sara Ashley. 2020. "Here's Why Amazon and Instacart Workers Are Striking at a Time When You Need Them Most." CNN, March 30, www.cnn.com/2020/03/30/tech/instacart-amazon-worker-strikes/index.html.

O'Connor, James. 1998. "Socialism and Nature," in *Natural Causes: Essays in Ecological Marxism*. New York: Guilford, 255–66.

Oelsner, Andrea, and Mervyn Bain. 2009. "Latin America," in Christian W. Haerpfer, Patrick Bernhagen, Ronald F. Inglehart, and Christian Welzel (eds), *Democratization*. Oxford: Oxford University Press, 290–308.

Offe, Claus. 2013. "Participatory Inequality in the Austerity State: A Supply-Side Approach," in Armin Schaefer and Wolfgang Streeck (eds), *Politics in the Age of Austerity*. Cambridge: Polity, 196–218.

Ollman, Bertell. 1998. "Market Mystification in Capitalist and Market Socialist Societies," in Bertell Ollman (ed.) *Market Socialism: The Debate among Socialists*. New York: Routledge, 81–121.

Olson, Mancur. 1971. *The Logic of Collective Action: Public Goods and the Theory of Groups*. Cambridge, MA: Harvard University Press.

Ophuls, William. 1976. *Ecology and the Politics of Scarcity: Prologue to a Political Theory of the Steady State*. San Francisco: Freeman.

Oppel, Richard A., Dionne Searcey, and John Eligon. 2020. "Black Americans Face Alarming Rates of Coronavirus Infection in Some States." *New York Times*, April 7, www.nytimes.com/2020/04/07/us/coronavirus-race.html.

Packard, Vance. 2011. *The Waste Makers*. Brooklyn, NY: ig Publishing.

Pampel, Fred C. 2007. *Sociological Lives and Ideas: An Introduction to the Classical Theorists*, 2nd edn. New York. Worth Publishers.

Panayotakis, Costas. 2006. "Working More, Selling More, Consuming More: Capitalism's 'Third Contradiction,'" in Leo Panitch and Colin Leys (eds), *Coming to Terms with Nature: Socialist Register 2007*. London: Merlin Press, 254–72.

———— 2011a. *Remaking Scarcity: From Capitalist Inefficiency to Economic Democracy*. London: Pluto Press.

———— 2011b. "Youth in Revolt." Truthout, June 10, www.truth-out.org/news/item/1567-youth-in-revolt.

———— 2012. "The Struggle in (and over) Greece." *Capitalism Nature Socialism*, 23(2): 1–3.

———— 2013. "The State of Anti-Austerity Struggles in Greece." *New Politics*, 15(2): 16–21.

———— 2014a. "Capitalism, Meritocracy, and Social Stratification: A Radical Reformulation of the Davis–Moore Thesis," *American Journal of Economics and Sociology*, 73(1): 127–50.

———— 2014b. "The Trouble with 'Solution-Driven Unionism': Labor's Crisis of Ideas and the Promise of Economic Democracy," *WorkingUSA: The Journal of Labor and Society*, 17(1): 93–104.

Panitch, Leo. 1994. "Globalization and the State," in Ralph Miliband and Leo Panitch (eds), *Between Globalism and Nationalism: Socialist Register 1994*. London: Merlin Press, 60–93.

———— 2000. "Reflections on Strategy for Labour," in Leo Panitch, Colin Leys, Greg Albo, and David Coates (eds), *Working Classes, Global Realities: Socialist Register 2001*. New York: Monthly Review Press, 367–92.

Panitch, Leo, and Ralph Miliband. 1992. "The New World Order and the Socialist Agenda," in Ralph Miliband and Leo Panitch (eds), *New World Order? Socialist Register 1992*. London: Merlin Press, 1–25.

Pashkoff, Susan. 2014. "Women and Austerity in Britain." *New Politics*, 14(4): 57–62.

Payiatsos, Andros. 2017. "The Rise and Fall of Syriza." Socialist Alternative, July 7, www.socialistalternative.org/2017/07/07/rise-fall-syriza.

Peet, Richard, and Elaine Hartwick. 2009. *Theories of Development: Contentions, Arguments, Alternatives*, 2nd edn. New York: Guilford.

Perano, Ursula. 2020. "Fauci Says 100,000 to 200,000 Americans Could Die from Coronavirus." Axios, March 29, www.axios.com/fauci-coronavirus-deaths-america-aa3c1c66–329b-49a6-bcc4–50484ace46ed.html.

Petchesky, Rosalind. 1979. "Dissolving the Hyphen: A Report on Marxist-Feminist Groups 1–5," in Zillah R. Eisenstein (ed.), *Capitalist Patriarchy and the Case for Socialist Feminism*. New York: Monthly Review Press, 373–89.

Petermann, Anne, and Orin Langelle. 2010. "Crisis, Challenge and Mass Action," in Ian Angus (ed.), *The Global Fight for Climate Justice: Anticapitalist Responses to Global Warming and Environmental Destruction*. Black Point, NS: Fernwood Publishing, 186–95.

Pitcheta, Rob, and Stephanie Halasz. 2020. "Hungarian Parliament Votes to Let Viktor Orban Rule by Decree in Wake of Coronavirus Pandemic." CNN, March 30, www.cnn.com/2020/03/30/europe/hungary-viktor-orban-powers-vote-intl/index.html.

Piven, Frances Fox, and Richard A. Cloward. 1987. "The Contemporary Relief Debate," in Fred Block, Richard A. Cloward, Barbara Ehrenreich, and Frances Fox Piven (eds), *The Mean Season: The Attack on the Welfare State*. New York: Pantheon Books, 45–108.

Plumer, Brad. 2018. "You've Heard of Outsourced Jobs, but Outsourced Pollution? It's Real, and Tough to Tally Up." *New York Times*, September 4, www.nytimes.com/2018/09/04/climate/outsourcing-carbon-emissions.html.

Polanyi, Karl. 2001 [1944]. *The Great Transformation: The Political and Economic Origins of Our Time*. Boston: Beacon Press.

Pollin, R. 2013. "Austerity Economics Is Bad Economics." *New Labor Forum*, 22(1): 86–89.

Post, Charles. 2012. "Why the Tea Party?" *New Politics*, 14(1): 75–82.

Postman, Neil, and Steve Powers. 2011. "The Commercial," in Jerome H. Skolnick and Elliott Currie (eds), *Crisis in American Institutions*, 14th edn. Boston: Allyn and Bacon.

Przeworski, Adam. 1985. *Capitalism and Social Democracy*. Cambridge: Cambridge University Press.

Refugees International. 2020. "Responding to the Covid-19 Crisis while Protecting Asylum Seekers." March 19, www.refugeesinternational.org/reports/2020/3/19/responding-to-the-covid-19-crisis-while-protecting-asylum-seekers.

Resnick, Stephen A., and Richard D. Wolff. 2002. *Class Theory and History: Capitalism and Communism in the USSR*. New York: Routledge.

Rifkin, Jeremy. 1996. "New Technology and the End of Jobs," in Jerry Mander and Edward Goldsmith (eds), *The Case against the Global Economy and for a Turn toward the Local*. San Francisco: Sierra Club Books, 108–21.

Riley, Charles. 2020. "Get Ready for Wartime Levels of National Debt and Tough Choices ahead." CNN, April 3, www.cnn.com/2020/04/03/economy/coronavirus-debt-deficits/index.html.

Ritzer, George. 2005. *Enchanting a Disenchanted World: Revolutionizing the Means of Consumption*, 2nd edn. Thousand Oaks, CA: Pine Forge Press.

———— 2008. *Sociological Theory*, 7th edn. Boston: McGraw-Hill Higher Education.

Robbins, Richard H. 2005. *Global Problems and the Future of Capitalism*, 3rd edn. Boston: Pearson.

Robertson, James. 1990. *Future Wealth: A New Economics for the 21st Century*. New York: Bootstrap Press.

Roemer, John E. 1988. *Free to Lose: An Introduction to Marxist Economic Philosophy*. Cambridge, MA: Harvard University Press.

———— 1994. *A Future for Socialism*. Cambridge, MA: Harvard University Press.

Rogers, Katie, Lara Jakes, and Ana Swanson. 2020. "Trump Defends Using 'Chinese Virus' Label, Ignoring Growing Criticism." *New York Times*, March 18, www.nytimes.com/2020/03/18/us/politics/china-virus.html?searchResultPosition=1.

Roodman, David Malin. 1996. *Paying the Piper: Subsidies, Politics, and the Environment*. Washington, DC: Worldwatch Institute.

Roosevelt, Frank, and David Belkin (eds). 1994. *Why Market Socialism? Voices from Dissent*. Armonk, NY: M. E. Sharpe.

Rose, Richard. 2009. "Democratic and Undemocratic States," in Christian W. Haerpfer, Patrick Bernhagen, Ronald F. Inglehart, and Christian Welzel (eds), *Democratization*. Oxford: Oxford University Press, 10–23.

Rosenberg, Erika L. 2003. "Mindfulness and Consumerism," in Tim Kasser and Allen D. Kanner (eds), *Psychology and Consumer Culture: The Struggle for a Good Life in a Materialistic World*. Washington, DC: APA Press, 107–25.

Rossi, Federico M., and Donatella della Porta. 2009. "Social Movement, Trade Unions, and Advocacy Networks," in Christian W. Haerpfer, Patrick Bernhagen, Ronald F. Inglehart, and Christian Welzel (eds), *Democratization*. Oxford: Oxford University Press, 172–85.

Rostow, W. W. 1990. *The Stages of Economic Growth: A Non-Communist Manifesto*. Cambridge: Cambridge University Press.

Rueschemeyer, Dietrich, Evelyne Huber Stephens, and John D. Stephens. 1992. *Capitalist Development and Democracy*. Chicago: University of Chicago Press.

Russell, James W. 2009. *Societies and Social Life: An Introduction to Sociology*, 2nd edn. Cornwall-on-Hudson, NY: Sloan Publishing.

Saad-Filho, Alfredo, and Deborah Johnston (eds). 2005. *Neoliberalism: A Critical Reader*. London: Pluto Press.

Sachs, Wolfgang. 1999. *Planet Dialectics: Explorations in Environment and Development*. London: Zed Books.

Sackrey, Charles, and Geoffrey Schneider (with Janet Knoedler). 2002. *Introduction to Political Economy*, 3rd edn. Cambridge, MA: Economic Affairs Bureau.

Sader, Emir. 2005. "Toward New Democracies," in Boaventura de Sousa Santos (ed.), *Democratizing Democracy: Beyond the Liberal Democratic Canon*. London: Verso, 447–68.

Sanger, David E., Maggie Haberman, and Zolan Kanno-Youngs. 2020. "After Considering $1 Billion Price Tag for Ventilators, White House Has Second Thoughts." *New York Times*, March 26, www.nytimes.com/2020/03/26/us/politics/coronavirus-ventilators-trump.html?searchResultPosition=1.

Santos, Boaventura de Sousa (ed.). 2005a. *Democratizing Democracy: Beyond the Liberal Democratic Canon*. London. Verso.

———— 2005b. "Participatory Budgeting in Porto Alegre: Toward a Redistributive Democracy," in Boaventura de Sousa Santos (ed.), *Democratizing Democracy: Beyond the Liberal Democratic Canon*. London: Verso, 307–76.

Sarkar, Saral. 1999. *Eco-Socialism or Eco-Capitalism? A Critical Analysis of Humanity's Fundamental Choices*. London: Zed Books.

Sassoon, Donald. 1996. *One Hundred Years of Socialism: The West European Left in the Twentieth Century*. New York: New Press.

Satz, Debra. 1996. "Status Inequalities and Models of Market Socialism," in Erik Olin Wright (ed.), *Equal Shares: Making Market Socialism Work*. London: Verso, 71–89.

Schaefer, Armin. 2013. "Liberalization, Inequality and Democracy's Discontent," in Armin Schaefer and Wolfgang Streeck (eds), *Politics in the Age of Austerity*. Cambridge: Polity Press, 169–95.

Schaefer, Armin, and Wolfgang Streeck. 2013. "Introduction: Politics in the Age of Austerity," in Armin Schaefer and Wolfgang Streeck (eds), *Politics in the Age of Austerity*. Cambridge: Polity Press, 1–25.

Schaeffer, Robert K. 1999. "Success and Impasse: The Environmental Movement in the United States and around the World," in Walter L. Goldfrank, David Goodman, and Andrew Szasz (eds), *Ecology and the World-System*. Westport, CT: Greenwood Press, 189–211.

Schmitt, John, and Kris Warner. "The Changing Face of US Labor, 1983–2008." *WorkingUSA: The Journal of Labor and Society*, 13(2): 263–79.

Schnaiberg, Allan. 2005. "The Economy and the Environment," in Neil J. Smelser and Richard Swedberg (eds), *The Handbook of Economic Sociology*, 2nd edn. Princeton, NJ: Princeton University Press, 703–25.

Schor, Juliet B. 1991. *The Overworked American: The Unexpected Decline of Leisure*. New York: Basic Books.

Schorske, Carl E. 1955. *German Social Democracy, 1905–1917: The Development of the Great Schism*. Cambridge, MA: Harvard University Press.

Schumpeter, Joseph A. 1942. *Capitalism, Socialism, and Democracy*. New York: Harper.

———— 2000 [1943]. "Capitalism in the Postwar World," in Harry F. Dahms (ed.), *Transformations of Capitalism: Economy, Society, and the State in Modern Times*. New York: New York University Press, 1–30.

Schwartzman, David. 2009. "Response to Naess and Hoyer." *Capitalism Nature Socialism*, 20(4): 93–97.

Schweickart, David. 1996. *Against Capitalism*. Boulder, CO: Westview Press.

———— 1997. "A Democratic Theory of Economic Exploitation Dialectically Developed," in Kai Nielsen and Robert Ware (eds), *Exploitation*. Atlantic Highlands, NJ: Humanities Press International, 49–68.

Scott, Alan. 1990. *Ideology and the New Social Movements*. London: Routledge.

Scott, John, and Gordon Marshall. 2005. *Oxford Dictionary of Sociology*. Oxford: Oxford University Press.

Seccombe, Wally. 1980. "The Expanded Reproduction Cycle of Labour Power in Twentieth-Century Capitalism," in Bonnie Fox (ed.), *Hidden in the Household: Women's Domestic Labour under Capitalism*. Toronto: Women's Press, 217–66.

Sen, Arup Kumar. 2016. "Politics of Social Democracy in a Communist-Ruled State in India," in Ingo Schmidt (ed.), *The Three Worlds of Social Democracy: A Global View*. London: Pluto Press, 201–17.

Sheth, D. L. 2005. "Micro-Movements in India: Toward a New Politics of Participatory Democracy," in Boaventura de Sousa Santos (ed.), *Democratizing Democracy: Beyond the Liberal Democratic Canon*. London: Verso, 3–37.

Shiva, Vandana. 2001. "The World on the Edge," in Will Hutton and Anthony Giddens (eds), *Global Capitalism*. New York: New Press, 112–29.

Simms, Andrew. 2005. *Ecological Debt: The Health of the Planet and the Wealth of Nations*. London: Pluto Press.

Sirianni, Carmen. 1991. "The Self-Management of Time in Postindustrial Society," in Karl Hinrichs, William Roche, and Carmen Sirianni (eds), *Working Time in Transition: The Political Economy of Working Hours in Industrial Nations*. Philadelphia: Temple University Press, 231–74.

Sitrin, Marina, and Dario Azzellini. 2014. *They Can't Represent Us! Reinventing Democracy from Greece to Occupy*. London: Verso.

Slater, Don. 1997. *Consumer Culture and Modernity*. Cambridge: Polity Press.

Slotnick, David. 2020. "Boeing Is Expected to Get Billions of Dollars in Bailouts from the Senate, despite Backlash over the 737 Max Crisis and Past Stock Buybacks." Business Insider, March 25, www.businessinsider.com/boeing-bailout-coronavirus-crisis-controversy-2020–3.

Smith, Adam. 1909 [1776]. *An Inquiry into the Nature and Causes of the Wealth of Nations*. New York: Collier.

Smith, Helena. 2012. "German 'Hypocrisy' over Greek Military Spending Has Critics Up in Arms." *Guardian*, April 19, www.theguardian.com/world/2012/apr/19/greece-military-spending-debt-crisis.

Soederberg, Susanne. 2015. "The Student Loan Crisis and the Debtfare State: How the Government Helped to Make the Debt Trap the New Normal." *Dollars and Sense: Real World Economics*, 318: 9–14.

Solnit, Rebecca. 2009. "The Revolution Has Already Occurred." *The Nation*, March 23, www.thenation.com/article/revolution-has-already-occurred.

Solomon, Claire, and Tania Palmieri. 2011a. "Introduction," in Claire Solomon and Tania Palmieri (eds), *Springtime: The New Student Rebellions*. London: Verso, 1–9.

——— (eds). 2011b. *Springtime: The New Student Rebellions*. London: Verso.

Sorscher, Stan. 2013. "Trade Agreements Reveal How Life Will Be Organized in 2050." Huffington Post, October 30, www.huffingtonpost.com/stan-sorscher/trade-agreements-reveal-how-life_b_4090014.html.

Spinney, Laura. 2020. "Is Factory Farming to Blame for Coronavirus?" *Guardian*, March 28, www.theguardian.com/world/2020/mar/28/is-factory-farming-to-blame-for-coronavirus.

Spitzner, Meike. 2009. "How Global Warming Is Gendered: A View from the EU," in Ariel Salleh (ed.), *Eco-Sufficiency and Global Justice: Women Write Political Ecology*. London: Pluto Press, 218–29.

Stacey, J. 2002. "The Family Is Dead, Long Live Our Families," in Nancy Holmstrom (ed.), *The Socialist Feminist Project: A Contemporary Reader in Theory and Politics*. New York: Monthly Review Press, 90–101.

Steger, Manfred B., and Ravi K. Roy. 2010. *Neoliberalism: A Very Short Introduction*. Oxford: Oxford University Press.

Stiglitz, Joseph E. 2001. "Foreword," in Karl Polanyi, *The Great Transformation: The Political and Economic Origins of Our Time*. Boston: Beacon Press, vii–xvii.

——— 2003. *Globalization and Its Discontents*. New York: Norton.

Stockman, Farah, and Mike Baker. 2020. "Nurses Battling Coronavirus Beg for Protective Gear and Better Planning." *New York Times*, March 5, www.nytimes.com/2020/03/05/us/coronavirus-nurses.html?searchResultPosition=1.

Strange, Susan. 1996. *The Retreat of the State: The Diffusion of Power in the World Economy*. Cambridge: Cambridge University Press.

Streeck, Wolfgang. 2013. "The Crisis in Context: Democratic Capitalism and Its Contradictions," in Armin Schaefer and Wolfgang Streeck (eds), *Politics in the Age of Austerity*. Cambridge: Polity Press, 262–86.

——— 2014. "How Will Capitalism End?" *New Left Review*, 87: 35–64.

Sweezy, Paul M. 1942. *The Theory of Capitalist Development: Principles of Marxian Political Economy*. New York: Monthly Review Press.

Szelényi, Iván, Katherine Beckett, and Laurence P. King. 1994. "The Socialist Economic System," in Neil J. Smelser and Richard Swedberg (eds), *The Handbook of Economic Sociology*. Princeton, NJ: Princeton University Press, 234–54.

Tanuro, Daniel. 2010. "Climate Crisis: 21st Century Socialists Must Be Ecosocialists," in Ian Angus (ed.), *The Global Fight for Climate Justice: Anticapitalist Responses to Global Warming and Environmental Destruction*. Black Point, NS: Fernwood Publishing, 237–82.

Tavernise, Sabrina, Audra D. S. Burch, Sarah Mervosh, and Campbell Robertson. 2020. "'We Have Lost It All': The Shock Felt by Millions of Unemployed Americans." *New York Times*, March 27, www.nytimes.com/2020/03/27/us/coronavirus-unemployed.html?searchResultPosition=2.

Taylor, Betsy, and Dave Tilford. 2000. "Why Consumption Matters," in Juliet B. Schor and Douglas B. Holt (eds), *The Consumer Society Reader* New York: New Press, 463–87.

Teorell, Jan. 2010. *Determinants of Democratization: Explaining Regime Change in the World, 1972–2006.* Cambridge: Cambridge University Press.

Thompson, Willie. 2011. *Ideologies in the Age of Extremes: Liberalism, Conservatism, Communism, Fascism 1914–91.* London: Pluto Press.

Ticktin, Hillel. 1998. "The Problem Is Market Socialism," in Bertell Ollman (ed.), *Market Socialism: The Debate among Socialists.* New York: Routledge, 55–80.

Tietenberg, Thomas H. 1996. "Managing the Transition to Sustainable Development: The Role for Economic Incentives," in Peter H. May and Ronaldo Serôa da Motta (eds), *Pricing the Planet: Economic Analysis for Sustainable Development.* New York: Columbia University Press, 123–38.

Tilly, Charles. 2007. *Democracy.* New York: Cambridge University Press.

Tilly, Chris, and Randy Albelda. 2002. "Toward a Strategy for Women's Economic Equality," in Nancy Holmstrom (ed.), *The Socialist Feminist Project: A Contemporary Reader in Theory and Politics.* New York: Monthly Review Press, 228–40.

Townsend, Terry. 2010. "Capitalism's Anti-Ecology Treadmill," in Ian Angus (ed.), *The Global Fight for Climate Justice: Anticapitalist Responses to Global Warming and Environmental Destruction.* Black Point, NS: Fernwood Publishing, 112–22.

Trainer, Ted. 2015. "The Degrowth Movement from the Perspective of the Simpler Way." *Capitalism Nature Socialism*, 26(2): 58–75.

Trigona, Marie. 2008. "Fasinpat (Factory without a Boss): An Argentine Experience in Self-Management," in Chris Spannos (ed.), *Real Utopia: Participatory Society for the 21st Century.* Edinburgh: AK Press, 155–68.

Union of Concerned Scientists. 2011. "Smoke, Mirrors and Hot Air: How ExxonMobil Uses Big Tobacco's Tactics to Manufacture Uncertainty on Climate Science," in Jerome H. Skolnick and Elliott Currie (eds), *Crisis in American Institutions*, 14th edn. Boston: Allyn and Bacon, 218–26.

Van Arsdale, David G. 2013. "The Temporary Work Revolution: The Shift from Jobs that Solve Poverty to Jobs that Make Poverty." *WorkingUSA: The Journal of Labor and Society*, 16(1): 87–112.

Van der Veen, Marjolein. 2014. "'Fewer! Fewer! Fewer!' A Step Too Far for the Ultra-Right in the Netherlands?" *Dollars and Sense: Real World Economics*, 312: 23–26.

Van Gelder, Sarah. 2011. "Wisconsin: The First Stop in an American Uprising?," in Erica Sagrans (ed.), *We Are Wisconsin: The Wisconsin Uprising in the Words of the Activists, Writers, and Everyday Wisconsinites Who Made It Happen.* Minneapolis: Tasora Books, 187–89.

Vattimo, Gianni. 2010. Weak Communism?," in Costas Douzinas and Slavoj Žižek (eds), *The Idea of Communism.* London: Verso, 205–8.

Wainwright, Hilary. 2003. *Reclaim the State: Experiments in Popular Democracy.* London: Verso.

Wallerstein, Immanuel. 1999. "Ecology and Capitalist Costs of Production: No Exit," in Walter L. Goldfrank, David Goodman, and Andrew Szasz (eds), *Ecology and the World-System.* Westport, CT: Greenwood Press, 3–12.

Wallis, Victor. 2011. "Workers' Control and Revolution," in Immanuel Ness and Dario Azzellini (eds), *Ours to Master and to Own: Workers' Control from the Commune to the Present.* Chicago: Haymarket Books, 10–31.

Warren, Elizabeth. 2015. "The Trans-Pacific Partnership Clause Everyone Should Oppose." *Washington Post*, February 25, www.washingtonpost.com/opinions/kill-the-dispute-settlement-language-in-the-trans-pacific-partnership/2015/02/25/ec7705a2-bd1e-11e4-b274-e5209a3bc9a9_story.html?utm_term=.e6bba74b68e2.

Watkins, Susan. 2016. "Casting Off?" *New Left Review*, 100: 5–31.

Weaver, Stuart. 1988. "The Political Ideology of Short Time: England, 1820–1850," in Gary Cross (ed.), *Worktime and Industrialization: An International History.* Philadelphia: Temple University Press, 77–102.

Weber, Max. 1958 [1905]. *The Protestant Ethic and the Spirit of Capitalism*. New York: Charles Scribner's Sons.

Weinbaum, Batya, and Amy Bridges. 1979. "The Other Side of the Paycheck: Monopoly Capital and the Structure of Consumption," in Zillah R. Eisenstein (ed.), *Capitalist Patriarchy and the Case for Socialist Feminism*. New York: Monthly Review Press, 190–205.

Weiner, Lois. 2018. "Walkouts Teach US Labor a New Grammar for Struggle." *New Politics*, 17(1): 3–13.

Welzel, Christian. 2009. "Theories of Democratization," in Christian W. Haerpfer, Patrick Bernhagen, Ronald F. Inglehart, and Christian Welzel (eds), *Democratization*. Oxford: Oxford University Press, 74–90.

Wen, Dale, and Minqi Li. 2006. "China: Hyper-Development and Environmental Crisis," in Leo Panitch and Colin Leys (eds), *Coming to Terms with Nature: Socialist Register 2007*. London: Merlin Press, 130–46.

Williams, Chris. 2010. "Cap and Trade Schemes," in Ian Angus (ed.), *The Global Fight for Climate Justice: Anticapitalist Responses to Global Warming and Environmental Destruction*. Black Point, NS: Fernwood Publishing, 126–29.

Wolff, Richard D. 2010. "Regulations Do Not Prevent Capitalist Crises," in *Capitalism Hits the Fan: The Global Economic Meltdown and What to Do about It*. Northampton, MA: Olive Branch Press, 200–3.

——— 2012. *Democracy at Work: A Cure for Capitalism*. Chicago: Haymarket Books.

Wolff, Richard D., and Stephen A. Resnick. 1987. *Economics: Marxian versus Neoclassical*. Baltimore: Johns Hopkins University Press.

——— 2012. *Contending Economic Theories: Neoclassical, Keynesian, and Marxian*. Cambridge, MA: MIT Press.

Wolfson, Martin H. 1994. "The Financial System and the Social Structure of Accumulation," in David M. Kotz, Terrence McDonough, and Michael Reich (eds), *Social Structures of Accumulation: The Political Economy of Growth and Crisis*. Cambridge: Cambridge University Press, 133–45.

Wright, Erik Olin (ed.). 1996. *Equal Shares: Making Market Socialism Work*. London: Verso.

Wright, Erik Olin, and Joel Rogers. 2011. *American Society: How It Really Works*. New York: Norton.

Xenos, Nicholas. 1989. *Scarcity and Modernity*. London: Routledge.

Yates, Michael D. 2009. "Why Unions Still Matter." *Monthly Review*, 60(9): 18–28.

Yeginsu, Ceylan. 2018. "What's Housework Worth? $1.6 Trillion a Year in UK, Officials Calculate." *New York Times*, October 4, www.nytimes.com/2018/10/04/world/europe/uk-housework-value.html.

You, Jong-Il. 1995. "The Korean Model of Development and Its Environmental Implications," in V. Bhaskar and Andrew Glyn (eds), *The North, the South and the Environment: Ecological Constraints and the Global Economy*. New York: Saint Martin's Press, 158–83.

Žižek, Slavoj. 2010. "How to Begin from the Beginning," in Costas Douzinas and Slavoj Žižek (eds), *The Idea of Communism*. London: Verso, 209–26.

Zweig, Michael. 2001. *The Working Class Majority: America's Best Kept Secret*. Ithaca, NY: ILR Press.

Zygoulis, Fotis, and Elina Zagou. 2014. "The Problems in the Greek Public Sector Cannot Be Solved Simply by Reducing the Size of Salaries and the Numbers of Staff." London School of Economics and Political Science, August 6, https://blogs.lse.ac.uk/europpblog/2014/08/06/the-problems-in-the-greek-public-sector-cannot-be-solved-simply-by-reducing-the-size-of-salaries-or-the-numbers-of-staff.

Index

EU authorised representative for GPSR:
Easy Access System Europe, Mustamäe tee 50,
10621 Tallinn, Estonia
gpsr.requests@easproject.com

www.ingramcontent.com/pod-product-compliance
Lightning Source LLC
Chambersburg PA
CBHW070247290326
41929CB00047B/2865